D0037563

DISCARD

Writing the Short-Story

A PRACTICAL HANDBOOK ON THE
RISE, STRUCTURE, WRITING AND
SALE OF THE MODERN SHORT-STORY

REVISED EDITION

BY

J. BERG ESENWEIN, A.M., LIT.D.

SOMETIME EDITOR OF LIPPINCOTT'S MAGAZINE
EDITOR OF THE WRITER'S MONTHLY

NOBLE AND NOBLE, *Publishers*
76 FIFTH AVENUE   NEW YORK

Printed in U. S. A.

TO MY WIFE

INSPIRER: CRITIC: FRIEND
THIS WORK IS INSCRIBED

TABLE OF CONTENTS

v

PART II.— THE STRUCTURE OF THE SHORT-STORY

Chapter I.— Choosing a Theme

Chapter II.— Gathering the Materials

Chapter III.— Fact in Fiction

Chapter IV.— Plot

PART IV.— THE MANUSCRIPT AND ITS MARKET

CHAPTER I.— WRITING THE STORY

CHAPTER III.— WHY STORIES ARE REJECTED — A COLLOQUY

PART V.— APPENDICES

PART VI.—SUPPLEMENTAL CHAPTERS

FOREWORD

The short-story, now the most popular literary form, is engaging the study of writers unnumbered, and the interest of an increasing host of readers. Its art is gradually crystallizing, its significance is deepening, and educators everywhere are giving courses for its study. This volume embodies the practical principles of short-story structure as recognized by American and British magazine editors, and as practised by authors whose products are judged to be of the first order. At the same time, the body of sound scholarship has not been lost sight of in considering the popular and marketable short-story, so that the treatise is peculiarly adapted to the needs of college and senior secondary-school classes, as well as suited to inspire and guide the individual writer, amateur or professional, who wishes to improve his art. Its preparation has involved a critical examination of practically every great short-story now available in print, and many thousands of manuscripts read in the course of editorial service. Its conclusions, therefore, are seasoned with an intimate knowledge of the short-story at its best — and at its worst — to-day. The invaluable assistance of brother editors, and especially that rendered by the editorial staff of *Lippincott's Magazine,* is gratefully ac-

knowledged; as is also the discriminating criticism of
Professor Albert E. Hancock, of Haverford College,
who kindly reviewed the proofs.

THE AUTHOR

NOTE FOR THE SIXTEENTH EDITION

The former revisions given to this treatise have all been in
order to greater accuracy of statement as well as to up-to-date-
ness. In this fuller revision, however, there have been added
references to recent stories, the fullest extant bibliographies of
treatises on the short-story and of general short-story collections, several supplementary chapters, and many important explanatory notes, thus making available to the student of the
short-story the latest consensus of editorial and critical opinions,
as the author has been able, through wide contacts, to formulate
them, together with his own more mature thought.

One important point has been held constantly in view—to
make it absolutely plain that the author does not believe that
anyone ever can give a genuine recipe for successful fiction
writing. All that we can do is to examine the methods of those
who have achieved admirably, and allow them to guide us in
so far as they fit our own natures, and no farther. The practice of any art can be taught by observation and intelligent practice, but it cannot be imparted. There are no rules, no formu-
laries, but to know the methods of great artists cannot fail to
help even an original genius.

THE AUTHOR

September 1, 1923.

NOTE FOR THE EIGHTEENTH EDITION

The chief changes incorporated in this edition are the addition
of a chapter dealing with punctuation for the story writer, and
references to bring the bibliographies up to the date of revision.

THE AUTHOR

January 1, 1928.

TO TEACHERS

THIS treatise is confidently commended to you for class-room use because of several important considerations: Its inspirational method and logical order are based upon the best pedagogical approach; it covers the entire ground of the subject fully yet concisely; it is the work, not of a doctrinaire, but of a successful editor whose scholarship previously commanded attention in the college class-room and whose profession it has been for years to examine, purchase, edit and publish the short-story, as well as other literary forms; its analytical method at once reveals the road by which the author reaches his conclusions, and leaves a clear impression upon the student; its suggestive questions and exercises following each chapter are not confined merely to the text, but will inspire and direct the student in original research, as well as suggest to the teacher other profitable lines along which such study may be followed, both in and out of the class-room; its comprehensive table of contents, and analytical summaries at the close of each chapter, present a clear view of the contents in whole and in part; its appendices and bibliographies are the most complete and helpful of any similar ones published; its *" Laboratory Method for the Study of the Short-Story"* is original, and constitutes the foundation for a future volume expanding this method, on which the author is already at work;[1] its typographical arrangement, paragraphing, references and indexing, present the whole subject and its related parts in so clear a manner as to facilitate lesson assignments, recitations and individual research; it actually teaches short-story writing, and not merely facts about the short-story—there is not a theory in the whole volume but has stood the exacting double-test of teaching value and of the best editorial practice.

THE PUBLISHERS

[1] *Studying the Short-Story*, by J. Berg Esenwein, was published in 1912.

HISTORICAL INTRODUCTION
THE RISE OF THE SHORT-STORY

Brief tales there have been since the world began, since the art of the story-teller was first attempted, since the Cave-men filled the long evenings around the smoking fire with narratives of the mysterious deeds of the strange creatures of their own primitive fancy, since the earliest travelers who ventured abroad brought back episodic accounts of one or another of their misadventures, commingled of fact and of fiction.— BRANDER MATTHEWS, *The Short-Story.*

It is easy to understand why primitive men loved the short-story and why the teller of such stories had a crowd about him in the streets of Bagdad and Damascus; and why medieval men and women delighted in the uncritical, loosely constructed tales included in the *Gesta Romanorum.* To the earliest men experience preceded reflection, the story of life began to unroll itself before there were any glossaries or commentaries; the things which happened were the only real things; and when the imagination began to open the windows and look out on the landscape of life, it saw everything from the standpoint of what had already happened.— HAMILTON W. MABIE, *Stories New and Old.*

WRITING THE SHORT-STORY

HISTORICAL INTRODUCTION

I. THE RISE OF THE SHORT-STORY

1. *The Story-Teller*

The story-writer is the lineal descendant of the story-teller. Before the earliest tale was committed to tablet or papyrus, the spinner of yarns was recounting the deeds of gods and heroes, celebrating the glories of ancestors, and inciting warriors to valor. It was the spoken story that whiled away the tedium of the winter camp, made supportable the heat of the summer market-place, and enlivened long evenings in the homes of prince and peasant.

What manner of stories were these first attempts at narration? The childhood of the race is precisely pictured for us in the tendencies of the young folk of our times. The tale of incident and action appealed strongly to men in whose lives reflection was not yet a force; fantasy could fly unhampered by the sober limits of fact; wonder-stories wedded the unknown to the known. To our early forebears the world seemed peopled with uncouth forces, mysterious presences, and supernatural beings, all delightfully free from present-day limitations. Every natural object, every natural power, hid — or disclosed — some god-like personality who might do the most surprising things upon the instant. So, born of this condition are most of the Greek, Roman and Oriental myths.

With such materials ready to hand, with such fears, faiths and fancies thronging the mind and coloring life, what imaginative soul could refrain from weaving all this into story? The border-land between the known and the imagined was wide and its confines debatable, and if the primal story-teller had himself traveled, or warred, or suffered, he found within himself — just as does the yarn-spinner of to-day — an added spring from which to draw joyous draughts of invention. Indeed, the twentieth-century narrator might well envy his early predecessor the marvel-world in which he lived and more or less consciously gathered his materials; but the modern will find compensation in the wider and deeper worlds of fantasy and of spirit which were closed to the uninstructed eye of the primitive story-teller.

2. The Epic

Loose and free and of slow growth, the epic poem was for centuries the dominant story-form. It took the wealth of material in which the ancient world abounded and strung the scattered stories upon a strand of personality. Thus a Ulysses or an Æneas became the hero of tales originally told of many another. From prehistoric times down to the years when the printed page spread the tale open before every eye, the resident or the traveling story-teller was almost the only purveyor of fiction, and he was " as welcome as is a visitor with recent magazines to a lighthouse on some distant and lonely island."

Sometimes the story-teller dealt in prose forms, sometimes he chanted the sonorous lines of long heroic poems, linking for a succession of days the several parts of his story. Often, in later centuries, his story took what I may call the continued-ballad form, and, in feudal Europe, Trouvere, Troubadour and Jongleur enlivened court and camp with accounts of some favorite hero's exploits.

So we find many really great stories in the famous epics[1] of all tongues, as well as in other poetic types, though in form they are primitive when compared with the developed modern short-story. Not until the spoken story was set down in writing,[2] polished, revised, re-revised, and printed, did we get the forms to which we are able accurately to trace our present artistic product. The modern short-story was long " a-borning," and its line of ancestry is ancient and honorable.

[1] For a concise classified list see the *Standard Dictionary*. *The Book of the Epic,* H. A. Guerber, contains a condensed yet sufficiently full prose narration of the essential stories or plot-action of all the prominent epics.

[2] The oldest recorded story is that found in *The Westcar Papyrus*.

NOTE: Not until Part II, Chapter I, are the types of short fiction discriminated and broadly defined.

3. *The Ancient and the Medieval Tale* [3]

Professor Baldwin [4] has pointed out that ancient and early medieval tales are of three kinds: the simple anecdote, the scenario (or mere summary), and, very rarely, the real short-story. To this classification might be added the tale that strings together a group of anecdotes, sometimes lengthening out indefinitely. Their chief difference one from another is length. With here and there a notable exception, the tales written previous to the nineteenth century lack the qualities which, as we shall see, constitute the chief merits of the modern short-story. And even when they were cast in that mold, there is no indication that they were especially admired, and certainly there was no attempt at reproducing their kind more and more perfectly, as the conscious literary artist does to-day.

Beginning with the Egyptian papyrus stories, ranging from 4000 to 1000 B. C., down through the Hebrew, Greek, Oriental, and Roman tales of from 1000 B. C. to 500 A. D., we observe the same general characteristics. The same is true of the tales of the Dark Ages, between the decline of the classical era and the dawn of the Renaissance, which gave us all the fantastic legends and devotional tales so typical of the early French; and after that, the stories of the Renaissance period, and the modern tale prior to Poe. The modern short-story is allied

---

[3] For a full discussion, with exhaustive lists and some specimens in translation, see Jessup and Canby's *The Book of the Short Story*. Also the Introduction to *The Short-Story*, Matthews.

[4] *American Short Stories*, p. 26.

to all of these by ancestry, in that they are preëminently simple, direct, and generally devised solely to tell a story. As specimens of pure narration they are often admirable, but "short-stories" they are not, as will presently appear.[5]

4. *The Sacred Books of the East* [6]

The short-story of to-day draws rich life-blood also directly from the sacred writings of the Orient. Many of these narratives have, in varying forms, been current for centuries, their original source remaining by most readers unsuspected. The rich color, the fascinating movement, the mystical beliefs of the East, permeate these more-or-less religious tales and invest them with a charm often quite the equal of that which we feel in the familiar *Arabian Nights*.

The Bible contains some of the purest specimens of art to be found anywhere, whether ancient or modern. When we examine the dramatic account of "The Prodigal Son," and the idyllic story of "Ruth," we must confess that modern art is powerless to approach their simple beauty and effectiveness. Quite apart from the reverence which these and other Biblical narratives inspire in many minds, it is a source of constant marvel that such venerable stories should have contained in large part the forecast of what writers are to-day striving after as standards. Undisputed, they take their place at the head of that small grou⌐ of stories of all languages which,

[5] See chap. i.
[6] For a summary of "The Sacred Books of the East" (the Bible excepted), see *Summaries of Noted Books,* in Charles Dudley Warner's *Library of the World's Best Literature.*

though they are the product of earlier centuries, remain to-day the best examples of their sort. They prophetically antedated the schools to which, by an elastic phrase, they may be said to belong.

Among the honored forebears of the short-story we must not fail to name also

5. *The Drama*

Primitive men, in common with children and adults who live much in their feelings, naturally dramatize — act out — their thoughts and emotions. Indeed, the drama must ever act out a story, and through thousands of years — for the drama is almost as old as the tale — the growth of dramatic art has tremendously contributed to the vividness, the intensity, the compressed power, the ingenuity of plot, and the emotional appeal of prose fiction both long and short. The printed play and the stage have neither time nor place for nonessentials — no more has the modern short-story; but it took yarn-spinners centuries to find this out; and many still refuse to learn the lesson. It must be left to a later chapter to dwell upon the service which the play and the playwright may render to the story-writer.

6. *The Novel*

It is no more exact to say that the novel is the father of the short-story than it is to allege, as did Bret Harte,[7] that the American short-story is " the germ of American

[7] *Cornhill Magazine,* July, 1899.

literature to come." To assert either is to assert too much. But it must appear to all that the short-story and the novel meet at more points than any other two forms of narration. Of course they owe much to each other, but certainly the novel has influenced the short-story more than the short-story has thus far helped the novel. But the critic a hundred years hence will scarcely so pronounce. Already the characteristics of the best short-story form are apparent in current novels — often to their advantage, sometimes to their hurt. The two must not come too close, however, lest each lose its individual savor.

Not only are the novel and the short-story more nearly alike than any other two fictional forms, but for this very reason the novel has more strongly influenced the modern short-story than has any other literary type, not excepting the drama. While the short-story is essentially by far the older, the novel came to its own long before the short-story was recognized as a distinct species. Irving, Poe and Hawthorne; Maupassant, Balzac and Mérimée; Stevenson, Barrie and Kipling; and all that brilliant Continental school that made luminous the literary history of the nineteenth century, drew inspiration and instruction from earlier novelists, more — incomparably more — than they ever did or could have done from all the writers of tales who preceded them. Upon the other hand, most of these and other nineteenth-century writers began the arduous climb of the novel-mountain by first essaying the scarcely less precipitous ascent of the short-story foothills.

7. *Other Literary Forms*

Doubtless, in greater or less degree all of the older literary forms have contributed to the short-story; but doubtless, too, those already adverted to have come more full-handed than any and all the others. The essay, for example, exhibits few points in common with the short-story, yet many short-stories (some of Hawthorne's, for instance, and some of Irving's tales) contain much essay material, while now and then an essay is cast in story form. The Spectator essay really embodied, now and again, so much narrative material as to make it a suggestive theme for study to-day. But all in all the kinship of the essay with the short-story is only that of a cousin.[8]

The lyric also has made its gift of direct personal appeal, and all poetry has set up standards of lofty thought, deep feeling and graceful expression. History, for its share, has given accuracy, while the photoplay has shed a clearer light on plot, setting and character.

8. *The Perfecters of the Short-Story*

A full study of this topic would involve too much space here,[9] but a few words may serve to point out the seven-league strides taken by story-writers during and since the second quarter of the nineteenth century.

In 1819 Irving published "Rip van Winkle"—gen-

[8] See *The Book of the Short Story,* Jessup and Canby, p. 17.
[9] For fuller discussions see the Introduction to *Representative American Short Stories,* Alexander Jessup, 1923.

erally, but not universally, admitted to be a short-story rather than a tale. In 1832 Poe published "Metzengerstein," and in 1842, writing on Hawthorne,[10] he impliedly claimed for the short-story the right to be regarded as a distinct species. Though more or less perfect short-stories had been produced at intervals for many centuries, Poe's keen criticism incited many to follow Irving, Hawthorne, and the critic himself, thus originating a distinctive type of American short-story.

In France, Nodier, Mérimée and Balzac — and in a less degree Gautier and Musset — were rendering much the same service for the French short-story, though on somewhat different lines.

Excepting the highly fantastic stories of E. T.W. Hoffman, in Germany, the modern short-story developed later elsewhere on the continent and in Great Britain than in France and in America, so that the honor of perfecting the present *genre* must be accorded to America, France and Germany — in the order named, if we consider the importance of the work produced and the clear working-theories evolved.

II. ITS PRESENT PLACE AND POWER

The short-story needs no apologist. It has won for itself an honorable and honored place among literary forms and, what is more valuable, in the public heart. Evidently it has come to stay, and to stay in a class by itself.

---

[10] *Graham's Magazine,* May, 1842.

1. *The Short-Story and the Novel*

Irving said that he found the short-story a more difficult form of composition than the novel [11]— though he never published a real novel.

A distinguished American critic concludes that " The work of the writer of the short-story differs from theirs (novelists') neither in quality nor in completeness; it differs only in magnitude. It involves, if possible, a firmer grasp of situations, a surer touch, a more sensitive feeling for dramatic values." [12]

It is the opinion of Professor Brander Matthews that, " Although as a form of fiction the Short-story is not inferior to the Novel, and although it is not easier, all things considered, yet its brevity makes its composition simpler for the 'prentice hand." [13]

In concluding his admirable brochure, *The Short Story,* [14] Mr. Henry Seidel Canby says:

" Except in one instance, which is the vivid expression of single incidents or detached movements in life, the Short Story is not to be chosen before the novel; but in its capacity for perfection of structure, for nice discrimination in means, and for a satisfying exposition of the full power of words, it is much superior to the novel, and can rank only below the poem. But the novel and the Short Story are distinct instruments, differently

[11] *Life and Letters,* Vol. II, p. 227.
[12] Hamilton W. Mabie, in the Introduction to *Masterpieces of Fiction.*
[13] *The Philosophy of the Short-Story* p. 51.
[14] *Yale Studies in English.*

designed, for diverse needs. And with such a point of view it is impossible not to grant to the latter a separate use and classification."

These opinions are representative, and indicate the position to which the short-story has attained in seventy-five years. Indeed, it may be said that there has grown up a clearer critical conception of the ideal short-story, and a more general agreement among experts as to its essential characteristics, than have yet been reached regarding the ideal novel. Naturally, attainment in the short-story form has been correspondingly higher among contemporary writers.

2. *Reasons for Popularity*

It is a different mood, perhaps even a different temperament, that prefers the short-story to the novel. The swift human appeal and the concise directness of the former suit it not only to our energetic and easily jaded modern spirit, but to our keener modern insight as well. We are less willing than formerly to have the obvious pointed out and the commonplace analyzed, even when these services are performed in a masterly manner. This, of course, is the mood of the busy reader, and of the languid or the impatient observer as well. The novel only will satisfy the desire for sustained observation.

As touching the popularity of the short-story the multiplication of popular magazines is at once a cause and an effect. The increasing demand for short-stories has encouraged new magazine ventures, resulting in a wider market for story-writers, and a decrease in the demand for novels. Naturally, so much writing means much poor writing; still, the tendency is upward, and magazine editors are becoming more and more critical of the stories offered to them, though it must be admitted that when called upon to choose between popularity and literary quality the present-day editor is still likely to choose popularity. Writers of genius in increasing numbers find the rewards of short-story writing attractive, and this alone accounts for a marked advance in quality. When quality advances, appreciation broadens. Furthermore, the growing love for art in all its forms stimulates interest in the short-story. The same artistic sense which in the public rejoices in the sharp clearness of the cameo-like story, and the delicate coloring of the fictive miniature, inspires the writer to finer work — and so public and author unite to perfect this fascinating art.

In seeking for the reasons that underlie the remarkable popularity of the short-story we must not overlook the spirit of play which abounds in a world so devoted to work as is ours. In the humor of the short-story, as in its puzzles, its breathless adventures, and its love appeals, millions take daily recreation, and thus turn aside to a life of fantasy that softens the hard life of fact.

3. *The Influence of the Short-Story*

This beneficent mission of fiction makes more contemptible the pandering viciousness of those writers who debase their gifts by presenting distorted views of life.

placing false values upon the things of experience, and picturing unclean situations — all for the sake of gain. However, only a very small percentage of stories presented to magazine editors are of such objectionable character; the great majority of fiction-writers are above these sordid temptations. The writer's search to-day is for reality and truth, and this responsibility he bears as nobly as could any other professional class. The public takes its short-stories seriously — even when the author is a humorist. Any manifest warping of truth is resented at once, so that even the farce and the dime shocker must *seem* to tell the truth.[15]

The influence of the short-story upon the novel has already been touched upon. Its power is even more evident in the style of the daily newspaper, which serves up fact as fiction — and, it is alleged, fiction as fact. In the reporter's parlance everything is a "story," and the newspaper follows as closely as possible the methods of the breezy short-story writer. It may be answered that our most vivid fictionists were themselves trained in the newspaper field. But the fact remains, whatever be cause and what effect. Even the contemporary essay, the travel sketch, and the hybrid magazine article, have nursed at the short-story bottle, and are sprightly "in precise proportion." Thus the latest literary form to come to its own is contributing generously to our literature and our life. In the words of Professor Albert E. Hancock, "it now holds chief attention and consumes

[15] See chapter on *Fact in Fiction.*

most energy." The most polished fictionists engage in its production, the most respected magazines make room for it in their pages, it is welcomed by a myriad readers, and vast commercial concerns are interested in its sale.

OUTLINE SUMMARY

I. THE RISE OF THE SHORT-STORY
  1. *The Story-Teller*
  2. *The Epic*
  3. *The Ancient and Medieval Tale*
  4. *The Sacred Books of the East*
  5. *The Drama*
  6. *The Novel*
  7. *Other Literary Forms*
  8. *The Perfecters of the Short-Story*

II. ITS PRESENT PLACE AND POWER
  1. *The Short-Story and the Novel*
  2. *Reasons for Popularity*
  3. *The Influence of the Short-Story*

PART I
THE NATURE OF THE
SHORT-STORY

Clear cut, with occasional plastic inspirations and moments of exquisite descriptive genius, Maupassant made himself the foremost master of the art of short-story writing in a group of writers who seemed to know instinctively the limitations and the resources of a literary form which exacts the nicest perceptions and the surest skill. He almost unerringly selected a single situation, related one or two characters vitally to it, suppressed all detail that did not contribute to portraiture, sketched a background with a few telling strokes, knit plot, character, situation, and denouement strongly together to secure unity of effect.— HAMILTON W. MABIE, *The Outlook*, April 25, 1908.

In the short-story of the first rank, power, skill, and invention combine to produce, with few materials, an effect similar in definiteness and intensity to that which lies within reach of the masters of fiction alone. It deals, as a rule, with an episode rather than a complete movement of experience; with a situation rather than with a series of events; with a single character rather than with a group; it must be condensed without sacrifice of shading or atmosphere; it must move swiftly to its climax, without any appearance of haste; it must omit the great mass of details, and yet leave nothing essential unsaid. It is not a study for a longer tale, nor is it a long story abbreviated; it is a work of art which has its own laws, its special qualities, its individual sources of charm; it must stand complete in itself.— HAMILTON W. MABIE, Introduction to *Masterpieces of Fiction.*

PART I

THE NATURE OF THE SHORT-STORY

CHAPTER I

WHAT IS A SHORT-STORY

Now a story is something more than incidents and descriptions. It is a definite thing. . . . It is such a reality that a man who reads it would carry away a definite impression.— F. HOPKINSON SMITH, quoted in Barrett's *Short Story Writing*.

A definition is a dangerous thing. The more vital and growing and resilient a thing is, the more difficult to fence it about, to fix its limitations by statute. The short-story formed itself experimentally; it was not invented. Poe and Hawthorne were heirs of all that had gone before. So we may arrive at an understanding of the short-story form rather by observation than by definition. This principle governs our whole inquiry.

Certain things, clearly, the short-story cannot be, and because these are most often the very things inexperienced writers produce and label as short-stories, we shall first inquire,

I. WHAT A SHORT-STORY IS NOT

But here a word of caution. To deny that a certain sort of literary composition is a short-story is not to

condemn it. It may be altogether admirable of its
kind. Emerson's mountain made a very pretty squirrel
track, but it couldn't crack a nut. It wasn't intended to.
If an author prefers to write something other than
short-stories, let him do so; he may write that one
thing better than any other has yet done it, but he
must not complain when he fails to sell his product as a
short-story. There may be a market for his wares,
but it is not the short-story market.

The greatest sources of misapprehension on this score
are — to imagine two illustrative cases — the contents
of a given volume of some famous author's collected
writings, and a copy of any popular magazine. The
young student of the short-story takes up either of these
miscellanies and finds, let us say, several types of ficti-
tious narrative, all admirable, all artistic, but only one
of which is really a short-story. Now, no one has explicitly labeled the sketch a sketch, the anecdote an anecdote, and the tale a tale, so the uninstructed reader may
mistake any or all for what their authors never designed
them to be, and what the editors knew perfectly well
that they were not — short-stories. Not all black-feath-
ered birds are ravens: to find a literary narrative in a
high-class magazine, signed by a famous author, does not
imply that it purports to be a short-story. What shall
we do, then? Simply press our inquiry as to what a
short-story is and what it is not, using our own judgment
when we come to decide upon the form best for our individual use. It is folly to ruin a delicate sketch or a
capital tale in order to meet a pedant's definition.

1. *The Short-Story Is Not a Condensed Novel*

Several popular magazines to-day publish complete novelettes monthly, which differ from novels only in their length, though both theme and method of handling are necessarily limited by the number of words permitted. Twenty-five thousand words is probably a fair average for these little novels — some longer, some shorter — while nowadays the full-grown novel runs from eighty to a hundred thousand words. Many are still shorter, whereas only a few reach the old ordinary length of one hundred and fifty thousand words and upward. The day of the two- and three-volume novel happily seems to be past.

But if the true novelette were compressed yet more — say to within half its present compass — it would still be a condensed novel and not a long short-story.[1] The real difference is in kind, not in length.

(a) *The short-story produces a singleness of effect denied to the novel.* In his essay, "Hawthorne's Tales,"[2] Poe writes as follows:

[1] The matter of nomenclature is always difficult when names have long been loosely used. There is one sort of so-called novel which in character is really only a long short-story. *The Port of Missing Men,* by Meredith Nicholson, and *The Filigree Ball,* by Anna Katharine Green, may serve as examples. This sort has scarcely any of the characteristics of the novel, and all of the nature of the short-story — except compression, both of plot and of scope. It lacks the breadth of the one without attaining to the concentration of the other. The greater number of "novels" published to-day are of this type — light, ephemeral, rapid-fire stories of plot, intended to while away four idle hours. Quite the same is true of most novelettes.

[2] *Graham's Magazine,* May, 1835.

"As it (the novel) cannot be read at one sitting, it deprives itself, of course, of the immense force derivable from totality. Worldly interests intervening during the pauses of perusal modify, annul or contract, in a greater or less degree, the impressions of the book. But simply cessation in reading would, of itself, be sufficient to destroy the true unity. In the brief tale,[3] however, the author is enabled to carry out the fullness of his intention, be it what it may. During the hour of perusal the soul of the reader is at the writer's control. There are no external or extrinsic influences — resulting from weariness or interruption.

"A skilful literary artist has constructed a tale. If wise, he has not fashioned his thoughts to accommodate his incidents; but having conceived, with deliberate care, a certain unique or single *effect* to be wrought out, he then invents such incidents — he then combines such events as may best aid him in establishing this preconceived effect. If his very initial sentence tend not to the out-bringing of this effect, then he has failed in his very first step. In the whole composition there should be no word written of which the tendency, direct or indirect, is not to the one pre-established design. And by such means, with such care and skill, a picture is at length painted which leaves in the mind of him who contemplates it with a kindred art a sense of the fullest satisfaction. The idea of the tale has been presented unblemished, because undisturbed;

---

[3] By "brief tale" Poe doubtless means what in this treatise is called uniformly the *short-story*.

and this is an end unattainable by the novel.[4] Undue brevity is just as exceptionable here as in the poem; but undue length is yet more to be avoided."

Growing out of this need for simplicity, for totality of effect, is this further demand upon the short-story:

(b) *It must differ from the novel in scope and in structure.* Speaking broadly, the novel is expansive, the short-story intensive. The great novelists sought " the all-embracing view " of life, the short-story writer looks upon a special — and often an exaggerated — character, incident, or experience. The canvas on which the true novelist paints is broader, accommodating more characters, who stand out upon a larger and more varied background. Thus in the real novel the reader is enabled " to see life whole," in Matthew Arnold's expressive phrase. Such a broad fictional outlook was Balzac's, rather than Poe's. Not any number of short-stories, however comprehensive and however skilfully related, could compass the universal life-record essayed by Balzac in his *Comédie Humaine.*

The plot of the novel is often complicated by episodes and contributory sub-plots, whereas the short-story exploits a single predominating incident, to which the

[4] Certain novels also leave a single compact impression upon the mind. Compare " The Fall of the House of Usher"—which leaves a weird impression of a decaying family come to its final disaster — with *Romola,* whose general impression is simply the degeneration of Tito Melema. Both create unified impressions, but the novel also presents a broad cross-section of life. The unity of the one is composed of an infinite and wonderfully organized diversity, while that of the other is simple. The one is a diamond of many facets, the other a pearl.

other incidents — few, if any — must be subordinate and directly contributory.[5]

Finally, the greater canvas and the more involved plot of the novel naturally mean a more leisurely movement than is possible in the short-story, though many sensational novels of the romantic type (not typical novels, and certainly not models in any sense) crowd incident upon incident with tremendous speed. But usually the realistic novelist takes plenty of time to make his characters philosophize on questions germane to the period, or to advocate a cause, or to expose a condition.

Not so the short-story. Since it must " move swiftly to its climax," all its mechanism is simplified and divested of clogging parts. At first this necessity for compression may seem to hamper the writer, but in reality it offers greater freedom. Themes too slight for the sustained spirit of the novel, light bits of fantasy, intense but brief incidents of life, all make admirable grist for the short-story mill. Love, which permeates nearly all novels, whether romantic or realistic, is not a necessary accessory of the short-story. The details of life, character and setting, which the novelist paints in with minute attention, the short-story writer delineates with a few swift strokes — which must be all the more deft because they are so few.

Thus, in its singleness of effect, in its more minute

---

[5] In his interesting *Philosophy of the Short-Story*, p. 16, Prof. Brander Matthews says: " A Short-story deals with a single character, a single event, a single emotion, or the series of emotions called forth by a single situation." This is a suggestive but extreme statement.

scope, and in its simplicity of structure, the short-story
proves itself to be something quite different from a mere
condensed novel.

2. *The Short-Story Is Not an Episode*

We have seen that the novels of the eighteenth lacked
the plotted unity of the works of the later century —
that they differed from the tale chiefly in length and in
the introduction of more episodes. Excerpt from *Rod-
erick Random, The Vicar of Wakefield,* or *Tom Jones,*
almost any one of the complete episodes with which they
abound, and the extract might be called a short tale. Do
likewise with many a complete episode from some modern novels and you have the same. In neither case,
however, would the episode exhibit the plot, the sense
of coming to a point, of ending up, which is necessary
to the short-story. To make a first-class short-story
longer would be to spoil it. The reader *feels* the conclusion and would not turn the page of the magazine
to see if there is anything more. While the episode fits
in with the rest of the novel, into which it was paren-
thetically inserted to illustrate some phase of character
or of conduct, the short-story is *not* meant to dovetail
into a novel which is to appear later.

To be sure, certain short-stories — notably detective
stories nowadays — are linked in series; but in each part
the story comes to a full stop, a satisfying resolution —
to use a musical figure. The connection with the other
stories of the series is in the detective, perhaps, or in the
lay expert, not in any relation of the plots.

3. *The Short-Story Is Not a Scenario, or Synopsis*

This is not very different from saying what has been said — that the short-story is not a condensed novel. Yet there is a distinction which a word will suffice to emphasize.

In plotting out a play or a novel the author may make a scenario. Or a synopsis may be made after the work has been completed. But such a skeleton would lack red blood as surely as it would be awkward and un-interesting, if not actually repellent. The play of char-acter, the pungency of conversation, the photography of description, would be absent. Many of the tales of the *Decameron* suffer for lack of these qualities. Compres-sion is essential, but it will not do to squeeze a story to death.

4. *It Is Not a Biography*

This would seem to be obvious, yet every editor re-ceives a surprising number of life-stories, complete from birth to burial, with no central incident, no unified ef-fect, to justify their writing. " Johnny Shark " [6] is such a biography — albeit the life of a diverting fish. " Marse Chan," by Thomas Nelson Page, one of the finest of our modern fictions, is a fictive biography rather than a short-story—which contains a plot.

Here I must again emphasize the importance of *not* concluding that a tale or a fictive biography may not be of the highest literary quality, and absorbingly interest-

[6] From *The Strife of the Sea,* by T. Jenkins Hains

ing, because it is not a real short-story. Stevenson's "Will o' the Mill" must be generally considered as quite the equal of "Marse Chan," yet it is not purely, or even chiefly, a short-story—magnificent work of fiction as it is: it is a sketch done in short-story form.

5. *It Is Not a Mere Sketch*

Sketch-qualities many admirable short-stories possess, but not *mere* sketch-qualities—short-stories are more than sketches. A fictional sketch is a picture, usually a condensed picture, of a character or characters caught at a highly interesting time. It tells no complete story, it has no plot. The sketch may suggest a story, but it does not narrate that story. Sometimes it is a picture of a character in a highly suggestive setting, as that of an old man visiting the grave of his soldier son. Again, it is a picture of wonderment, of mirth, of hatred, or any dramatic emotion whatsoever. But, let it be repeated, in the sketch the emotion, the setting, the relation of the characters, the personality sketched does not develop into a story, but remains a picture. Whatever movement there may be in the sketch, therefore, is not plot-action.

Just so, whatever value word-sketches of character and atmosphere may possess—and many do have an incomparable value as impressionistic records, as suggestive studies—they are not short-stories, for in them nothing happens; they have neither essential beginning nor necessary ending; they leave no single completed impression; they lack the effect of totality on which Poe so constantly insisted. What more exquisite piece of descriptive prose narrative does the English language hold than Lafcadio Hearn's " Chita "? And it perfectly illustrates the fictional sketch which is not a short-story.

6. *The Short-Story Is Not a Tale*

Once more the matter of nomenclature raises a difficulty. The terms " tale " and " short-story " are commonly used interchangeably. Poe so uses them, Mr. Henry James loosely refers to novels as tales, and Professor Brander Matthews now and then indulges a free transfer of the expressions. Indeed, it will not do to be too precise here, for the tale readily drifts over into the short-story, and the latter into the former. However, for the purposes of a treatise of this scope it seems necessary to make between these close kindred a discrimination which is more than academic, for to deny the distinction entirely is not to class the short-story as a separate literary species.

Something concerning the tale — particularly as to its origin — has been said in the Historical Introduction to this volume, but now we need a definition:

A tale is a simple narrative, usually short, having actually no plot, developing no essential change in the relation of the characters, and depending for its interest upon incidents rather than upon plot and the revelation of character.

Here is an attempt at a grouping of

KINDS OF TALE [7]

(Classified as to Purpose)

Didactic	Fable Parable Allegory Moral
Entertaining	Sporting Adventure Strange Experience Humorous
Either Didactic or Entertaining	Myth Legend Anecdote Travel Historical True Story

Whether designed to teach a lesson or to tell a story for entertainment, all of the foregoing general themes, when cast in the form of the tale, will be found to be simple narrative. Fundamentally they do not conform to Poe's

[7] This classification must not be understood as implying that all short fictions on these general themes are tales and not short-stories.

important law, that the short-story should march in all its parts directly and swiftly toward a single impression. The tale admits of digressions, moral or amusing reflections, and loosely-connected episodes *ad libitum*. The reader feels it to be, not a skilfully organized and compact unity, but a mere incident taken out of a larger experience, more of which of similar kind might be related if the narrator would.

Now it must be borne constantly in mind that the magazines to-day are printing many excellent tales, which touch in one, two, or three points the peculiar *genre* of the short-story, and in proportion as they do this more fully they become less the tale and more the short-story, until sometimes the " middle wall of partition " becomes like a hair — too thin to split.

The best examples of tales which consciously seek the methods and the effects which we now credit to the short-story, are those of Washington Irving. Here and there, too, the same may be said of Chaucer's poetic *Canterbury Tales* and the stories of Boccaccio. In his Introduction to the *Tales of a Traveler,* Irving says: " For my part, I consider a story merely as a frame upon which to stretch my materials. It is the play of thought, and sentiment, and language; the weaving in of characters, lightly, yet expressively delineated; the familiar and faithful exhibition of scenes in common life; and the half-concealed vein of humor that is often playing through the whole — these are among what I aim at, and upon which I felicitate myself in proportion as I think I succeed."

In that exposition of his art, Irving erected the first critical half-way house between the tale and the short-story.

Mr. Henry Seidel Canby [8] has thus summed up this distinction :

" It might be asserted that what is loosely called the modern Short Story seems to differ from the old tale by a very scientific adaptation of means to end, which end may be called vividness, and by a structure which, in its nice proportions and potentiality for adequate expression, is a more excellent instrument than anything the old tale can show; and by an interest in situation, as a rule, rather than in simple incident. Also through the source, which is an impression or impressions, usually of a situation; and the purpose, which is to fitly convey these impressions as well as to tell a story. ' Ruth ' [9] will do very well as an example of the tale, ' The Purloined Letter ' [10] as a tale done into Short Story form, and ' Markheim,' [11] ' A Coward,' [12] or ' Without Benefit of Clergy,' [13] for the typical Short Story. If it is necessary to say what characterizes all of the shorter stories now being written, I should suggest that it is an attempt at greater vividness, and this attempt is made largely through those practices in composition which the endeavor to convey fitly an impression has brought into common use."

[8] Introduction to Jessup and Canby's *The Book of the Short Story.*
[9] Bible.
[10] Poe.
[11] Stevenson.
[12] Maupassant.
[13] Kipling.

II. WHAT A SHORT-STORY IS

Having seen in what respects other narrative forms —
the novel, the episode, the scenario or synopsis, the biography, the sketch, and the tale — differ from the short-
story, it will be a much briefer task to assemble its positive qualities.

The true short-story is marked by seven characteristics:

1. *A Single Predominating Incident.*
2. *A Single Preëminent Character.*
3. *Imagination.*
4. *Plot.*
5. *Compression.*
6. *Organization.*
7. *Unity of Impression.*

All of these either have been discussed in the negative
exposition or will be touched upon later. Perhaps, then,
it is time to attempt a definition:

*A Short-Story is a brief, imaginative narrative, un-
folding a single predominating incident and a single
chief character,* [14] *by means of a plot, the details of which
are so selected, and the whole treatment so organized,
that a single impression is produced.*

In proportion as the short-story embodies and combines its seven parts artistically, that is to say harmo-

---

[14] Note the word *chief.* When two "chief" characters are
strictly coördinate, as is rarely the case, the exception will
merely sustain this element in the definition.

niously and effectively, it is great. Not all great short-stories are great at all points. Though no unnecessary point should be included, and no important factor omitted, still its brilliant qualities may atone for its defective parts. Thus criticism must be flexible and unprejudiced. Suppose the London publishers had declined Dickens's novels because they exhibited grave defects!

Do not forget that the whole is greater than the sum of all its parts. The completed result must possess a spirit all its own, it must be almost a living personality. And who will analyze *that* for us and lay bare its vital secret? At every stage of our inquiry we must feel how impossible it is to saw up a story and find anything more than lumber, or to nail and glue its parts together and have aught other than a grinning wooden clown. The story, the yarn, is the big thing. Unless the writer have a story to tell the telling of it is foolish contradiction.

" But "— I hear some young writer say — " if the short-story is *not* all this and *is* all that, I am in despair. How shall I work with freedom within the bounds of so many fences? "

For reassuring reply look at the painter of pictures. Having passed through the times of thou-shalt-not and thou-shalt, he is all the freer to express his ideals with individuality. The body of rules he has learned is not so much with him consciously while he works, as that *it has formed his standards and cultivated his ability to criticise himself.* Beyond that, rules have no value, and, when slavishly adhered to, produce wooden results.   The definitions in this chapter are merely analyses—they are *not* recipes for "how to write a story."

OUTLINE SUMMARY

I. WHAT A SHORT-STORY IS NOT
   1. *Not a Condensed Novel*
      (*a*) Singleness of Effect
      (*b*) Differs in Scope and Structure
   2. *Not an Episode*
   3. *Not a Scenario*
   4. *Not a Biography*
   5. *Not a Mere Sketch*
   6. *Not a Tale*

II. WHAT A SHORT-STORY IS
   Seven characteristics, and definition.

QUESTIONS AND EXERCISES FOR CLASS OR INDIVIDUAL STUDY

1. Should an editor decline to publish a brief story solely because it does not conform to the standards of short-story form as set forth in such a treatise as this? Give reasons supporting your answer.

2. Do you think that all writers of technically perfect short-stories are conscious of their art, or do some intuitively conform to good usage?

3. Does a knowledge of rules help or hinder an original genius? Show how.

4. Set down the points of likeness and of difference between the short-story and the novel.

5. What is a picaresque novel? An episode? (See dictionary.)

6. Is there any difference in method between *The Vicar of Wakefield* and *The Memoirs of Sherlock Holmes?*

7. Is Irving's "The Legend of Sleepy Hollow" a tale, or a short-story? "Rip Van Winkle"? Why?

8. Define the terms: (a) didactic, (b) a fable, (c) a parable, (d) an allegory, (e) a myth, (f) a legend, (g) an anecdote. (See Dictionary.)

9. Is it always possible to put into words the final impression of a short-story? Illustrate.

10. Write (a) a brief fairy story, (b) a parable, (c) a fable, (d) an anecdote, (e) a tale in imitation of a myth.

11. Write a tale based upon (a) an adventure, (b) or travel, (c) or a legend, (d) or a psychic experience.

12. Write a sketch showing (a) a phase of character, (b) or a bit of home life, (c) or an emotion.

NOTE: Just now, do not bother about the later instructions of this volume, but write according to your present standards. All written work should be preserved, so that rewriting and development may be called for in connection with later study.

NOTES ON THE SHORTER FICTIONAL FORMS: Once in a large number of instances an episode—an illustrative story introduced within a longer story—may be said to be a short-story in form, as is Sir Walter Scott's *Wandering Willie's Tale,* from the novel *Redgauntlet,* diffuse though it is. However, it is almost universally true that episodes take the form of the expanded anecdote or the tale. Those that approximate the short-story in form were, of course, not written *as* short-stories but to amplify parts of the longer story.

A simple illustration will help us to distinguish between the typical short-story and the sketch, and the short-story and the tale. Here are a watch, a chain and an engraved "charm." The charm is engraved with the picture of an oriental monarch riding over his prostrate subjects. It suggests autocracy and fanatical servility, but it tells no complete story. It may stand for the sketch. The chain has many curious links of varying size, but cut it or lengthen it and it would still be a chain. It has connection and variety, but no organization. That suggests the tale. The watch, however, is all organization. Wheels turn in every direction, hidden springs exert their quiet force, and levers move hither and yon—all with the purpose of directing the hands as the maker designed them to move: inevitably toward the appointed hour. That is the short-story.

CHAPTER II

Narrow as are its limits and exacting as are its requirements, the short-story holds up as many kinds of mirrors as life demands for the reflection of its numberless aspects and experiences. It affords, too, ample opportunity for subtle and penetrating analysis; for close and merciless study of morbid temperaments or vitally sympathetic portraitures of great natures contending with tragic conditions; for the segregation of a bit of significant experience and a finished presentation of its aspects and effects; for the detachment of a single figure from the dramatic movement, and a striking sketch of its features and gestures; for the dissection of a motive so searching and skilful that its deepest roots are laid bare; for effectiveness in bringing a series of actions into clear light in a sudden and brief crisis, and telling a complete story by suggestion; for the delicate impressionism which by vividness or charm of phrase and diffusion of atmosphere, magically conveys the sense of landscape; for the touch of humor concentrated on a person or an incident, and for the touch of tragedy resting like a finger of fate on an experience or a character.— HAMILTON W. MABIE, *Stories New and Old.*

It is as impossible as it would be useless to compile a descriptive catalogue of all the kinds of short-story. He who does not recognize the fundamental kinds can scarcely produce anything worthy of the name. Besides, kinds of story may mate in unsuspected variety — much to their profit. The army-story may be breathed upon by the spirit of sport and yet tickle the reader to tears. As to general sorts, either realism or romance consists with pretty nearly every kind of story; so do farce, comedy, tragedy, melodrama, and the tones that sound between; while love will consort with almost all known varieties. Thus these broad types must be regarded as *general spirits,* rather than individual species.

The following grouping — by no means exhaustive — may serve to stimulate the writer to invent fresh combinations of motive, scope and setting. I may say in passing that the various kinds in large measure apply to the sketch, the tale, and the novel quite as closely as to the short-story.

A SHORT-STORY CLASSIFICATION [1]

	Children	for Children for Adults
I. *Stories Based on Types of Humanity.*	Youth	School College Adventure Start in Life
	Women	Home and Family Love
	Men	Politics War Adventure

[1] Whitcomb, in *The Study of a Novel,* appendix, differentiates over two hundred "types of prose fiction," without classifying them, however.

2. *Based on the Moral Nature.*
- Character
  - Crisis
  - Deterioration
  - Development
  - Revelation
- Motive
- Problem
- Religious

3. *Based on Occupations.*
- Labor
- Trades
- Business
- Professions
  - Learned
  - Arts
  - Science
    - Real
    - Pseudo
- Army and Navy
- Recreations
  - Travel
  - Sports and Games
  - Theatre

4. *Based on Locality.*
- Dialect
- Country
- City
- Sectional
- National
- Foreign
- International

5. *Based on Wonder.*
{
Fantastic
Weird
Horror
Ghost
Occult
Psychic
Detective
Adventure
}

6. *Based on Social Classes.*
{
Rich
Society
Middle
Poor
Lower
Criminal
}

7. *Based on the Emotions.*
{
Love
Friendship
Heroism
Hate
Jealousy
Revenge, etc.
}

QUESTIONS AND EXERCISES FOR CLASS OR INDIVIDUAL STUDY.

1. (a) Select at least three short-stories from current issues of magazines and tell to what kinds they belong. (b) Point out the characteristics which led you to your decision.

2. Which of the stories, if any, showed marks of more than one kind of story?

3. Would they be helped or marred by conforming more closely to a single type?

4. (a) Try to add several kinds of short-stories to the classification given in this chapter. (b) Criticise the classification.

5. Construct at least five combinations from the foregoing list, thus: A character-trades-comedy; a children's-adventure-fairy story.

6. Which of the five seems most promising in material? Which next?

7. Draw up a short plan for such a story.

8. From memory—what kind of stories does Kipling generally write? W. W. Jacobs? "O. Henry"? Mary Wilkins Freeman? Henry James? "Anthony Hope"? "Mark Twain"?

9. Name your favorite short-story writer and tell the sort of stories he or she writes.

10. Why do you like that particular sort?

11. What kinds of stories predominate in the magazines nowadays?

12. Does this seem to you to be a bad or a good sign, and why?

13. Examine three or four issues each of three widely varying magazines and try, in three short sentences, to state the kinds of stories that predominate in the several magazines.

14. What kind of stories does John Galsworthy usually write? Edith Wharton? Margaret Deland? Scott Fitzgerald? Alice Brown? Richard Washburn Child? James Oliver Curwood? Fannie Hurst? Joseph Hergesheimer? Octavus Roy Cohen? Will Levington Comfort? Melville Davisson Post? Select four for your answer.

PART II

THE STRUCTURE OF THE
SHORT-STORY

In literary as in all other art, structure is all-important, felt, or painfully missed, everywhere — that architectural conception of work, which foresees the end in the beginning and never loses sight of it, and in every part is conscious of all the rest, till the last sentence does but, with undiminished vigor, unfold and justify the first — a condition of literary art, which . . . I shall call the necessity of *mind* in style.— WALTER PATER.

I do not believe in hard and fast rules for the construction of stories. Methods of work must vary with individual temperaments. My own way of work naturally seems to me the most logical, but I realize that this is a question which each writer must decide for himself. Personally, I find it necessary to know the general course of a story, and above all to know the end before I can begin it.— ARLO BATES.

PART II

THE STRUCTURE OF THE SHORT-STORY

CHAPTER I

CHOOSING A THEME

First of all (I would say), my young friend, you should choose a truly American subject. All the critics say that this is essential. Americanism is what the age demands; and it must be produced even if we have to invent a machine to do it. Do not go abroad for your theme. Do not trifle with the effete European nightingale or ramble among Roman ruins. Take a theme from the great Republic; something that comes close to the business and bosoms of the Democracy; something unconventional and virile. Take, for example, the Clam — the native, American, free-born, little-neck Clam. We all know it. We all love it. Deal originally and vividly with the Clam.— HENRY VAN DYKE, *Some Reflections on the Magazines:* a humorous address delivered before the Periodical Publishers' Association of America, Washington, D. C., April 17, 1904.

The short-story is a vital force in the modern world, but more especially in the life of the American people. Multiform and complex as are the interests of our land, this latest form of literature is adequate to their expression; and we have only begun the development of its infinite resources. There are no limits to the range of theme suitable to the short-story, except only propriety

41

and bigness. One might fill volumes in attempting to name the unending varieties of life, and their infinite interplay, which offer inviting subjects for the interpreter's pen. Subtle analysis of motive, swift synthesis of character, merciless dissection of temperament, brilliant portraiture of types, humorous sketching of crudities, satirical thrusts at foibles, tragic march of fatality, delicate tracing of fancy, sure unfolding of emotions, robust depicting of achievement — all the free and unmeasured sweep of a myriad-sided nation dwelling in a young land of swiftly-changing color comes to the American story-artist, clamoring for delineation. There is no lack of fresh themes. (See IMPORTANT NOTE, p. 50.)

But from this embarrassment of riches how does the writer select a theme? Doubtless, no two just alike; yet all methods of selection may roughly be included under either of two. For some writers

1. *The Theme Is Born Spontaneously*

That is, it may just " pop into your mind." Now and then this experience is so vivid as to amount to the joy of a great discovery. You may be doing anything or nothing, waking or sleeping, alert or apathetic, when suddenly a spirit arises before you from nowhere and cries: " Sir, Madame, I am a Story. Write me up!" Then there is no rest until the story is shaped and spread upon paper.

Naturally, a well-furnished mind is the most likely to produce story-germs in this manner, hence all the pother in the succeeding chapter about "gathering materials." It would be an interesting psychological study to try to determine just how far this spontaneous birth of a theme is the result of suggestion from without, operating upon the mass of materials already a part of the author's mental, moral, and emotional equipment.

At other times we may readily trace the inspiration to its source-spring. A look, a word dropped in conversation, an incident on the street, a paragraph in the newspaper, an apt retort, an emotional mood, a clever sentence in a book — from any of a thousand and one points of contact may flash the gleam of conviction: There is a story in this!

Again, the germ will develop more slowly — much more slowly — and months, even years, elapse before the tiny suggestion becomes a full-fledged story-theme, ready for elaboration. Wise is that writer who patiently awaits the hour of full-coming before attempting to write; for with the fresh, inspiring, self-born theme fully matured in the mind, and — I want to add — in the heart, half the battle is won.

But inspiration is not always on call. Who was it that likened his mind to a mule which habitually ran when he wished it to stop and as regularly balked when he longed for it to run? So, if a story is due at the editor's on Tuesday after next, and no obliging theme has presented itself, or those which have applied have not been found worthy, then the author has no other recourse than to seek out a theme.

2. *The Theme Sought Out*

Here invention is put to it for originality. Writers of wide acceptance have freely confessed that they have driven a host of ideas from Dan to Beersheba until one has yielded up the coveted theme. Then the seven sources of material [1] are tried in order — and seventy-seven others, in disorder. Still no theme. Every possible motive, every impossible emotion, every conceivable situation, every inconceivable complication — all tried and all pronounced " stale, flat and unprofitable." At last (why is the head more inventive when under a hat in the open air?) a walk abroad brings the decision to a focus: the theme is found!

" I know one writer," says George W. Cable, " who even for a short story has sat for weeks in feline patience and tension at the mouse-hole of his constructive powers, knowing only that the inspiration was in there and had to come out." [2]

The author's brain is like a magician's top hat, into which he puts all manner of things only to take out, for the delight of an audience (not always large or select, but always worthy of study) a store of altogether surprising things, altogether transformed.[3] " The Piece of String " (Maupassant), " The Gold Bug " (Poe), " A

[1] See the next chapter.
[2] *Afterthoughts of a Story-Teller, North American Review,* January, 1894.
[3] Naturally, the writer's purpose in telling a story — whether to please, instruct, chastise, tickle the public, or just to express something worthy of expresssion — will bear strongly upon his theme selection. See p. 284.

Church Mouse " (Mary Wilkins Freeman), and " The Leather Funnel " (Doyle), are not only clever titles of stories drawn from master necromancers' hats, but, as titles, indications of the ideas that may have suggested the stories. How fascinating it would be if each of a dozen well-loved writers would give us the intimate life-history of his best fiction, from inspiration down to publisher's check; yes, and through the years afterward, when its grip upon the readers had surely yet impalpably drawn them to open up their heart of hearts in confession, in thanks, in protest, in — what not!

3. *Themes Barred*

Since nearly all the short-stories that attain to print are published in newspapers and periodicals, it would seem that an author who is anxious to see his story in type should consider the limitations set by the public — the real masters of the editor. Yet, on various pleas authors persist in offering for publication stories on themes entirely unsuited to publication in any periodical of general circulation. Occasionally one is accepted, either by mistake or from sheer determination to print the story because it is " good stuff," however Mrs. Grundy may view its subject. But the doubtful theme usually has but little chance with an editor.

Only a general grouping of subjects which are taboo can be attempted here.

(a) *Trite Themes.* Hackneyed subjects now and then are treated in so original a manner as to bring the whole story above the commonplace level, but that is a performance too unusual for even a genius to dally with often. Editors and public tired long ago of the poor boy whose industry at last brought him the hand of his employer's daughter; the pale-faced, sweet-eyed young thing whose heroism in stamping out a fire enabled her to pay off the mortgage; the recovery of the missing will; the cruel step-mother; answering a prayer which has been overheard; the strange case of mistaken identity; honesty rewarded; a noble revenge; a child's influence; and so on to a long-drawn-out end. Naturally, nothing but a fair acquaintance with the short-stories of the last two decades, together with a nice sense of values, will save the writer from choosing trite subjects. I know of no printed list of hackneyed themes; the surest teachers are common sense, a wide reading, a friendly critic, and the printed rejection slip.

(b) *Improper Themes*. The buyer of a book may know for a certainty whether it discusses matters which he prefers his children should not read — the reviewer, or his friends, or his book-seller, will tell him. But this is rarely so when he buys a magazine. If he has subscribed for it, he has bought twelve cats in a bag and he has a right to expect that they should prove to be of similar parentage. If he buys a single copy, nothing but the titles, the authors' names, and the reputation of the magazine can guide his selection. Now it is this very question of reputation that bars certain themes from certain magazines, and it is quite as important for the writer to recognize these magazine reputations as it is for the reader.[4]

It is not for me to decide as to whether the short-story should deal with the intimate subjects of self and sex. Some of the most effective French stories handle these topics with .utmost freedom, and certainly it requires some bravery to say certain needful things in the form of fiction; but the better sort of American magazine handles sex themes with restraint, leaving clinical subjects to the "frank" modern novelist. True, a theme of great and serious intimacy may be treated with frankness and yet not give offense, while a conventional subject may be handled with nasty suggestiveness. The magazines that will accept the former sort are few, but unmistakably high class; those that print the latter are few and—unspeakable. One thing is quite intolerable: to treat a "broad" subject with levity.

Speaking to this subject, Dr. Frederic M. Bird says:

"Then there is the improper tale, which is of two classes. In one the author means to be bad, and in most cases goes about it delicately: in the other, ladies of the highest character write, from the purest motives, to expose the evils of free love, or the wickedness of men, or the dangers to which working girls are exposed, or some other abuse of sexual attractions or affections. The public, which takes less account of intentions than

[4] See Part IV, chap. ii.

of results, is apt to merge these in one common con-
demnation, confounding the salacious with that which
is meant to be merely monitory." [5]

(c) *Polemic Themes*. The novel may freely take up
the cudgel in defense of a sect, a party, a cult, or a
" crankism," but the short-story writer had better avoid
polemics. " Genius will triumph over most obstacles,
and art can sugar-coat an unwelcome pill; but in nineteen
cases out of twenty the story which covers an apology for
one doctrine or an attack upon the other has no more
chance (with the periodicals) than if it were made up of
offensive personalities." [6]

(d) *Unfamiliar Themes*. By this I mean themes with
which the author is not on intimate terms. The number
of writers who fly from familiar subjects to themes they
know not of, is legion. The beginner rushes in where
genius fears to tread. If you are really anxious not to
waste your time, don't attempt too much. Time spent on
studying your subject will come back with compound interest when you actually write. Find your own field.
Cultivate every square inch of it. Don't be tempted to
try the field next door without first finding out all about
it. It is necessary to be interested in your theme, but distinguish between superficial curiosity and an interest
that is genuine. The stay-at-home cannot write battle
scenes — usually. The recluse cannot depict society-
life — usually. You may be the exception, but the

[5] *Lippincott's,* Nov., 1894.
[6] *Magazine Fiction,* Frederic M. Bird, *Lippincott's,* Nov., 1894.

chances are that you are not. It is better to write well of what you know than badly of what you do not know. Some things you can imagine, some things you cannot. Don't confuse the two. One of the most damning criticisms of the editorial office is — "this writer doesn't know his field."

OUTLINE SUMMARY

CHOOSING A THEME

1. *The Theme Born Spontaneously*
2. *The Theme Sought Out*
3. *Themes Barred*
    - (*a*) Trite
    - (*b*) Improper
    - (*c*) Polemic
    - (*d*) Unfamiliar

QUESTIONS AND EXERCISES FOR CLASS OR INDIVIDUAL STUDY

1. Extemporaneous. Set down as many themes as "pop into your mind" in ten minutes. (Naturally, you must not expect startlingly original ideas to bloom in this way.)

2. Select two of these and perfect the statement of them in not more than a sentence or two each, preserving them for use in connection with the chapters on plot.

3. Examine the chains of ideas to discover, if possible, what gave rise to the themes.

4. Make a list of themes which seem to you to be hackneyed.

5. Have you seen any of these used lately? Where?

6. Select one hackneyed theme from any magazine or story-collection.

7. Is it well handled?

8. If possible, show how a fresher treatment would make it more readable.

9. Does the moral impropriety of a theme consist in the theme itself or rather in its handling? Discuss.

10. Make a list of polemic themes which seem to you unsuited to the short-story form. Be prepared to give your reasons in each instance.

11. Set down a theme for a story that came to you from a photoplay, but do not imitate the theme of the moving picture.

IMPORTANT NOTE: The word "theme" has both a popular and a technical meaning. Popularly, it means *subject, that which is written or spoken about;* and in this sense it is used in this chapter. Considered technically, however, the theme of a short-story is more specific. It is *the gist of the plot, the condensed argument, the subject-idea, of the story;* out of the theme the plot is to grow. (See pp. 72-3). For example, the theme of Maupassant's *The Necklace* might be stated as: *How a poor but socially ambitious woman mortgaged ten years of her life to redeem the loss of a borrowed necklace—with an amazing outcome.* When so understood, the formulation of a short-story theme becomes a vital matter to the writer, for the ability to build an effective plot is largely the result of being able to conceive of, and to state briefly and clearly, the essential basis of the story.

Some themes—called "thesis-themes"—contain only the seed of the story proper, the idea that is later to be exemplified in the story. Thus, the thesis-theme of Stevenson's *A Lodging for the Night* is: *Every man has his own code of honor, warped though it may be;* but all the real invention would lie ahead for the author who first conceived his story in this form—as some authors actually do. So when the story-germ comes to the writer in such a general form, his first task is to develop it into workable shape.

While the plot-germ comes to some writers as a partially or fully complete theme, to others it comes as a dramatic "situation" —which is explained in a note on page 92.

CHAPTER II

Of an eminent master in eloquence and letters this is said: "He habitually fed himself with any kind of knowledge which was at hand. If books were at his elbow, he read them; if pictures, engravings, gems were within reach, he studied them; if nature was within walking distance, he watched nature; if men were about him, he learned the secrets of their temperaments, tastes, and skills; if he were on shipboard, he knew the dialect of the vessel in the briefest possible time; if he traveled by stage, he sat with the driver and learned all about the route, the country, the people, and the art of his companion; if he had a spare hour in a village in which there was a manufactory, he went through it with keen eyes, and learned the mechanical processes used in it."— HAMILTON W. MABIE, *Essays on Books and Culture.*

The writer is first of all a citizen of the world, with eyes alert to explore its delights, its sorrows, and its mysteries. No other ever has a yarn to spin. Next, he turns his gaze inward. Lastly, he studies books. If you must omit one of these three processes, let it be the last.

Once convinced that somewhere in you are a theme, a story, and the spirit of a story-teller, the first step would seem to be simply the telling of the story. Logically, yes; practically, no. To do so would be to ignore the fact that skilful story-telling is now a fine art, and badly-told stories had better remain untold — as they generally remain unprinted. Before giving forth, you must prepare by taking in, even if that preparation should be quite unconscious.

The general question of the author's preparation for his work must be discussed in succeeding chapters,[1] but it should be said here that a primary requisite for successful authorship is the fixed habit of both training and furnishing the mind for the author's work. All things must be looked at with an eye to their possible literary use, so that daily life may become a daily storing up of materials, whether with a single story in view or merely to enrich the treasure house against the day when some chosen theme will call forth its utmost resources. So bear in mind, in all that follows, that your gathering will have either a particular or a general object.

In this process the first and longest step is

1. *Observation*

Get the facts. If you can, get them at first hand. They will hit you harder, and, through you, hit your readers harder, if you have gone straight to the original for your knowledge. Ruskin took a common rock-crystal and saw hidden within its stolid heart a world of interest. Thoreau sat so still in the shadowy woods that birds and insects came and opened up their secret lives to his eye. Preyer for three years studied the life of

[1] Part III.

his babe and so became an authority upon the child-
mind. Sir Walter Scott, in preparing to describe Guy
Denzil's cave, in *Rokeby*, observed " even the peculiar
little wild flowers and herbs that accidentally grew round
and on the side of a bold crag." When Lockhart laughingly wondered at this minuteness of study, the Wizard
replied that " in nature herself no two scenes were exactly alike, and that whoever copied truly what was
before his eyes, would possess the same variety in his
descriptions, and exhibit apparently an imagination as
boundless as the range of nature in the scenes he recorded; whereas — whoever trusted to imagination,
would soon find his own mind circumscribed, and con-
tracted to a few favorite images." [2]

" Whoever has done literary work," says Arlo Bates,[3]
" is likely to have discovered how constantly the literary
mind must be on the alert. The daughters of the horse-
leech that in the Scriptures are said continually to cry
' Give! Give! ' are less insatiable than is the greedy
pen of the professional writer. Like the grave, it has
never enough. He who makes literature a profession
must take for his model the barnacle at high tide. As
that busy and tireless unpleasantness grasps ceaselessly
with finger-like tentacles, so the mind of the writer must
be always reaching out — grasping, grasping, grasping
— until the accumulation of ideas, of facts, of impressions, with the realization that this is literary material,
becomes a second nature."

[2] Lockhart's *Life of Scott*, Vol. IV, p. 20.
[3] *Talks on Writing English*, p. 147.

And Professor Genung has given us this:

"The spirit of observation, as applied to the world in general, outer and inner, is practically identical with what is called . . . the scientific spirit in the large sense, with all the enthusiasm, the sense of values, the accuracy, the verifying caution, that characterize the born observer." [4]

But the story-writer will find quite as much suggestive material in observing human nature as in studying the lower orders of creation. With the works of the great analysts to serve as models and stimulate the writer to emulation, surely no further word is needed. Here indeed is a field for applied psychology, second to none other. Myriads of interesting men and women are waiting for some master hand to pluck out the heart of their mystery. Holman Day, Mary Wilkins Freeman, and "O. Henry," have not "used up" all the unique characters in America.

It may be urged that all this elaborate and minute observation would serve rather to equip the novelist than the writer of short-stories. Not so. No one can compress into a few bold strokes the essentials of a portrait who has not first taken in with precision all the nonessentials. The work of literary selection is really a work of rejection.

2. *Experience*

"Mark Twain deliberately threw away his [European] street-car ticket fifteen times, and each time was

[4] *The Working Principles of Rhetoric*, p. 397.

required to pay his fare. He made five hundred dollars from the story which he based upon this simple incident"[5] In *Vawder's Understudy,* James Knapp Reeve tells the story of an author who entered open-eyed into a platonic friendship for the purpose of observing results. The results were observable. In *Tommy and Grizel,* Tommy the sentimentalist-author. makes a number of startling essays at the laboratory method of gathering literary material.

Doubtless all these and similar experiences are exceptional rather than typical. Experience may be deliberately sought, and often should be, as in the cases of the authors of *The Workers,*[6] *The Woman Who Toils,*[7] and similar books; but for the most part the really valuable experience is that into which our daily walk leads us. There we shall find an abundance of the " literatesque,"[8] without more than an occasional prolonged

[5] *The Short-Story,* Albright, p. 15.
[6] Professor Walter Wyckoff.
[7] Marie Van Vorst and Mrs. John Van Vorst.
[8] " There should be a word in the language of literary art to express what the word 'picturesque' expresses for the fine arts. *Picturesque* means fit to be put into a picture; we want a word *literatesque,* 'fit to be put into a book.' An artist goes through a hundred different country scenes, rich with beauties, charms and merits, but he does not paint any of them. He leaves them alone; he idles on till he finds the hundred-and-first — a scene which many observers would not think much of, but which he knows by virtue of his art will look well on canvas, and this he paints and preserves. . . . Literature — the painting of words — has the same quality, but wants the analogous word. The word ' *literatesque* ' would mean, if we possessed it, that perfect combination in the *subject-matter* of literature, which suits the *art* of literature. . . . As a painter must not only have a hand to execute, but an eye to distinguish — as he must go here and there through the real world to catch the picturesque man, the picturesque scene, which is to live on his canvas — so

excursion into atmospheres far removed from our own.

Growing out of observation and experience, as sources of literary materials, is

3. *Self-study*

" Sir Philip Sidney had a saying, ' Looke in thy heart and write '; Massillon explained his astute knowledge of the human heart by saying, ' I learned it by studying myself '; Byron says of John Locke that ' all his knowledge of the human understanding was derived from studying his own mind. ' " [9]

One peril lies along this path, however, and to it the famed author of *Childe Harold* fell a victim; its avoidance is a mark of real greatness. All that Byron ever wrote was so tinctured with his own personality that the reader must see the author's portrait in his characters. They all do and think and say very nearly what Byron would, under like conditions. Maupassant fell into the same trap, as did Poe and Hawthorne, though in less degree.[10] All morbid and self-centered artists are peculiarly liable to study self so exclusively that self becomes their microcosm. A certain amount of this self-centric spirit is inevitable, but to dress and undress one's soul too persistently leads to mania, and may be allowed to epoch-making geniuses rather than to the rank and

the poet must find in that reality, the *literatesque* man, the *literatesque* scene which nature intends for him, and which will live in his page."— Bagehot, *Literary Studies,* Vol. II, pp. 341, 343, 345.

[9] From the Author's *How to Attract and Hold an Audience* p. 55. (Noble and Noble, New York.)

[10] See p. 248.

file. Yet what marvellous short-stories have Poe, Hawthorne, and Maupassant given to the world by their
morbid introspection! The golden middle-path, as
Horace put it, is better for the average writer — if such
a person there be.

4. *Reflection*

Here we have a calmer, saner mental habit than morbid self-scrutiny. Reflection is a rich word, which carries its meaning in a figure. How placid and clear the
mind must be to summon to its magic mirror images
of past days and find them projected there in all their
pristine color, form and detail. Memory is the soul
of reflection, just reason its limbs and members. This
ability to withdraw oneself from the hurly-burly and
reflect — re-image — gives us a palpable connection between the real and the fancied. Imagination calls up
its phantom-world out of the mirror of past experience,
adding to the real the touch of fantasy, and even creating beings and cycles the like of which " never was on
sea or land." Reflection and imagination both need to
be nurtured with the food of solitude and humored by
oft-practice; and both repay the time and care be-
stowed.

In *Afterthoughts of a Story-Teller*,[11] George W.
Cable says: " No author, from whatever heaven, earth,
or hell of actual environment he may write, can produce
a living narrative of motives, passions and fates without

[11] *North American Review,* 158:16.

having first felt the most of it and apprehended it all, in his own inner life." You see, experience may in a sense be vicarious — the " inner life " may apprehend experiences that the body has never realized.

5. *Reading*

" Reading maketh a full man," said much-quoted Bacon; but it depends upon the reader as to what he will be full of — other men's ideas, or a dynamic store of fact and fancy. Writers do not read too much; they digest too little. A prodigious diet of reading, assimilated into brain and heart, cannot but be of vast assistance in all future creation. But to be the slavish imitator of those whom you read is the sign-manual of inferiority.

Here is an enthusiastic word from Professor Phelps,[12] supported by a warning from Emerson.

" Voltaire used to read Massillon as a stimulus to production. Bossuet read Homer for the same purpose. Gray read Spenser's ' Faerie Queene ' as the preliminary to the use of his pen. The favorites of Milton were Homer and Euripides. Fenelon resorted to the ancient classics promiscuously. Pope read Dryden as his habitual aid to composing. Corneille read Tacitus and Livy. . . . With great variety of tastes, successful authors have generally agreed in availing themselves of this natural and facile method of educating their minds to the work of original creation.'

[12] *Men and Books,* p. 303.

" Books are the best of things, well used; abused, among the worst. What is the right use? What is the one end which all means go to effect? They are for nothing but to inspire. I had better never see a book than to be warped by its attraction clean out of my own orbit, and made a satellite instead of a system." Emerson here [13] uses the enthusiast's license to exaggerate, but it is a wholesome hyperbole and will not frighten the sensible reader out of a respect for the information as well as the inspiration to be found in books.[14] In the same essay, a little farther on, he adds another pungent word: " One must be an inventor to read well. As the proverb says ' He that would bring home the wealth of the Indies must carry out the wealth of the Indies.' There is then creative reading as well as creative writing."

There remains yet another potent field for the gathering of short-story material:

6. *Discussion*

Hawthorne's notebooks refer again and again to talks over plots, incidents, and characters, held with literary friends. Sometimes he definitely credits certain material to a suggestion received in such discussions. Many a little restaurant table, many a " Bohemian " garret, could tell fascinating tales of how stories were born and brought unto strength by a helpful exchange of suggestion and

---

[13] *The American Scholar.*
[14] See Part III, chap. i.

criticism. As there is nothing so blinding to a writer as to read his manuscript to adulating friends, so there is nothing so illuminating as the good-natured slashes of a discerning critic — the entrance of such cutting words giveth light. It was Francis Bacon who discoursed upon the educational value of asking questions from the man who knows, and Li Hung Chang who put the advice into effective use.

But how shall we preserve for ourselves the results of observation, and experience, and self-study, and reflection, and reading, and discussion? The answer is too obvious to need elaboration:

7. *Taking Notes*

Let it be scrap-book, card-index, index-rerum, envelope system, or filing cabinet; only in some way — loosely or precisely, on your cuffs or in elaborate records — preserve your own random thoughts and the facts and ideas you get from every source. See what even a newspaper item may mean to you:

" A short-story should have for its structure a plot, a bit of life, an incident such as you would find in a brief newspaper paragraph. . . . He [Richard Harding Davis] takes the substance of just such a paragraph, and, with that for the meat of his story, weaves around it details, description and dialogue, until a complete story is the result." [15]

[15] *How to Write Short Stories.* An Interview with F. Hopkinson Smith in the Boston *Herald,* quoted in *Current Literature,* June, 1896.

OUTLINE SUMMARY

GATHERING THE MATERIALS

1. *Observation*
2. *Experience*
3. *Self-Study*
4. *Reflection*
5. *Reading*
6. *Discussion*
7. *Taking Notes*

QUESTIONS AND EXERCISES FOR CLASS AND INDIVIDUAL STUDY.

1. After one glance out of a window, set down as many different objects as you remember seeing, going minutely into detail.

2. Take a longer look and correct your paper.

3. In what respects do two — any two — of your friends differ (a) in dress, (b) manner, (c) disposition? Be precise and minute.

NOTE: Interesting tests of the powers of observation may be made by asking the pupils to tell the color of a friend's eyes, how many rungs are in the front of his chair, how many steps lead up to the piazza, the kind of numerals on the face of his watch, and the like — all without specially looking.

4. Search for evidences of superficial observation in the short-stories of any current magazine.

5. Write out any unusual experiences which seem to you to be "literatesque."

6. Discussion: Should the writer deliberately go out after adventures and experiences, or simply be observant of what he meets in the usual course? Give reasons "pro and con."

7. Write about two hundred words showing how "self-awareness" is a good source of fictional material.

8. Write several paragraphs reporting accurately what you are now thinking. Continuously press in upon yourself the question, *What am I now thinking?*

9. Do an hour's deliberate reading, following your own choice, and report the result, carefully noting such materials as

suggest incidents, characters, scenes, sayings, and plots, for short-stories. Do not seek for quantity, but for quality.

10. General report: What kinds of reading proved most stimulating — history, essays, poetry, drama, fiction?

11. Let the instructor assign to the students, individually, the task of suggesting how scrap-books, card-indexes, etc., may be kept.

12. Gather at least five newspaper cuttings which contain raw material for short-stories, pointing out their particular qualities.

CHAPTER III

FACT IN FICTION

Prefer an impossibility which seems probable, to a probability which seems impossible.— ARISTOTLE.

It may be said boldly that *fiction is truer than fact.* Half the difference of opinion on the whole subject rests upon a mental confusion between two things, fact and truth — fact, the mass of particular and individual details; truth, that is of general and universal import — fact, the raw material; truth, the finished article into which it is to be made up, with hundreds of chances of flaws in the working.— R. G. MOULTON, *Four Years of Novel Reading.*

All fiction is fabricated from fact. Running through its every part are strands of reality without which, as warp and woof, it would fall apart at the reader's touch. If only some master of fiction would frankly speak out and tell us in what precise proportions fact and figment should be mixed in weaving the short-story. But the wisest author cannot prescribe a fixed formula. It is a problem that more or less consciously arises with the telling of every story, and personal observation must guide the judgment. Doubtless actual happenings do occur once in a long time in precisely the order, proportion, and setting, to make a good story without alteration; but is there just enough expressive conversation, local color, and incident, to allow the actualities to be photographically reproduced and yet result in a good short-story? Rarely — perhaps never. It is the old question of nature and art. The one is not a respecter of persons, the other is. Fact takes things as they come, fiction makes a mainstay of judicious selection.

1. *The Stream of Fiction*

naturally divides into the branches of realism, romanticism, and idealism; but it is both difficult and undesirable to dam up all the sociable little water-courses that insinuate their way across Mesopotamia and lightly mingle the divided waters. Romance gains when tinctured with realism, which in turn gives the color of verity to romanticism, while an entire absence of idealism **tends** to make both sordid.

The short-story writer, like the novelist, may in theory adhere to any of these schools, for his temperament will naturally determine his preferences; but in practice the utmost he may safely do is to give preëminence to his favorite form. He appeals to a ready-made audience that is naturally intolerant of fads and frills for mere theory's sake.

It is quite apart from the purpose of this treatise to discuss the claims of the several schools; it will be enough to summarize each position briefly.

(a) " *Realism,*" [1] says Mr. Howells, " is nothing more

---

[1] For adequate studies of Realism see *A Study of Prose Fiction*, Bliss Perry, chap. ix; *The Limits of Realism in Fiction*, Edmund Gosse, in *Questions at Issue; Criticism and Fiction*, W. D. Howells; *Le Roman Experimental*, Emile Zola.

or less than the truthful treatment of material." [2]   This statement is inadequate, but add Zola's utterances [3] and we get a clearer view of the realist's position.   This he defines as " the negation of fancy " and as " the exclusion of the ideal."   Realism " paints men as they are " and denies that the author should present his own point of view in a story, or even attempt to interpret the words and actions of his characters, who should be neither championed nor denounced by the author, but judged by the reader solely from what they think, do, say, and evidently are.   " That fiction which lacks romantic atmosphere," says Professor Perry,[4] is realistic.   No material is too high, or low, or commonplace, or beautiful, or dirty, for the realist, so long as he makes a faithful transcript of contemporary life.

(b) *Romanticism* [5] is as untrammeled as realism is circumscribed.   It builds castles in the air of what material it will, being well content with only a general seeming of reality.   With one of its accepted apostles it says, " Fiction is not nature, it is not character, it is not imagined history; it is fallacy, poetic fallacy, pathetic fallacy, a lie if you like, a beautiful lie, a lie that is at once false and true — false to fact, true to faith." [6]

Thus, to gain verisimilitude, romance either lays a

[2] *Criticism and Fiction*, p. 73.
[3] In *Le Roman Expérimental.*
[4] *A Study of Prose Fiction*, p. 229.
[5] See the chapter on The Romantic Novel, in *The Evolution of the Novel*, Francis Hovey Stoddard; *The Domain of Romance*, Maurice Thompson, *Forum*, 8 : 328.
[6] *The New Watchwords of Fiction*, Hall Caine, *Contemporary Review*, April, 1890.

foundation of truth and rears a true-appearing super-
structure of more or less impossible fancies, or else lays
down a fantastic substructure and (in the main) builds
truthfully thereupon. This latter method is illustrated
by Eugene Sue. In Poe's criticism of *The Mysteries of
Paris,* he remarks that the incidents which follow upon
the premises are perfectly credible, but the premises themselves are laughably impossible. Yet this very device
has made the success of many a wonder-story, for in its
truthful progress the reader forgets the unlikely ground-
work.

Of romance, Evelyn May Albright says,[7] " But a com-
moner interpretation of the term seems to include an element of remoteness of place or time ; or an element of the
abnormal or unusual in experience, of the frankly impossible; or the element of the supernatural, including
the weird or the uncanny, and the simple but intangible
spiritual truths."

The story that deals with spiritual truths might more
properly be included under the next category.

(c) *Idealism.* Idealistic fiction,[8] as its name implies,
is born of an ideal, which it seeks to express. A character is conceived of as living and moving under certain
conditions. Now what, in the circumstances, might,
would, could, or should that character be and do and say?
The answer is governed not so much by a strictly im-
partial (realistic) examination of living men and women,

[7] *The Short-Story,* p. 180.
[8] See *The Influence of Idealism in Fiction,* Ingrad Harting,
Humanitarium, Vol. VI.

as by the ideals held by the author. Idealism pictures life as the author thinks it should be in certain circumstances, and is in that respect didactic.

(d) *Composite Method.* It must be emphasized that even in the novel — so much more leisurely and full than the short-story — we seldom find any one of these types purely exemplified; and almost never in the short-story, which, in its best form, embodies something of all three elements. From realism it takes its faithful delineation of color and character, from romanticism it gains the fascinating touch of fantasy, from idealism it receives the instructive spiritual conception of how certain imagined conditions would operate on a character, or how a character would mould his own final environment. (See page 231.)

An almost perfect realistic short-story is " Twenty-Six and One," one of Maxim Gorky's vagabond series.[9] A typical romantic story is Rudyard Kipling's " The Man Who Would Be King." A fine idealistic specimen is " A Christmas Carol," by Charles Dickens, for as the story goes on ideal conditions more and more prevail.

So much for distinctions, for a thorough study of which references have already been given. It is time now to consider the practical handling of fact in fiction.

2. *The Use of Facts*

Every editor knows these sentences by heart: " This is a true story — it occurred exactly as I have written it,

[9] Translated in the volume of the same title (J. F. Taylor & Co., New York).

the names only are changed;" "I can vouch for the absolute exactness of the football incident, it happened to my brother;" "The elopement scene is not at all overdrawn as I took careful notes at the time a neighbor's daughter ran away with the hired man."

Thus ambitious realists think that the single quality of fidelity to fact must give any incident a passport to roam at will in the field of fiction. But, barring the extreme realists, authors and critics agree that while the letter (fact) killeth, the spirit (truth) maketh alive. Unless your mind's eye is telescopic as well as microscopic your vision will be distorted. The important thing in fiction is that your story should *seem* to be true. Of course, fiction of a gory, gushy, ghoulish sort which is as shocking as it intends to be, "succeeds" in proportion as it departs from truth, and glories in its degeneracy. But whether you will or not, your story is a teaching power. Your obligation to tell the *essential* truth — that is, to leave a final impression which is faithful to the realities of life — is immeasurably profound. If you trifle with it you ought to fail in fiction, and probably you will. Even farce must not mislead morally in its efforts to entertain. Let it be never so uproariously funny, still beneath the solemn cassock, or the suit of heroic armor, it must slyly disclose its cap and bells, as if to say, "See, I am only fooling!" "Mark Twain" is never so philosophical as when he is side-splitting.

Speaking now of serious fiction: "When anybody's work lacks verisimilitude — when it impresses you as beyond the bounds of life, of nature, of possibility, or reasonable probability — it matters not what the author's talent, we have little use for it: imaginary persons must think and feel and talk and act as such persons would in real life." [10]   When Shakespeare wrote the orations of Antony and Brutus he wrote history.   Not that in any sense he copied the words of these orators; he would not have so copied them had their words been extant; but in that with consummate understanding he wrote out the spirit of the orators.   This it is to " found the story on fact," to " hold the mirror up to nature," to " speak truth as though it were fiction and fiction as though it were truth."

Figment and fact, then, must become a composite — neither of them so prominent as to spoil the story.   Only the characteristic, the delineative, the salient in situation, in emotion, in character, in conversation, in denouement, must be selected in the most highly selective of all arts — the art of the short-story.

Finally, the writer of the short-story, in combining fact with fiction to produce a convincing semblance of reality, must vitalize fact with emotion and with fantasy. In the words of Mr. Mabie:

" He must invest his story with an atmosphere which shall enfold his reader and lay a spell on his senses as Poe has done in ' The Pit and the Pendulum,' or compress the tragedy of a lifetime into a few pages, as De Maupassant does in ' The Necklace,' or secure all the force and swiftness of a tumultuous current of narrative,

[10] *Fact in Fiction,* Frederic M. Bird, *Lippincott's,* July, 1895.

as Mr. Kipling has done in ' The Man Who Would Be King,' or stir the deepest emotions in a tale of love, as he has done in ' Without Benefit of Clergy,' which an American critic of high standing has declared to be the best short-story in English." [11]

OUTLINE SUMMARY

Fact in Fiction

: The Main Stream of Fiction
  (a) Realism
  (b) Romanticism
  (c) Idealism
  (d) Composite Method
2. The Use of Facts in Fiction

QUESTIONS AND EXERCISES FOR CLASS OR INDIVIDUAL STUDY

1. Discussion: Is the practice of realistic writing robbing the world of romance?

2. Paper: Has realism added to the interest of fiction?

3. Discussion: Is idealism a practical philosophy of life?

4. Discussion, or paper: Ought a short-story writer take sides for or against his characters, or ought he remain neutral? (See Part II, chap. xi.)

5. Describe, in fiction form, the street you live on, with realistic attention to detail.

6. Write an absolutely realistic short-story illustrating homely life.

7. Rewrite 5 and 6 in a romantic spirit.

8. Rewrite them in an idealistic spirit.

9. Make a list of facts which might be used in fiction.

10. Construct an incident from one of these and embellish it in romantic form.

[11] Introduction to *Masterpieces of Fiction.*

CHAPTER IV

PLOT

My model is **E**uclid, whose justly celebrated book of short stories, entitled *The Elements of Geometry,* will live when most of us who are scribbling to-day are forgotten. Euclid lays down his plot, sets instantly to work at its development, letting no incident creep in that does not bear relation to the climax, using no unnecessary word, always keeping his one end in view, and the moment he reaches the culmination he stops.— ROBERT BARR, *The Bookman,* March, 1897.

We need constant reminder that our theme admits of few positive rules and limitations, though the student of the short-story is able to recognize many clear general tendencies of the art. For this reason the analyses presented in the several chapters are not to be regarded as dogmatic and final, but rather as attempts at plain and comprehensive exposition. Necessarily, in a subject whose parts are so intimately related as are those of the short-story, there will be considerable over-lapping of chapters. This is peculiarly true of the topic now to be discussed.

I. WHAT IS A SHORT-STORY PLOT

In its simplest, broadest aspect, plot is the scheme, plan, argument or action of the story. But these are general terms and cover so many varieties of plot as to be more

brief than illuminating. Professor Bliss Perry says,
rather vaguely, that plot is " that which happens to the
characters." [1] Some one else has loosely called it " design
applied to life."   To hazard an exact definition : *Plot in
fiction is the climactic sequence of events in relation to the
characters.*   More simply, it is the unfolding of the story
— it is the very story itself, divested of all its description,
characterization and conversation.   Not that a bare plot
could stand alone as a short-story, but that without plot
there could be no short-story in the precise sense in which
that term is used in this treatise, for the notion of plot
is at the basis of the modern short-story, and, if we except plot in the drama, is itself a recent development. [2]

The plot in fiction differs from the ordinary drift of
events in life in one important respect : the events which
go to make up a fictional plot are artificially arranged so
as to bring about a particular result.   Thus stories of
the purest realism do not have complicated plots, but the
drift of events is made (artificially) to follow a simple
course which seems real because it is natural.   The artificial touch may be no more violent than a mere hasten-
ing of natural events, or a re-arrangement of their
sequence, still the artifice is there.

In this treatise the word " plot " is regarded as having
a narrower meaning than that of the word " theme," [3]
which always stands for the subject-idea of the story,
without any elaboration.   It is out of the theme that the

---

[1] *A Study of Prose Fiction,* p. 129.
[2] See p. 28.
[3] See Part II, chap. i.

plot must grow, so the theme is really the elemental, embryonic, or potential plot.

How the plot differs in scope and detail from the mere stated theme I shall now illustrate. The theme of " The Reformation of Calliope," by " O. Henry," [4] may be stated as, *How the " Terror," Calliope Catesby, came to serve as city marshal.* This tells us little more than does the title. Indeed, at a pinch the title might serve as a compact statement of the theme.

Compare this with the full statement of the plot — which, however, could be outlined in fewer words:

" Calliope " Catesby is a Westerner — at best a nuisance, at worst a " terror "— who habitually hangs out " danger-signals of approaching low spirits," and these the denizens of Quicksand are prompt to observe. " The different stages of his doldrums " reach their climax in drink, and in the peculiar yell that has given Calliope his nickname. After shooting up the town, he is attacked by the city marshal, Buck Patterson, and a posse. Calliope takes refuge in the railway station, whither Buck follows and is shot. Just now the westbound train comes in and a little old lady alights. She is Calliope's mother, unexpectedly come to visit him. In a flash the Terror removes Buck's glittering city marshal's badge and pins it on his own shirt. He then pretends to his mother that he is city marshal and has shot Buck in the performance of his duty. The mother bathes the prostrate man's temple, which the shot has merely grazed.

[4] *Heart of the West,* Doubleday, Page & Co.

As Buck revives, she pleads with him to give up his reckless habits. With a glance of understanding at Calliope, Buck promises. The old lady then leaves the waiting-room to look after her trunk, and Buck, assured of the real Terror's willingness to reform, saves Calliope's reputation with his mother by allowing him to pose as city marshal during the week of her visit, and goes out to post the "boys" as to this novel state of affairs.

But now we must look for one essential feature of a true plot—complication, by which I mean not complexity, but a mix-up, or twist. Strictly, narratives without twists are without plots, and, as has been said, are tales rather than short-stories. In the former, events take a simple course; whereas in the latter this course is interrupted by a complication. Something happens, and that happening starts, or sometimes actually constitutes, the plot. The rival interferes with the lover, or the "villain" carries out his scheme, or an accident happens, or a hidden condition is disclosed; whereupon things are tied up, and the reader remains more or less in suspense until the denouement—the untying, as the word really signifies, of the knot tied by the complication.

Unless something happens, whether outwardly or inwardly, we can have no plot, and no short-story. You might as well speak of the plot of a sermon, because it has a well-constructed plan, as to apply the term to the realistic tales and sketches which are mere photographic records of life without any complication and without the element of fantasy. Read the most subtle of Mr. Henry

James's analyses, or the most adroit of Mr. Howells's sketches, and you may delight in them, but that delight is not likely to be due to the existence of a plot. It must be attributed, rather, to your satisfaction in recognizing, say, the characters the literator has so skilfully delineated, and in observing the movement of their lives in natural channels. In the typical story of plot your interest is of an entirely different sort. If it is not aroused by, it is at least greatly increased by, the complication in the plot, by the crisis in the affairs of the characters, and you eagerly wait for the unfolding. All the writer's skill in characterization, in description, in all the literary devices, is used largely if not solely to lead up effectively to this climax, and to handle the denouement with equal art.

In his criticism, *The American Drama,* Poe has pointed out the necessity for compact unity in the true plot. He says:

" A mere succession of incidents, even the most spirited, will no more constitute a plot than a multiplication of zeros, even the most infinite, will result in the production of a unit. This all will admit — but few trouble themselves to think further. The common notion seems to be in favor of mere *complexity;* but a plot, properly understood, is perfect only inasmuch as we shall find ourselves unable to detach from it *or disarrange* any single incident involved, without *destruction* to the mass. This we say is the point of perfection — a point never yet attained, but not on that account unattainable. Practically, we may consider a plot as of high excellence when no one of its component parts shall be susceptible of *removal* without *detriment* to the whole."

II. KINDS OF PLOT

Various critics have said that all plots may be reduced to a few general classifications, ranging from four — those based upon Love, Identity, Hunger and Death [5] — to thirteen, which need not be named here. However this may be, it is certain that the kinds cross each other in unending combinations for which writers are duly grateful. Six kinds — doubtless an imperfect grouping — will now be briefly examined: Plots based upon *Surprise; Problem; Mystery; Mood or Emotion or Sentiment; Contrast;* and *Symbolism.* Let it be remembered that these are only general groupings, and that a story is likely to exhibit more than one element as well as any one of a thousand minor variations.[6] The danger is that the beginner takes a convenient grouping of this sort as a hard and fast classification. Nothing could be more unwise and nothing more deadening to invention.

---

[5] Credited by Mr. Leslie Quirk, in *The Editor,* Mar., 1908, to Mr. Charles Leonard Moore, in *The Dial.*

[6] Many stories are thoroughbred mongrels, sired by the short-story writer and damned by the critic. But, like the common cur, they possess most lovable characteristics. A live mongrel is better than a dead prize-winner — but there is always the live prize-winner to serve as the standard for points; and there are ribbons at the show for every breed, from Terrier to Great Dane.

I. *The Surprise Plot*

Here we have the simplest device of plot construction. The pride of the beginner is to produce the unexpected, frequently with a most unnatural result. That is the danger. It requires the exercise of sound sense to devise a genuine surprise for the reader and yet make the denouement perfectly natural, as in "Marjorie Daw," [7] for example. In the following simple surprise plot the old device of two men and a woman—the three-cornered plot —is used: [8]

A young woman falls in love with a man, but, being worldly-minded, she refuses his addresses because of his poverty. She leaves the country, and years pass. One day, a distinguished-looking man is introduced to her. "My old lover!" is her instant thought, and her heart goes out to him irresistibly. He has grown rich and thereafter they are much together, though neither mentions former days. At length he proposes, and she accepts him, when it transpires that her *fiancé* is not her old lover at all, but his twin brother, of whose existence she did not know.[9] The jilted brother appears on the scene, and she does not hold the love of either.

[7] *Atlantic.* 31 : 407.
[8] The chapter on Plot in Barrett's *Short Story Writing* contains some interesting examples of the prevalence of the three-cornered, or "three-leaved clover," plot.
[9] Mistaken identity is a very old device.

2. *The Problem Plot*

This is a self-explanatory term. The magazines are full of problem stories — some serious, some humorous. Though not as popular as surprise stories they offer a more attractive field for the skilful writer, particularly for the psychologist.

Sometimes the writer leaves the reader wondering how the characters met the issue — a dangerous device. Not every one can carry off a situation as Stockton did with " The Lady or the Tiger." [10] For months after that ingenious hoax was perpetrated upon the public, smart writers bombarded weary editors with one imitation after another until newspaper notices began to appear, warning young story-tellers that no such plots could be considered.

Now and then the author tackles a problem which is too big for him. Then in self-defense he kills off the characters — a poor way to beg the question.[11]

The three great dangers in choosing problem plots are : that the problem may not strike the reader as being vitally interesting; that the solution is likely to be apparent from the beginning; and that the author's solution may be unsatisfying. Let the tyro read Balzac's " La Grande Brétèche "— here are both surprise and problem handled by the master.

The problem plot often takes up a character and con-

[10] *Century,* 25 : 83.
[11] In *Rupert of Hentzau* any other ending than the death of Rudolf would have forced an unpleasant decision upon the reader.

centrates a white light upon some typical life-crisis, with
a swift suggestion of the upward or the downward path
leading away from the crossroads of decision. Sometimes the problem is shown in the background, with the
decision made long ago, or even just reached. Then the
plot works out the after-effects — as in " The Delusion
of Gideon Snell." [12]   Most stories dealing with the accus-
ing conscience, or with retributive justice, belong to this
class.

3. *The Mystery Plot*

The detective story, the ghost story, and the plain
mystery story, all deserve a fuller treatment than can
here be given.

Whether Poe modeled Monsieur Dupin's deductions
upon the reasoning of Voltaire's clever Zadig is open
to question, but it is certain that present-day writers
acknowledge Poe as their preceptor in the realm of mystery.   They all introduce the detective, amateur or professional, for the purpose of unraveling the mystery before the reader's very eyes and yet concealing the key-
thread until the last.   Sometimes the web of entangle-
ment is woven also in full sight — with the author's
sleeves rolled up as a guarantee of good faith; and the
closer you watch the less you see.

As a character, the detective cannot be much more than
a dummy.   That is, his individuality cannot be brought
out in a single short-story, except by a few bold strokes
of delineation; but when he figures in a series of stories,

[12] James Raymond Perry, *Lippincott's,* June, 1908.

as does Sherlock Holmes, the reader at length comes to know him quite well.

In the detective plot, the author seems to match his wits against the detective's, by striving to concoct a mystery which presents an apparently impossible situation. It adds to his problem that he must leave the real clue in full sight, yet so disguised that the reader cannot solve the mystery before some casual happening, or the ingenuity of the detective, shows it to the reader at the proper moment. Of course, the detective always plays the winning game against all comers, and this pleases the reader.

If a murder is to be committed, the victim must not be permitted to win the reader's sympathy too fully, else the story becomes revolting. Then, too, the clues generally point to an innocent person, who is so interesting as to cause the reader to fear lest he or she should turn out to be the criminal. But you know the conventional situations well enough; to invest the old problems with new forms is the province of invention.

The ghost-story calls for a single comment, and that shall be in the words of Mr. Julian Hawthorne:

". . . a ghost story can be brought into our charmed and charming circle only if we have made up our minds to believe in the ghosts; otherwise their introduction would not be a square deal. It would not be fair, in other words, to propose a conundrum on a basis of ostensible materialism, and then, when no other key would fit, to palm off a disembodied spirit on us.

Tell me beforehand that your scenario is to include both worlds, and I have no objection to make; I simply attune my mind to the more extensive scope. But I rebel at an unheralded ghostland, and declare that your tale is incredible." [13]

As for the plain mystery story, its name is its exposition. It enjoys all the freedom possible to any short-story, its only requirements being those of ingenuity, interest, and denouement concealed until the close by hiding the real intrigue of the plot.[14]

4. *The Plot of Mood, Emotion, or Sentiment*

Do not forget that plot may deal with the internal man as really as with the external. There is an action of the soul more vital and intense than visible action ever could be. When the inner finds expression in the outer, you have a powerful combination. Here is a fine field for delicate treatment. Hawthorne and Poe are the masters in America, as yet unapproached; Maupassant has never been equalled among the French. In stories of this type the plot is constructed so as to show setting, characters, and incidents, all colored by a dominant mood — like the sense of inevitable downfall in Poe's " The Fall of the House of Usher ; " or an emotion — like fear, in " A Coward," [15] by Guy de Maupassant; or a sentiment — like the quest of success, in Hawthorne's " The

[13] " Riddle Stories," Introduction to *Mystery and Detective Stories,* Appendix A, 8. Expanded into *Lock and Key Library.*
[14] See p. 206.
[15] In *The Odd Number,* Harper.

Great Carbuncle." All of these great stories, and most others by this trinity of fictionists, conform to Poe's requirement that the author should begin with a clear idea of the unified impression he desires to leave upon the reader, and then subordinate everything to this purpose. Naturally, plot and action will have a smaller place in the story of mood or sentiment than in the story of incident.

5. *The Plot of Contrast*

is a favorite with many able writers because it yields such excellent opportunities for character drawing. In Bret Harte's " The Outcasts of Poker Flat," two gamblers and two dissolute women, having been driven out of Poker Flat, a western mining camp, fall in with an unsophisticated young man and the young girl whom he is about to marry. They are all snowed in by a terrible blizzard, and the story of how their privations reveal their best and their worst qualities, even down to the last unavailing struggle with death, is a masterpiece of contrast, and one of the finest of American shortstories.

Contrast of characters may serve as foundation for contrasting environment and incident. The sharp distinctions of extremes, as well as the more delicate contrasts noticeable in closely related ideas and things, will be found full of suggestiveness to the writer whose eye is open to see them as they really are.

6. *The Plot of Symbolism*

The lofty ground taken by Hawthorne in his short-stories is nowhere more evident than in his symbolic fictions — in which he makes things, events, or char-acters stand for abstract truths. Yet this purpose in Hawthorne " is saved from abstractness by being conveyed through appropriate physical images . . . [as] the bright butterfly in ' The Artist of the Beautiful,' and the little hand on the cheek of Aylmer's wife (' The Birth-mark '). Such an idea is jotted down in its most general form :—

" ' To symbolize moral or spiritual disease by disease of the body; as thus — when a person committed any sin, it might appear in some form on the body — this to be brought out.' " [16]

The plot of symbolism always results in a didactic story — one which plainly seeks to teach a lesson. To be worth reading it must be very well done indeed. Few writers possess the skill, sincerity and power of Bunyan and Hawthorne. While the public is commonly supposed to be more ready to take its medicines when sugar-coated as fiction, still most symbolic short-stories are failures. Speaking generally, it is better to let the story teach its lesson by inference, unless the symbolism is very delicately suggested. Kipling's " They " may safely be taken as a model for the symbolic short-story.

[16] American Note Book, 2: 59, quoted in *The Short-Story*, Albright, p. 43. See this author's suggestive chapters on " The Motive as the Source of Plot," and " Plot."

III. WHAT CONSTITUTES A GOOD PLOT

By this I mean a plot that meets the demands of art, is adequate to the purpose of the author, and satisfactorily impresses the reader. Judged by this standard good plots might seem to be few, but this is not the case. Without doubt most short-stories fail of acceptance because of some defect other than that of an unsatisfactory plot. Usually, plot is better than workmanship.

A good short-story plot must possess

1. *Simplicity*

Complexity serves well for the novel, but in the short-story it bulks too big for its vehicle. One hundred words are enough in which to compact a statement of the plot of almost any first-rate short-story. You cannot atone for the feebleness of situation by multiplying incident. Avoid wheels within wheels (sub-plots, they are called), for they divert from the power of the main situation. But, it is objected, some of the greatest artists triumphantly use sub-plots, double-plots, and episodes. Granted, but not because they know no better. Genius gloriously offends, making a virtue out of a weakness. Only swift runners take handicaps — and then sometimes lose. Be sure of your strength before you adopt a pet weakness.

Remember that there is more than one meaning to the word " simple." In constructing your plot be certain to follow the right one. " The plot," says Dr. Bird, " may be so cleverly handled that we read with pleasure — and then at the end are disgusted with ourselves for being pleased, and enraged at the writer for deluding us; for we thought there would be something beneath his graceful manners and airy persiflage, and lo, there is not." [17] A simple plot is not a silly plot, a " blind lane " that gives promise of leading to a fascinating climax but which only turns the reader back in his tracks, hoaxed, ashamed and irritated.

Simplicity consorts with unity. They are boon companions. Let unity — unity of conception, unity of treatment, unity of effect — wholly possess your plot.

2. *Plausibility*

Arlo Bates has reminded us that a writer of fiction must be like the White Queen in *Through a Looking Glass,* who by practice was at length able to believe so many as six impossible things before breakfast. Some authors reserve this state of mind until after dinner, but it is a useful attainment for the romancer at all hours. Even if the author would not take oath that his tale is true, still to him as he tells it it must *be* true. If little fishes are made to talk, as Goldsmith remarked in commenting on Dr. Johnson's literary methods, they should talk like little fishes, not like whales.

Plausibility makes the skilful liar and the adept fictionist. Under the Merlin-touch of both all things are believable, and the most skeptical are silenced, even if

[17] *Magazine Fiction, Lippincott's,* Nov., 1894.

unconvinced. In ancient times tales dealt with the impossible,[18] then they took up possibilities, next they essayed improbable situations, later they depicted the probable, and nowadays Messrs. Anderson, Lewis & Co. insist upon limiting our themes to the inevitable. Whether this change from romance to realism is or is not progress is beside the question. It is a tendency to be reckoned with in story-telling. You must fabricate with due regard for what seems probable. No matter how impossible your romance, cock one eye toward plausibility of plot. In proportion as your theme leaves romance and walks toward realism your plot must clasp hands with truth and truth-seeming.

But have a care at this point. The primary necessity for plausibility does not lie in the promises of a wonder-story, but rather in what follows. When the author asserts that Mars is peopled with such beings as H. G. Wells has invented, the reader good-naturedly accepts the premise. So far, all is easy. But now these Martians must behave in such a manner as to justify themselves and become realities. There is no objection to creating a wonder-island, or a human being who can fly, or an invisible hero, but there is objection to constructing a plot which involves such things without causing events to follow plausibly. The four-armed giant must perform deeds suited to his prowess.

Upon the other hand, it will not do to introduce a

---

[18] A modification of Professor Brander Matthews' statement, that, "Fiction dealt first with the Impossible, then with the Improbable, next with the Probable, and now at last with the Inevitable."

wonder-plot into an atmosphere which is not suited thereto. Once establish any "impossible" condition, and you are free to carry out your plot to its logical conclusion.

Re-read Julian Hawthorne's words on page 80.

The idea of plot is inherent in the human mind. Fiction found its germs in nature. In nature, cause points to effect, character results in conduct, conduct leads to destiny — these are cherished beliefs among civilized peoples. Mere chance can no more rule in the serious story than it can ultimately in life. Now and then accident, or what seems such to be, crops up, but the general reader does not want to feel that chance is making puppets of the characters in the story. In extravaganza he forgives incongruity, but otherwise he demands a plausible progress of incidents. You may be clever at carpentering a plot, but the convincing plot is a GROWTH. Get hold of this truth with both hands.

The great literators recognized this necessity for consistent truth-seeming when they let fall significant words in their story-telling which, read in the light of the final issue, were really well-concealed forecasts—or, at least, portents. Such, in real life, were the words of Jesus which his followers afterwards knew to have had reference to coming events.

3. *Originality* [19]

"It is not sight the story-teller needs, but second sight." [20] Give us something new, is the ever-increasing

[19] See chapter on Originality, Part III, chap. i.
[20] *After-thoughts of a Story-Teller,* George W. Cable, *North American Review,* Jan., 1894.

cry. Nor is this impossible, even with the field so well-tilled as it truly is. In his essay, *The American Drama*, Poe says:

" Originality, properly considered, is threefold. There is, first, the originality of the general thesis; secondly, that of the several incidents or thoughts by which the thesis is developed; and, thirdly, that of the manner or *tone,* by which means alone an old subject, even when developed through hackneyed incidents or thoughts, may be made to produce a fully original effect — which, after all, is the end truly in view.

" But originality, as it is one of the highest, is also one of the rarest of merits. . . . We are content perforce, therefore, as a general thing, with either of the lower branches of originality mentioned above."

Professor Saintsbury has called our attention to the remarkable basic similarity among Hall Caine's plots for novels.[21] Yet that entertaining romancer writes for a steadily increasing army of readers. He follows the spirit of Poe's dictum just quoted.

[21] *Fortnightly Review,* LVII N. S., p. 187. Also compare the plots of these three short-stories: (a) "The Cask of Amontillado," by Poe, in which a revengeful man lures his enemy to some ancient wine vaults and walls him up in a niche alive. (b) "La Grande Brétêche," by Balzac, in which a husband learns that an intruder is hiding in a closet and has him walled up alive before his wife's eyes. (c) "The Duchess at Prayer," by Edith Wharton, in which a cruel and neglectful husband learns that his wife has been intriguing with a cousin in a crypt of the family chapel, and entombs the cousin alive. Conan Doyle ("The New Catacomb") and many lesser writers have also used the same basic idea.

Mr. Leslie W. Quirk cites in *The Editor* some interesting cases of alleged plagiarism arising from several authors' using the same newspaper account as material for stories.[22]

4. *Climax*

There is a great divide in every perfect plot. Toward its summit the story must steadily progress, directly and without episode or digression. On that summit the reader lingers in suspense for a longer or shorter moment. From thence the plot swiftly falls away to its full close. This great divide we call the climax.[23]

5. *Interest*

The good plot must be interesting, it must touch the reader in a vital spot. The remote, out-of-date, feeble, tempest-in-a-teapot theme begets a story of like sort. Remember that when an editor takes up your manuscript or a reader your printed story, the chances are generally against you — you must *win* interest, it is not waiting for you ready-made. Your story is in competition with others. Your judge knows a good story when he meets it and is looking for good points in yours — with an eye open for defects as well. But be sure of this: what virtues soever your story may possess, it fails if it does not grip and hold the reader's interest, and the big interest in fiction is human interest. Even when animals play parts in the fictive drama they make up in partial

[22] March, 1908, p. 117.
[23] For a fuller treatment of Climax, see Part II, chap. x.

human guise — like "Br'er Rabbit" and "Br'er Fox." Make up your mind that human interest cannot be "faked." Don't try to write about that which does not lay hold of your own soul mightily. Get close to the pulsating life about you, know it, feel it, believe in it, sympathize with it, do something for it, live it, and as it pours through the channels of your own being it will qualify you to picture that life for others interestedly and interestingly. Take Wilkie Collins's prescription for fiction-writing, "Make 'em laugh; make 'em cry; make 'em wait." At the same time, "mix your paint with brains." The great life-forces which compel men's interest in real life — sacrifice, courage, genuineness, devotion, love, and all the rest — will grip your readers with convincing power. First transmute life into fiction, then fiction will awake to life.

OUTLINE SUMMARY

I. WHAT IS A SHORT-STORY PLOT

II. KINDS OF PLOT
  1. *Surprise Plot*
  2. *Problem Plot*
  3. *Mystery Plot*
  4. *Plot of Mood, Emotion, or Sentiment*
  5. *Plot of Contrast*
  6. *Plot of Symbolism*

III. WHAT CONSTITUTES A GOOD PLOT
  1. *Simplicity*
  2. *Plausibility*
  3. *Originality*
  4. *Climax*
  5. *Interest*

QUESTIONS AND EXERCISES FOR CLASS OR INDIVIDUAL STUDY

1. What differences and similarities do you see between a plot which is a design against a person, and a fiction-plot?

2. Do you see any peculiar fitness in Robert Barr's comparison of a plot with a theorem, on page 71.

3. Construct a simple plot from one of these themes: (a) The long self-reproach of a man who thinks he has committed a crime but at length discovers that appearances deceived him. (b) How the double meaning of a remark caused a humorous complication in the affairs of a conceited man. (c) How her projected injury to a neighbor caused such a change in the thought and bearing of a woman that she finally believed she had actually committed the injury. The consequences.

4. Select from the current magazines at least four stories illustrating the different kinds of plot named on page 90. Briefly summarize the plots, in the manner shown in Appendix C.

5. Which of the six kinds of plot do you find the most common? How many stories, and what magazines, did you examine in coming to a conclusion?

6. Do certain magazines seem to prefer certain kinds of plot? If so, specify; and assign reasons.

7. Name as many minor kinds of plot as you can which might be included under the six general kinds.

8. Point out the main complication (crisis) in each of the first four plots in Appendix C. Try to substitute a different complication in each plot.

9. Do you see any weak points in any of these four plots?

10. Try to find a story that has no complication in the course of its events, briefly outlining its plan. Is it a tale, a sketch, or a short-story?

11. Would a complication mar or improve the interest of the story for you?

12. Suggest a possible complication and say how it would act on the interest of the plot — if you think there is a real plot.

13. Criticise the plot of a story selected from a current

magazine, with regard to simplicity, plausibility, originality, climax, and interest.

14. Is the plot of "An Error of Judgment," p. 214, plausible?

15. Construct a simple plot for a short-story of incident.

16. Can you name (a) a recent long story (generally called a novel) whose plot is really an overgrown short-story plot? (b) A short-story whose plot is too big for the short-story form?

IMPORTANT NOTE: Plot-germs come to the writer not only in theme form (p. 50), but also as *plot situations,* or *dramatic* situations. A "situation" is a state of affairs that seems bound to result interestingly. It is full of possibility. The state of affairs may exist between two or among several persons, between a woman and her environment, or between a man and his conscience, or his past life, and so on. The essential point is this: The states of affairs that produce vital stories contain the issues that are joined in real life. They are like doors that threaten to open and disclose a momentous secret, rivers that menace a flood, bombs that in innocent hands are about to explode—the comparisons are endless. Situations are not confined, of course, to those that serve as foundations for the plot, but may occur all through the story .

In Galsworthy's *The First and the Last* we have this foundation situation: A lawyer who is in line for a judgeship and is also about to make a brilliant marriage is shown in his comfortable bachelor quarters contemplating his good fortune. (Thus far we have no drama. We have a state of affairs, but nothing threatens to tangle the threads.) Suddenly the attorney's ne'er-do-well brother comes in, disheveled. "Why, Brother, you look as if you had just killed a man!" says the annoyed barrister.

"That is just what I have done!"

Thus the peaceful mountain becomes a volcano. Something *must* issue, both spiritual and physical. Think of all the problems that now confront the lawyer, and you will see the many possibilities that a single situation may present. This it is that challenges invention to find the most unusual yet the most convincingly natural outcome from even a commonplace situation, for a situation need not be startling to be full of promise.

CHAPTER V

PLOT DEVELOPMENT

Let him [the fiction writer] choose a motive, whether of character or of passion; carefully construct his plot so that every incident is an illustration of the motive, and every property employed shall bear to it a near relation of congruity or contrast;—and allow neither himself in the narrative nor any character in the course of the dialogue, to utter one sentence that is not part and parcel of the business of the story. . . . And as the root of the whole matter, let him bear in mind that his novel is not a transcript of life, to be judged by its exactitude; but a simplification of some side or point of life, to stand or fall by its significant simplicity.—ROBERT LOUIS STEVENSON, *A Humble Remonstrance.*

The foregoing quotation from the great Scottish master may serve to link the preceding chapter on "Plot" with the present one on "Plot Development."

I. THE SOURCES OF PLOT

The chapters on "Choosing a Theme," "Gathering the Materials," and "Fact in Fiction" have pointed out the general sources of literary material, still it seems worth while to look somewhat closely at three special plot-sources, as being fundamental to plot construction.

1. *The Characters* [1]

Here arises the old question as to whether circumstances govern men or men control circumstances. As to fiction, Mr. Howells holds to the latter view. "The true plot," he says, "comes out of the character; that is, the man does not result from the things he does, but the things he does result from the man, and so plot comes out of character; plot aforethought does not characterize." A more moderate view, it seems to me, is that events ordinarily modify characters, and that in certain instances men actually make events. When circumstances are too much for the struggling will, and events pile up, irresistibly driving man on to his destiny, we have tragedy.[2] But not all life is tragic. Now and again the hero's hand disposes of affairs and he arises victorious.

"To many men, doubtless, there is far more fascination in conceiving a group of characters — and then setting to work to discover a narrative which will give them the freest action — than in toiling over the bare idea, and the subsequent plot, followed by a series of actors and actresses who work out the denouement." [3]

When Thackeray planned *Vanity Fair* the characters gave form to the plot. In writing to his mother he says: "What I want is to make a set of people living without God in the world (only that is a cant phrase), greedy,

---

[1] See chap. xi, *Characters and Characterization.*
[2] A study of Professor Moulton's *Shakespeare as a Dramatic Artist* will abundantly repay the student.
[3] *How to Write Fiction,* anon., p. 46.

pompous men, perfectly self-satisfied for the most part, and at ease about their superior virtue." [4]

To conceive of a character as subject to the limitations of heredity, or of environment, at once opens up the book of life, whose lightest word is weighty with meaning. What a field is here disclosed, replete with the most absorbing problem plots! [5] A dissolute but good-natured man comes into a fortune, but it is to be his contingent upon his entire reformation: how does he act? A man born without timidity, at middle age suddenly finds fear obsessing his every thought: how would he attempt to maintain his place among his associates? A light woman suddenly awakens to the fact that she has forfeited the respect of her grown daughter: what means will she take to regain it?

The combinations are endless.

In the great majority of instances the characters in the short-story will disclose themselves by means of

2. *Dramatic Situations*

Marion Crawford has called the novel a pocket stage.[6] The same may be said even more truly of the short-story. It is patent to the observer that these two are now influencing each other profoundly. The dramatist and the short-story writer labor with the same materials, under nearly like conditions, and often seek similar effects.

[4] Introduction to *Vanity Fair,* Biographical Edition.
[5] See Hawthorne's *American Note Books* for many germ-plots based upon conceptions of character.
[6] *The Novel: What It Is.*

The drama exhibits "characters in action" [7]—so does
the short-story; the drama is plotted with a view to the
same requirements as govern the short-story—brief and
comprehensive introduction of characters and setting,
rapid rise of the complicating incident to the climax,
period of suspense, denouement, and swift close; both
are contrived to produce a preconceived and unified
effect; both are compressed, scenic, and usually contain
a touch of fantasy. Thus the points of likeness might be
multiplied and expanded. (See IMPORTANT NOTE, p. 92.)

One word, however, may be offered about the bearing
of the old dramatic unities—action, time and place.[8]
The unity of the short-story upon which Poe insists is
none of these; it is, as has already appeared, a unity of
effect, or impression. At the same time it is well to remember that unity of action, which Corneille called the
unity of intrigue, is essential to good plot. It is also
usually desirable to limit the time to a short period,
and the place to one general locality—of which more
later.

From the foregoing it will be plain that the characters and dramatic situations as well as the general
sources noted in previous chapters must generally be
used conjointly. This idea is amplified in the following:

"In his recently written preface to the revised *Portrait of a Lady,* Mr. Henry James quotes a remark of

[7] I am much indebted to Professor Bliss Perry's chapter on
"Fiction and the Drama," in *A Study of Prose Fiction.*

[8] For a thorough discussion of the dramatic unities see *Dramatic Art and Literature,* A. W. von Schlegel, p. 232.

Ivan Turgenev ' in regard to his own experience of the usual origin of the fictive picture.' It began for him, Mr. James reports, ' almost always with the vision of some person or persons, who hovered before him. . . . He saw them subject to the chances, the complications of existence, and saw them vividly, but then had to find for them the right relations, those that would most bring them out; to imagine, to invent and select and piece together the situations most useful and favorable to the sense of the creatures themselves, the complications they would be most likely to produce and to feel.' " [9]

3. *Impressionism*

One never tires of quoting Stevenson. The following words from Graham Balfour's *Life and Letters* of the great romancer admirably point out the three special sources of fictional plots — characters, dramatic incidents, and impressionism. Balfour is speaking:

" I remember very distinctly his saying to me : ' There are, so far as I know, three ways, and three ways only, of writing a story. You may take a plot and fit characters to it, or you may take a character and choose incidents and situations to develop it, or lastly — you must bear with me while I try to make this clear '— (here he made a gesture with his hand as if he were trying to shape something and give it outline and form) —' you may take a certain atmosphere [10] and get action

---

[9] *The Forum,* April–June, 1908. Compare p. 94.
[10] A brief discussion of " atmosphere " is given in chap. viii.

and persons to express and realize it. I'll give you an
example — *The Merry Men*. There I began with the
feeling of one of those islands on the west coast of Scot-
land, and I gradually developed the story to express
the sentiment with which the coast affected me.' "

Stevenson's experience is what Mr. H. S. Canby [11]
calls (as he himself laments, for want of a better term)
" impressionism," but in Stevenson's case the impression
gained totality only when the story grew out of his somewhat vague " feeling " of atmosphere. He first received
an impression, and then sought to convey that impression
by means of the story — and he did. [12]

Of course the general impression of atmosphere is
not the only one the author may wish to convey through
the medium of the short-story. The more specific feeling
aroused by a picture, an incident, a situation, a problem,
a character — what not — may be just as effectively
conveyed to the reader. Mr. Canby thus dwells upon
this theme in his brochure, *The Short Story:*

" So the nucleus of ' The Luck of Roaring Camp ' may
have been the glimpse of a lank, rough figure, with a
tiny baby in its arms, and, in spite of the excellent plot,
a feeling akin to the pleasurable emotion which would
follow upon such a scene in real life remains longest

[11] *The Short Story,* Yale Studies in English, p. 15.
[12] The same results may be attained in the sketch, as witness
Kipling's Indian sketches — half pictures, half anecdotes, altogether atmospheric. *The Smith Administration* papers are examples in point.

with the reader. According to this theory [impression-ism] the process, if one should attempt to write a Short Story, might be something like this: I leave my room and meet a drunken beggar reeling from the gutter. As I turn to avoid him, he pulls himself together and quotes huskily a dozen lines of Virgil with a bow and a flourish, and stumbles off into the darkness. I make him into a story, and, be the plot what it may, the effect upon the reader that I shall strive for will be a vivid impression of incongruity, not far different from that which I felt when the drunkard turned scholar and relapsed. Not all short stories can be analyzed back to their basic ele-ment as easily as this one may be built up, but with many the process is easy and obvious. Nearly every *conte* of Maupassant is a perfect example; his titles ' Fear,' ' Happiness,' ' The Coward,' would lead you to suspect as much. In the *motifs* and suggestions for stories, some utilized later, some not, which may be found in quantity scattered through Hawthorne's *American Note-Books,* there is often enough such an impression noted at the moment of its inception. Here in the *American Note-Books,* II. 176, is ' The print in blood of a naked foot to be traced through the streets of a town,' which seems to inspire ' Dr. Grimshaw's Secret,' and again, N.B. I. 13, ' In an old house a mysterious knocking might be heard on the wall, where had formerly been a doorway now bricked up,' which is applied in ' Peter Goldthwaite's Treasure;' also, ' A stranger, dy-ing, is buried; and after many years two strangers come in search of his grave and open it.' . . . In Henry

James's story, ' Flickerbridge,' which appeared in *Scribner's* for February, 1902, the action of the story can only be explained by the deep impression which the quaint, delightful lady of Flickerbridge makes upon the hero, which impression it is the intent of the author to convey to the reader; and so with many another."

II. ACTUAL PLOT DEVELOPMENT

Sir Walter Scott once said that in working out a plot he " took the easiest path across country." Doubtless this will account for the winding way by which the Wizard sometimes leads us. But not all masters of fiction found plot development so simple a process as a journey afield. To some it has always been the most arduous task of all the labor of fiction building.

Here is a concrete instance of how easily conversation may bring out a plot-germ : Several friends were seated on my piazza lately while the talk drifted.

" There is a professor of Psychology at ——— college," said one, " who has sold his head to a learned society for $15,000. His head is of unique form and," he chuckled, " the society thinks it may be even more valuable after his death than it is now."

" When is the money to be paid? " queried another of the group.

" The professor is already actually living on the $15,-000, and —"

" But," interposed a third, " what would happen if he should be lost at sea? "

"I wonder if the society has insured his life in their favor?" pondered the first gentleman.

And so the conversation went on. No one of the group has yet made a short-story out of the germ, but the query "what would happen?" holds several ingenious answers awaiting development.

At just such a stage as this, plot development must be taken up in earnest. Then, with Poe, whose words follow, we long for some practical demonstration of how the master workman sets about his task.

"I have often thought how interesting a magazine paper might be written by an author who would — that is to say, who could — detail, step by step, the processes by which any one of his compositions attained its ultimate point of completion. Why such a paper has never been given to the world, I am much at a loss to say — but perhaps the authorial vanity has had more to do with the omission than any one other cause. Most writers — poets in especial — prefer having it understood that they compose by a species of fine frenzy — an ecstatic intuition — and would positively shudder at letting the public take a peep behind the scenes, at the elaborate and vacillating crudities of thought — at the true purposes seized only at the last moment — at the innumerable glimpses of idea that arrived not at the maturity of full view — at the fully-matured fancies discarded in despair as unmanageable — at the cautious selections and rejections — at the painful erasures and interpolations — in a word, at the wheels and pinions, the tackle for scene-shifting, the step-ladders and demon-traps, the cock's feathers, the red paint and the black patches, which in ninety-nine cases out of the hundred constitute the properties of the literary *histrio*." [13]

Several well-known authors have since done precisely what Poe here suggests, and I can do no better than devote the rest of this chapter to two personally conducted tours in which successful writers take us into their work-shops.[14] They are both novelists, it is true, but their words are full of meat for the short-story writer.

The first conductor is the fecund Wilkie Collins.[15] He is showing us how he wrote *The Woman in White*.

" My first proceeding is to get my central idea — the pivot on which the story turns. The central idea in ' The Woman in White ' is the idea of a conspiracy in private life, in which circumstances are so handled as to rob a woman of her identity, by confounding her with another woman sufficiently like her in personal appearance to answer the wicked purpose. The destruction of her identity represents a first division of her story; the recovery of her identity marks a second division. My central idea next suggests some of my chief characters.

" A clever devil must conduct the conspiracy. Male devil or female devil? The sort of wickedness wanted seems to be a man's wickedness. Perhaps a foreign man.

---

[13] *The Philosophy of Composition.*
[14] In his *Philosophy of Composition* Poe himself circumstantially tells how he wrote *The Raven.*
[15] See his *Autobiography.*

Count Fosco faintly shows himself to me before I know his name. I let him wait, and begin to think about the two women. They must be both innocent and both interesting. Lady Glyde dawns on me as one of the innocent victims. I try to discover the other — and fail. I try what a walk will do for me — and fail. I devote the evening to a new effort — and fail. Experience tells me to take no more trouble about it, and leave that other woman to come of her own accord. The next morning before I have been awake in my bed for more than ten minutes, my perverse brains set to work without consulting me. Poor Anne Catherick comes into the room, and says, ' Try me.'

" I have now got an idea, and three of my characters. What is there to do now? My next proceeding is to begin building up the story. Here my favorite three efforts must be encountered. First effort: To begin at the beginning. Second effort: To keep the story always advancing, without paying the smallest attention to the serial division in parts, or to the book publication in volumes. Third effort: To decide on the end. All this is done as my father used to paint his skies in his famous sea-pictures — at one heat. As yet I do not enter into details; I merely set up my landmarks. In doing this, the main situations of the story present themselves in all sorts of new aspects. These discoveries lead me nearer and nearer to finding the right end. The end being decided on, I go back again to the beginning, and look at it with a new eye, and fail to be satisfied with it.

"I have yielded to the worst temptation that besets a novelist—the temptation to begin with a striking incident without counting the cost in the shape of explanations that must and will follow. These pests of fiction, to reader and writer alike, can only be eradicated in one way. I have already mentioned the way — to begin at the beginning. In the case of 'The Woman in White,' I get back, as I vainly believe, to the true starting point of the story. I am now at liberty to set the new novel going, having, let me repeat, no more than an outline of story and characters before me, and leaving the details in each case to the spur of the moment. For a week, as well as I can remember, I work for the best part of every day, but not as happily as usual. An unpleasant sense of something wrong worries me. At the beginning of the second week a disheartening discovery reveals itself. I have not found the right beginning of 'The Woman in White' yet. The scene of my opening chapters is in Cumberland. Miss Fairlie (afterwards Lady Glyde); Mr. Fairlie, with his irritable nerves and his art treasures; Miss Halcombe (discovered suddenly, like Anne Catherick), are all awaiting the arrival of the young drawing master, Walter Hartwright. No; this won't do. The person to be first introduced is Anne Catherick. She must already be a familiar figure to the reader when the reader accompanies me to Cumberland. This is what must me done, but I don't see how to do it: no new idea comes to me; I and my MS. have quarreled, and don't speak to each other. One evening I happen to read of a lunatic who has escaped from an asylum — a paragraph of a few lines only in a news-paper. Instantly the idea comes to me of Walter Hart-wright's midnight meeting with Anne Catherick escaped from the asylum. 'The Woman in White' begins again, and nobody will ever be half as much interested in it now as I am. From that moment I have done with my miseries. For the next six months the pen goes on. It is work, hard work; but the harder the better, for this excellent reason: the work is its own exceeding great reward. As an example of the gradual manner in which I reached the development of character, I may return for a moment to Fosco. The making of him was an afterthought; his canaries and his white mice were found next; and, in the most valuable discovery of all, his ad-miration of Miss Halcombe, took its rise in a conviction that he would not be true to nature unless there was some weak point somewhere in his character."

The second conductor shall be Sir Walter Besant.[16]

" Consider — say, a diamond robbery. Very well; then, first of all, it must be a robbery committed under exceptional and mysterious conditions, otherwise there will be no interest in it. Also, you will perceive that the robbery must be a big and important thing — no little shop-lifting business. Next, the person robbed must not be a mere diamond merchant, but a person whose loss will interest the reader, say, one to whom the robbery is all-important. She will be, say, a vulgar

[16] *On the Writing of Novels, Atlanta,* Vol. I, p. 372.

woman with an overweening pride in her jewels, and of course, without the money to replace them if they are lost. They must be so valuable as to be worn only on extraordinary occasions, and too valuable to be kept at home. They must be consigned to the care of a jeweler who has strong-rooms. You observe that the story is now growing. You have got the preliminary germ. How can the strong-room be entered and robbed? Well, it cannot. That expedient will not do. Can the diamonds be taken from the lady while she is wearing them? That would have done in the days of the gallant Claude Duval, but it will not do now. Might the house be broken into by a burglar on a night when a lady had worn them and returned? But she would not rest with such a great property in the house unprotected. They must be taken back to their guardian the same night. Thus the only vulnerable point in the care of the diamonds seems their carriage to and from their guardian. They must be stolen between the jeweler's and the owner's house. Then by whom? The robbery must somehow be connected with the hero of the love story — that is indispensable; he must be innocent of all complicity in it — that is equally indispensable; he must preserve our respect; he will have to be somehow a victim: how is that to be managed?

" The story is getting on in earnest. . . . The only way — or the best way — seems, on consideration, to make the lover be the person who is entrusted with the carriage of this precious package of jewels to and from the owner's house. This, however, is not a very distinguished rôle to play; it wants a very skilled hand to interest us in a jeweler's assistant — We must therefore give this young man an exceptional position. Force of circumstances, perhaps, has compelled him to accept the situation which he holds. He need not again be a shop man; he may be a confidential employé, holding a position of great trust; and he may be a young man with ambitions outside the narrow circle of his work.

"The girl to whom he is engaged must be lovable to begin with; she must be of the same station in life as her lover — that is to say, of the middle class, and preferably of the professional class. As to her home circle, that must be distinctive and interesting."

And so on to the end. This is enough, however, to turn the author's reasoning processes inside out for our examination.

OUTLINE SUMMARY
PLOT DEVELOPMENT

I. THE SOURCES OF PLOT
   1. *The Characters*
   2. *Dramatic Situations*
   3. *Impressionism*

II. ACTUAL PLOT DEVELOPMENT
   Methods of Wilkie Collins and Sir Walter Besant.

QUESTIONS AND EXERCISES FOR CLASS OR INDIVIDUAL STUDY

1. (a) Briefly describe at least three characters known to you, whose individualities suggest short-story plot possibilities. (b) Do the same from any one of Dickens' novels.

2. Construct a plot based upon one of the three, in cases a and b (foregoing).

3. Paper: Compare and contrast the dramatic form with the short-story form.

4. Can you discover any flaws in Sir Walter Besant's reasoning, or method, on p. 106.

5. Look over the outlines of chapters shown in the Table of Contents, and make a list of the sources of plot-material.

6. Which of these seem to you to be the most fertile? Why?

7. Build a simple plot from one such source.

8. Does environment limit plot? Give reasons.

9. Outline a plot, original or borrowed, the incidents of which could not have happened in any given locality you choose to name.

10. Outline one that could be set anywhere.

11. Rewrite "The Necklace," p. 326, setting the incidents in New York, or some other American city.

12. Construct a short-story plot from a newspaper account, adhering closely to facts.

13. Construct a plot from the same item, giving free play to the imagination.

14. Select any plot from Appendix C, and (a) entirely change the first half; (b) the last half.

15. Construct a plot from a situation presented in a painting, or engraving.

NOTE: Other exercises in plot-development may be devised by building plots of any or all the kinds grouped in the chapter on "Kinds of Short-Story." Perhaps the best practice-method would be to invent in each case a dramatic situation (see Notes, pp. 50 and 92) and work out the plot from that point of departure. The important thing about such a situation is not that it should be extremely strange—for example, in "The Necklace," it is not extraordinary that a woman should lose a borrowed jewel—but that the situation should be worked out in a fresh and absorbing way, to a striking climax—one that, if not surprising, is at least impressive.

CHAPTER VI

HOW STORIES ARE TOLD

The great adversary of Invention is Imitation.— POE, *The American Drama*.

How shall I tell my story? In any one of a dozen ways — if you can. The " if " is expressive of two conditions: your art and your viewpoint. (See NOTE, p. 124.)

Any way is good if it is artistic; but some ways are harder than others. That, however, is no argument against trying them, provided you fully realize how you hamper yourself by their adoption, not only as to difficulty but as to popular approval as well. Art can take a time-worn and prosaic method and breathe into it the breath of life. But are you an artist? In making your decision you must be frank with yourself: Are you a past-master of form? If not, is it safe to attempt the most difficult of all tasks — to handle an old method with such skill as to make it virtually new; to work over your story until you have invested its old style of narration with the charm of freshness? Are you ready to study the work of others — not in order to imitate, but to form your own judgments as to effects? If so, go ahead. Be individual. Employ any method that you can use with skill, but make certain of your skill before you handicap yourself by clinging to time-worn devices.

The second condition to govern your choice of how to tell your story is your own viewpoint as the story-teller. It is your story, and ten chances to one it possesses you, for the time being. If it doesn't, pigeonhole it until it does. But I assume now that you are full of your story. Look within yourself and see if there is not some form of narration that is within your range and peculiarly suited to the story itself. Give the same story to another writer and he would tell it differently, but as you visualize the pictures of your fiction, ask yourself how may you best present these pictures to the prospective reader. Do you naturally think of yourself as an actor in the scenes to be portrayed? Are you one of your characters, or merely an interested but impersonal on-looker? Are you the intimate friend of the actors in your little drama, or are you careless of what happens to them? [1]

Press home questions like these until you are aware of your precise relation to your story, its setting, its characters, its denouement. This once determined, try to maintain the same attitude throughout the story. Don't quarrel with your hero or fall in love with the villain unless you are willing to begin all over again and assume a fresh viewpoint. Don't indulge your sneaking preference for a minor character at the expense of the heroine, unless you give them both new places in the plot. You tacitly ask your readers to assume your chair as they read, and look at your creations through your spectacles. If you are a realist, you may deny this, but your very

[1] Compare p. 229.

methods of selection show that you wish the reader to
see your characters as you yourself do.

And the reader likes to adopt the author's viewpoint;
in fact he resents it when he is denied that privilege
because of the unfair, unnatural, morbid, silly, brutal,
or outlandish attitude taken by the author toward his
creations. A short-story is never more enjoyed than
when the author has quite captured the reader and their
sympathies harmonize.

So, having attained some skill in the art of narration in one style or more, your own attitude toward your
story will determine your manner of telling it — though
perhaps not on the instant; your decision may be the
result of experiment, with one method after another
tested until you have found the one best suited to your
story and to your abilities.

1. *Story-telling in the Third Person*

This is the commonest, probably the easiest, and surely
the safest form of narration. The author keeps entirely
in the background, unless, like Thackeray, he comes forward with his own platter to offer a moral morsel to the
reader. But in the short-story such homilies and personal expressions are looked upon askance. The beginner had better avoid them. To be sure, an author of
strong personality cannot help impressing his point of
view, but he does it mostly by means of the dialogue, and
by the same token the reader discerns it, feels it, more
surely than if it were written out declaratively. It needs

no expositor to point out the gentle spirit of sympathy and humor that pervaded the author of "The Joy of Youth" when she wrote her story. It stands out in the first paragraph and the reader willingly adopts the same viewpoint.

Emmeline Ames, going down the village street that winter afternoon, was conscious of a little uncomfortable lump in her right shoe. She was also conscious of an innocent bravado of shame as the lump worked from the hollow of her instep toward her toes. A soft red, and a delicious, silly smile, overspread her face. The lump was composed of some dried sprigs of the plant called boys'-love, or southernwood. Emmeline believed firmly in the superstition concerning it. She was sure that a girl with a sprig of boys'-love in her shoe would marry the first boy whom she met. In summer, when the plant with its long gray-green aromatic leaves flourished in the garden, she often wore a sprig in her shoe, and she had secretly pressed some in her own particular books, in order that she might be able to try the charm in the winter-time. Emmeline had too much credulity and imagination to be in a perfectly normal state; or, on the contrary, she may have been too normal, with all her human instincts dangerously near the surface, and as prone to injury as her great-grandmother's egg-shell china teacups.[2]

Some stories are so impersonal that they may be said to have no point of view. The author simply tells them "for what they are worth," for mere entertainment, as though someone had told him, or he had seen the happenings, and he impartially unreeled the yarn. The third-person style of narration is peculiarly suitable to this sort of story. The story itself is everything, the

[2] *The Joy of Youth,* Mary E. Wilkins Freeman, *Harper's,* Dec., 1907.

author nothing. Adventure, spirited action, and humor are types well suited to this form of story-telling. See how the author keeps out of sight in " Fleas is Fleas," by Ellis Parker Butler.[3]

Mike Flannery was the star boarder at Mrs. Muldoon's, and he deserved to be so considered, for he had boarded with Mrs. Muldoon for years, and was the agent of the Interurban Express Company at Woodcote, while Mrs. Muldoon's other boarders were largely transient.

"Mike," said Mrs. Muldoon one noon when Mike came for his lunch, "I know th' opinion ye have of Dagos, and niver a-one have I took into me house, and I think the same of thim meself — dirthy things, an' takin' the bread away from th' honest American laborin' man — and I would not be thinkin' of takin' one t' board at this day, but would ye tell me this :— is a Frinch-min a Dago?"

Flannery raised his knife and laid down the law with it.

"Mrs. Muldoon, mam," he said, "there be two kinds of Frinchmin. There be the respictible Frinchmin, and there be th' unrespictible Frinchmin. They both be furriners, but they be classed different. Th' respictible Frinchmin is no worse than th' Dutch, and is classed as Dutch, but th' other kind is Dagos. There is no harm in the Dutch Frinchmin, for thim is such as Napoleon Bonnypart and the like of him, but ye want t' have nawthing t' do with the dago Frinch. They be a bad lot."

A more subtle art is required to convey the impression that the narrator (in the third person) was a comrade in the enterprise, a witness of the drama, an intimate of the characters, and yet never explicitly say so, nor even for a moment emerge from the narrator's hazy background. Many of " O. Henry's " most diverting stories suggest

[3] *American Magazine*, Dec., 1907.

this intimacy of experience.   There is a fine sense of the author's close relation to his narrative in H. B. Dean's "Pluck Versus Diplomacy," a delicately sympathetic sketch.[4]

Some people said St. Margaret's Hospital was the coolest place in town. This might be true up in the large, dim wards with windows wide and awnings dropped, but below in the basement dispensary it was hot, sticky, and malodorous. From the ambulance courts six granite steps led down to a door opening on a large, low-ceilinged room, lighted and aired by two small windows. With its hard wooden benches, it was a weary waiting place that hot August day for those who came for treatment.

Some few talked in low tones to chance acquaintances of the dispensary, but the majority sat in silence, watching the glass door which led to an adjoining room. Occasionally this door would be opened by a nurse whose "Next!" lessened the waiters by one. Early in the day her voice was as crisp and fresh as the blue and white uniform she wore, but with the lengthened shadows in the court voice and gown became limp.

The benches were almost empty when a small boy, balancing his thin body on one leg, hopped down the granite steps and sank wearily on the nearest seat. The occupants of the benches gathered around with cries of sympathy. As their voices penetrated to the adjoining room, a white-coated young house-surgeon came out. At his approach the group parted, and the boy, raising his arms as if to a friend, whispered, "Say, doc, will youse give us a lift? My foot it's queered this time for keeps."

In creating the illusion of the author's close relation to his narrative there is a danger: the reader unconsciously demands that the narrator confine his statements to such things as could have been observed or learned

---

[4] *Lippincott's,* Oct., 1907.

naturally. The universal pass-key to the human sanctuary is denied him — he must use only his powers of inference and observation.

When the narrator keeps absolutely out of sight, by common consent we refrain from asking "how do you know?" Every one admits his right and his ability to peep into secret places and report the most private conversations and events. To him even the meditations of a maiden are an open page.

So here is a strong motive for the beginner to adopt this style of telling a story. He need not worry, he thinks, with trying to make his puppets disclose their inmost selves by word and deed, for in a single sentence he may furnish them with emotions and sentiments; furthermore, he knows that the latter method is the easier, even though immeasurably less artistic. For his inability to reveal character and feeling by dialogue and incident he consoles himself by remembering that his story must be short. Really, just here is the difference between superior and inferior story-telling.

2. *The First Person*

There are more varieties of the story told in the first person than in any other form.

First, there is the story told by the principal actor. In the hands of an expert the most convincing results are attained. (To what reality, to what personal approach, does Zola attain in "The Death of Olivier Becaille"![5]) If it is told seriously, the greatest care is

[5] See p. 376, No. 11.

needed to steer a middle course between an egotistic exhibition and an over-modest dullness. One recalls Emerson's *mot*: "I have the feeling that every man's biography is at his own expense."

When an adventurer tells of his own exploits we expect and amusedly tolerate the tone of bombast naturally adopted by the lovable knave, as in the exploits of the inimitable Gerard.[6] No narrator but himself could do justice to his superb aplomb. The bragging is part of the fun; underneath is the feeling of heart and valor.

But the first-person story may also be told by a minor actor — Poe's favorite device, as in "The Gold Bug."[7] This offers less dangers than the method just referred to. By a modest display of good qualities, and by subordinating himself to the principal character, the narrator escapes the imputation of egotism, while still allowing himself a considerable place in the action. In his Sherlock Holmes stories Conan Doyle has assigned such a part to Dr. Watson, though the physician's chief business is to glorify his astute friend. When well handled, no more convincing form of story-telling can be adopted — but don't overlook the qualifying clause.

Another variation is that in which a minor character tells of the deeds of his enemy, who is nevertheless the central figure in the story.

Again, the narrator may tell the story as an observer, with only the slenderest part, or no real participation, in the action. Such an attitude is gracefully assumed

[6] *The Adventures of Brigadier Gerard,* A. Conan Doyle.
[7] See p. 376, No. 11.

by Alphonse Daudet in the sketches and short-stories in *Letters From My Mill*.[8] Such also is the author's attitude in Edward Everett Hale's "The Man Without a Country."[9]

Two further varieties of the first-person story may be noted. In the one the narrator tells his story directly to the reader, addressing him as "you," and even reminding him of former experiences together, or of stories told on previous occasions. Here it would seem best to avoid extremes of intimacy with the reader. Few can carry them off with a natural air. Such familiarity will attract some readers, but others it will repel. In the second sort, the author tells his story either to a lay figure, or to some more active character in the plot.

A hackneyed device is to tell the story in the first person after having introduced the speaker by a second person, who really thus reports the story "as it was told to me." You may be sure of two things in this connection: a story begun in this style must possess unusual merit to offset the triteness of its introduction; and, it is a hard task to convince the reader that you could not have plunged into the story in the first person direct, relying upon the opening sentences to set the scene. Still, if you can do it exquisitely, go ahead. No rule in art is so good but that it may well be broken by a master stroke. Kipling occasionally delights to fly in the face of conventions of form, and does it so originally that we are grateful to him for showing us that there

8 See p. 376, No. 10.
9 See p. 376, No. 11.

are no really worn-out methods. One wonders, however, what would result if the same degree of ingenuity were trained upon a new device. I give space to the following lengthy introduction to "The Solid Muldoon," from Kipling's *Soldiers Three,* because it so fully displays both the merits and the demerits of the story within a story. Note the false starts, the digressive remarks, the atmosphere, the characterization — a jumble of good literary method and bad. In extenuation, it must be remembered that this story is one of a series.

This befell in the old days, and, as my friend Private Mulvaney was specially careful to make clear, the Unregenerate.

There had been a royal dog-fight in the ravine at the back of the rifle-butts, between Learoyd's Jock and Ortheris's Blue Rot — both mongrel Rampur hounds, chiefly ribs and teeth. It lasted for twenty happy, howling minutes, and then Blue Rot collapsed and Ortheris paid Learoyd three rupees, and we were all very thirsty. A dog-fight is a most heating entertainment, quite apart from the shouting, because Rampurs fight over a couple of acres of ground. Later, when the sound of belt badges clinking against the necks of beer-bottles had died away, conversation drifted from dog to man fights of all kinds. Humans resemble red-deer in some respects. Any talk of fighting seems to wake up a sort of imp in their breasts, and they bell one to the other, exactly like challenging bucks. This is noticeable even in men who consider themselves superior to privates of the line; it shows the refining influence of civilization and the march of progress.

Tale provoked tale, and each tale more beer. Even dreamy Learoyd's eyes began to brighten, and he unburdened himself of a long history in which a trip to Molham Cove, a girl at Pateley Brigg, a gauger, himself and a pair of clogs were mixed in drawling tangle. "An' so Ah coot's yead oppen from t' chin to t' hair an' he was abed for t' matter o' a month," concluded Learoyd, pensively.

Mulvaney came out of a reverie — he was lying down — and flourished his heels in the air. "You're a man, Learoyd," said he, critically, "but you've only fought wid men, an' that's an ivry-day expayrience; but I've stud up to a ghost, an' that was not an ivry-day expayrience."

"No?" said Ortheris, throwing a cork at him. "You git up an' address the 'ouse — you an' yer expayriences. Is it a bigger one nor usual?"

"'Twas the livin' trut'!" answered Mulvaney, stretching out a huge arm and catching Ortheris by the collar. "Now where are ye, me son? Will ye take the wurrud av the Lorrd out av me mout' another time?" He shook him to emphasize the question.

"No, somethin' else, though," said Ortheris, making a dash at Mulvaney's pipe, capturing it, and holding it at arm's length; "I'll chuck it across the ditch if you don't let me go!"

"You maraudin' hathen! 'Tis the only cutty I iver loved. Handle her tinder or I'll chuck you acrost the nullah. If that poipe was bruk — Ah! Give her back to me, sorr!"

Ortheris had passed the treasure to my hand. It was an absolutely perfect clay, as shiny as the black ball at pool. I took it reverently, but I was firm.

"Will you tell us about the ghost-fight if I do?" I said.

"Is ut the sthory that's troublin' you? Av course I will. I mint to all along. I was only gettin' at ut my own way, as Popp Doggle said whin they found him thryin' to ram a cartridge down the muzzle. Orth'ris, fall away!"

He released the little Londoner, took back his pipe, filled it, and his eyes twinkled. He has the most eloquent eyes of anyone that I know.

"Did I iver tell you," he began, "that I was wanst the divil av a man?"

"You did," said Learoyd, with a childish gravity that made Ortheris yell with laughter, for Mulvaney was always impressing upon us his merits in the old days.

"Did I iver tell you," Mulvaney continued, calmly, "that I was wanst more av a divil than I am now?"

"Mer-ria! You don't mean it?" said Ortheris.

"Whin I was corp'ril — I was rejuced aftherwards — but, as I say, whin I was corp'ril, I was a divil of a man."

He was silent for nearly a minute, while his mind rummaged among old memories and his eyes glowed. He bit upon the pipe stem and charged into his tale.

3. *The Letter Form* [10]

This well-worn scheme of the first-person story is sure to be adopted by the uninitiated. Sometimes the letters are written by but one character and tell the whole story; again the replies may be given, or a whole round of correspondents may contribute the narrative. Try this form if you will, succeed if you can, and all the more credit if you do, but by adopting it you take on a heavy handicap. When Richardson wrote *Pamela* the scheme was new.

I have rarely advised young writers against the letter-form but they have quoted such successful books as the Baroness von Hutten's *Our Lady of the Beeches* and the anonymous *The Lady of the Decoration.* Of course the argument is unanswerable. Yet ask any experienced manuscript reader how many failures are to be recorded as contrasted with the few modern successes in the letter form. However, if your work is good enough, some publisher will print it, and the public will buy it, in any form.

4. *The Diary Form*

A diary is an intimate letter to one's self. As a fictive form it has been employed with fine skill; but the

[10] See *The Technique of the Novel,* Horne, p. 245.

same warning holds as in the case of the epistolary style
— do it well or do it not at all. "Love in Old
Clothes," [11] by H. C. Bunner, is a fair sample of ingenuity in this line. Notwithstanding its archaic spelling
the effect is pleasing. A masterpiece is Maupassant's
"The Horla." [12] The genuinely humorous diary, after
the manner of Judge Shute,[13] is still unhackneyed. If
conversation is introduced, all the better. As a form,
however, the diary is best suited for character study, and
that is always dull reading in the short-story when un-
enlivened by dialogue.

5. *The Composite Form*

Many writers seek novel expression by combining the
various forms. For instance, the story of adventure is
begun in the first person and, in order to permit the narrator to die, a second narrator finishes the story — a feeble device no matter if masters do use it. Others tell the
story by casting it in several parts, each told by a different
character speaking in the first person. A story told entirely by telegrams is still another scheme. Brander
Matthews and H. C. Bunner wrought a rather ineffective
novelty in "The Documents in the Case," [14] a story told
by two-score exhibits made up of letters, telegrams, play-
bills, a pawn ticket, I-O-U's, legal documents, and the

[11] See p. 377, No. 19.
[12] See p. 376, No. 10.
[13] *The Real Diary of a Real Boy.*
[14] See p. 377, No. 18.

like.   The magazines will furnish examples of other novelty methods a-plenty.

Though merely an anecdote, the following incident will serve to illustrate the fictional possibilities of a telephone conversation heard at one end of the line, the imaginative reader being permitted to fill in the gaps.

This is the story of a balking mule named " Shoe," driven by an old negro named " Abe," and owned by a wholesale feed house.   One day Shoe balked on Broad Street and refused absolutely to be driven again.   After old Abe had spent his energies on Shoe for an hour in the vain endeavor to get him to start, he went into a store to telephone his employers.   The following is what a party of gentlemen near the telephone heard:

AS TOLD OVER THE TELEPHONE

" Please, marm, gimme number two hund'ed an' 'leven. Is dat you, Marse Henry? . . . Yessir, dis is Abe. I dun ring yer up, sir, ter tell you about Shoe. Shoe, he dun balk down yer on Broad Street, sir."

" _____ "

" 'Bout a hour, sir."

" _____ "

" Yessir, I bus' him in de head."

" _____ "

" I dun wear de whip handle out on him, sir."

" _____ "

" Yessir, I kick him in de belly 'bout eight times, sir."

" _____ "

" Marse Henry, I would ha' kick um some mo' but I hu't me big toe on um de las' time I kick um."

" _____ "

" Twis' he tail? No, sir, not dis nigger. A gemman from New York, he twis' he tail."

" _____ "

" No, sir, I don't think he dead. De doctor take him 'way in de amb'lance."

" _____ "

" Yessir, it was sure foolish."

" _____ "

" Marse Henry, I done set fire under Shoe."

" _____ "

" De harness? Dun bu'n de harness clean off um."

" _____ "

" De cart? Yessir, dun bu'n de cart too, sir, all 'cept one wheel, sir."

" _____ "

" Yessir, I git de feed out fust, sir."

" _____ "

" Marse Henry, is you want me to come back to de store and go to work, or mus' I wait fer Shoe to move?" [15]

Doubtless new forms are still to be devised and it is well to seek them out. In his *Lives of the Poets* [16] Samuel Johnson remarks: " The great source of pleasure is variety. Uniformity must tire at last, though it be uniformity of excellence. We love to expect; and, when expectation is disappointed or gratified, we want to be again expecting."

But permanent success in the short-story field must look for its secret to more than variety, more than novelty, more than ingenuity. Any one of the simpler forms of narration is still an uncovered field. There are more touch-downs to be won by straight football than by tricks.

[15] " L." in *Walnuts and Wine, Lippincott's,* Oct., 1906.
[16] Vol. I, p. 219.

OUTLINE SUMMARY

How Stories are Told

1. *In the Third Person*
2. *In the First Person*
3. *Letter Form*
4. *Diary Form*
5. *Composite Form*

QUESTIONS AND EXERCISES FOR CLASS OR INDIVIDUAL STUDY

1. Write a story of simple incident, in the third person.

2. Rewrite it in the first person, assuming the part of the leading character.

3. Rewrite it, assuming the part of one of the minor characters.

4. Which form yielded the most satisfactory results to you personally?

5. Write a story in the form of telegrams.

6. Write one side of a telephone conversation, telling a simple story.

7. Try to suggest a fresh form of telling a story.

NOTE: The technical and the common meanings of a term are often confused. In this treatise it has seemed necessary to use "viewpoint" and "point of view" in six distinct senses: (1) The author looks at his subject from the point of view, say, of a moralist. (2) He views one of his characters impartially, as a partisan, satirically, or with disapproval. (3) He describes a scene from a given viewpoint—nearby, distant, etc. In each of these three cases he, as a rule, expects the reader to adopt his— the author's—point of view. (4) The fictional characters cannot, without other information, see, hear or know anything outside of their own viewpoints. (5) The story may be told from the viewpoint of a certain character. Any shift to the point of view of another character must be made reasonable and clear. (6) The angle of narration must not shift awkwardly. These points are expanded in Chapter II, "Supplemental Chapters." See also pp. 158 and 275-9.

CHAPTER VII

THE OPENING OF THE STORY

Well begun is half done.— OLD PROVERB.

The last thing that we find in making a book is to know what we must put first.— PASCAL, *Thoughts.*

Most people have a very strong impulse to preface something in particular by at least a paragraph of nothing in particular, bearing to the real matter in hand a relation not more inherently intimate than that of the tuning of violins to a symphony. It is the mechanical misfortune of musicians that they cannot with certainty tune their instruments out of hearing. It is the mechanical luck of the writer that he need not show a bit more of his work than he chooses.— BARRETT WENDELL, *English Composition.*

All stories must have beginnings, but not all beginnings should be introductions. The fiction writer's immediate concern is to get a picture quickly and clearly set in the mind's eye of the reader — to establish the reader in a way of thinking or a way of feeling. How he shall go about this depends solely upon the nature of the story and the impression he wishes to make. The reader may require the knowledge of some fundamental facts before he can take in the details of the picture, and that means introducing the story more or less formally. Upon the other hand — the better hand, as I think — the story may be such that the reader should be plunged into the action at once. Between these extremes lie all sorts and gradations.

I. THE BEST USAGE

For this inquiry I have examined and broadly classified the openings of six hundred short-stories, including tales and sketches of the short-story type. The list takes in what critics and public regard as the world's greatest stories. The authors selected are nearly all well-known, and in most instances famous. Practically all the stories were written within the last seventy-five years, and a large majority since 1870. American stories preponderate, with French, British, German, Russian, Italian, Scandinavian, Polish, Hungarian, Spanish, and minor nationalities following in about the order named. Current fiction has been given due regard as compared with the short-story of the period preceding 1870. Altogether, the investigation seems well calculated to give us a fair view of how approved story-tellers begin their narratives.

It must be noted that many introductions — I now use the word as broadly covering the beginning of a story, whether the author formally introduces the setting or plunges directly into the thick of the action — exhibit more than one purpose. For example, in giving initial prominence to a character some details of the setting are often worked in; or, in electing to give the setting first, the author is likely at the same time to touch upon some character of the story. In attempting this classification the predominating phase of the introduction has been taken as determining its class.

1. *Stories That Open With Dialogue*

There is a general impression that a considerable number of short-stories begin in this manner. The actual proportion is surprisingly small, though the usage of the last ten years tends moderately in that direction, particularly among writers who produce fiction of the light and " clever " kind.

Of the six hundred stories examined, only fifty-one — less than ten per cent.— were found to begin with conversation, and these were rarely stories of great merit. Observe, however, that conversation occurs *very early* in a large proportion of the total number of stories ex‧ amined.

These fifty-one stories may be grouped in five subdivisions :

(a) *Twenty-six use the opening dialogue to give the setting.*[1] In the term " setting " are included the surroundings in which the action begins, the mood which dominates the situation, and the conditions under which the story opens. It may be compared to the scene which meets the eye when the curtain rises on the stage. As we see in the following example, the characters appear even while the stage is being set, and this on account of the dialogue form.

[1] See the next chapter ; also chap. **xii.**

"MANY WATERS"[2]

"Well?"

"True bill; I'm awfully sorry."

Thomas Fleming took his cigar out of his mouth, and contemplated the lighted end. He did not speak. The other man, his lawyer, who had brought him the unwelcome news, began to make the best of it.

"Of course, it's an annoyance; but —"

"Well, yes. It's an annoyance," Fleming said, dryly.

Bates chuckled. "It strikes me, Tom, considering the difference between this and the *real thing,* that 'annoyance' is just the right word to use."

Fleming leaned over and knocked off the ashes into his waste basket. He was silent.

"As for Hammond, he won't have a leg to stand on. I don't know what Ellis and Grew meant by letting him take the case before the Grand Jury. He won't have a leg to stand on!"

"Give me a light, will you, Bates? This cigar has gone out again."

Note how deftly the setting is conveyed by dialogue — a lawyer and his client are seated discussing the latter's indictment for an offense against the law. The lawyer's attitude and that of the client, their estimate of the case, and the names of their opponents, are all quickly brought before the reader. The situation made this handling possible. Few situations can be opened up in the same manner. You may read through a number of magazines without finding a single short-story of distinction, as " Many Waters " certainly is, which opens with a conversation.

(b) *Twelve use the opening dialogue to delineate the characters.* That is, the emphasis is placed on the char-

[2] Margaret Deland, *Collier's,* May 13, 1905.

aeters rather than on the atmosphere in which they
move — an easier performance always than that accomplished by Mrs. Deland.

THE AFFAIR OF THE BROWNS [3]

"Ah!" cried Wilberton, sitting up straight in his chair on
the year-round resort hotel veranda. "Here is where Dull
Monotony packs his things and hikes from the seaside."

"I should like to know why," commented Mrs. Wilberton
skeptically. "I am sure nothing has occurred —"

"Well, something will occur very shortly," her husband
assured her. "Why," he exclaimed, "things simply cannot be
quiescent with a woman as pretty as *that* in their midst."

He nodded. Mrs. Wilberton, letting her gaze follow the direction of the nod, saw a young woman following the valise-
encumbered porter toward the hotel entrance. She was a tall
young woman, and slender, and her tan traveling gown was
unquestionably in the latest style. By the hand she held a
very small boy who was having great trouble with a very large
straw hat.

"Your taste in women is constantly changing," Mrs. Wilberton averred in a tone which plainly conveyed her contempt for
such inconsistency. Mrs. Wilberton was fat, and she was not
tall, and her eyes were not gray. "Since when —"

"Oh, I always liked them tall and slender!"

"This one is positively *thin!*"

"And with dark hair and big gray eyes!"

"One can never be sure about hair."

"And clear, clean complexion, free of drugstore blush —"

"It is certainly absurd to regard *that* complexion as *real,* or
pretty, or even artistically *done.* And anyhow it will not last
two days in this sun and sea breeze."

"She walks well, a sort of queenly gait —"

"Very carefully studied from some second-rate actress, I dare
say — not at all natural, and *decidedly* — er — indolent."

"She doesn't seem to be very enthusiastic," agreed Wilberton.

[3] Harrison Clark, *Hampton's Broadway,* July, 1908.

(c) *Nine use the opening dialogue to suggest the spirit of the story.* The two openings which follow will make this clear.

A CASE OF IDENTITY [4]

" My dear fellow," said Sherlock Holmes, as we sat on either side of the fire in his lodgings at Baker Street, " life is infinitely stranger than anything the mind of man can invent. We would not dare to conceive the things which are really mere commonplaces of existence. If we could fly out of that window hand in hand, hover over this great city, gently remove the roofs, and peep in at the queer things which are going on, the strange coincidences, the plannings, the cross-purposes, the wonderful chain of events, working through generations, and leading to the most *outré* results, it would make all fiction, with its conventionalities and foreseen conclusions, most stale and unprofitable."

THE BLAST OF THE TRUMPET [5]

" De daid," asserted Aunt Janty Gibbs solemnly, " con-*tin*-ually do walk."

"Does dey walk all tuh wunst?" inquired her grandson, Gabriel Gibbs, a youth with an unquenchable thirst for information on all subjects.

" No, chile," returned his grandmother with a superior air, " dey walks sometimes in twos an' sometimes in threes, but mos'ly dey walks alone in de night-time."

" Dey's a time comin', Aun' Janty, when dey's all gwine tuh walk tuh wunst," remarked Brother Eli Wiggins with conviction.

" Whut yo' 'ludin' tuh, Brothah Wiggins, whut yo' 'ludin' tuh?" asked Aunt Janty as she hospitably replenished his cup, while Gabriel improved the opportunity to slip unnoticed from the room.

[4] A Conan Doyle. See p. 377, No. 14.
[5] Ella Middleton Tybout, *Lippincott's,* May, 1904.

"Dey's a time comin'," he replied, pouring the steaming tea into his saucer, "when ole Gabriel am gwine tuh soun' de note on he hawn good an' loud. Den de graves am gwine tuh bus' open an' de daid come fo'th tuh walk up an' down in de worl', tuh an' fro in hit. Y-a-a-s, Aun' Janty, dat's so."

Brother Wiggins paused and looked solemnly at his hostess.

"Aun' Janty," he said, his voice sinking to a sepulchral whisper, "dat time ain' so fuh off ez mos' folks b'lieves."

In this latter story, the opening dialogue, while giving us the spirit of the story, both sets the stage and brings on the characters.

(d) *Two use the opening dialogue to lead up to the story proper by fact or explanation.* This form is in fact a true introduction, yet only two stories out of the six hundred examined begin with dialogue used for this purpose. As for a reason, the style is antiquated. Writers prefer to pack preliminary statements into a few concise sentences rather than burden the dialogue with explanations which are as unnatural in the mouths of the characters as are similar " information speeches " on the lips of actors in " Act I. Scene 1 " of the ordinary play. A stronger reason for discarding this old form is that the crisp modern short-story does not begin in the past, but on the very threshold of the plot, if not in the middle, as one magazine editor used to put it.

(e) *Two use the opening dialogue solely to win attention.* This seems like a waste of good type and paper. Besides, it is difficult enough to start a conversation brilliantly and yet make it naturally lead up to something else, without making epigrams solely to gain a reading. The brilliant talk which opens one and another of An-

thony Hope's *Dolly Dialogues* is never mere fireworks,
but is full of delicate light and heat.

Think how fearful of his story Wilhelm Hauff must
have been when he essayed to catch the reader by this
transparent introduction; yet he had a good story to
tell.

THE SINGER [6]

"It is a strange occurrence, truly," said Councillor Bolnau to
a friend whom he met on Broad Street in B. "You must confess that this is a queer age we live in."

"You mean the affair in the North?" answered his friend.
"Have you important news, councillor? Has your friend, the
foreign minister, told you some important secret of state?"

"Oh, don't bother me with politics or state secrets; let them
go as they may. I mean now the affair of Mademoiselle
Bianetti."

To sum up: Of the fifty-one stories that begin with
dialogue, one-half devote the opening conversation to
the setting, one-fourth to characterization, less than one-
fifth to giving the spirit of the story, and one-twenty-fifth
each to introductory facts and to an effort to cajole the
reader's attention. The conversational opening is not
so common as is supposed. Many stories will be found,
however, in which the conversation begins in the second
or third paragraph. The dialogue opening is the most
difficult one to do well, and the easiest to do badly.

2. *Stories That Open Without Dialogue*

Five hundred and forty-nine stories of the six hundred
which were classified belong under this grouping. This

[6] See p. 377, No. 21.

clearly shows that expert writers regard the opening sentences of a story as of the highest value. They realize that they must compress into a few words the essence of all that the reader ought to know in order to take up the story with intelligent interest. This is the sense in which the word "introduction" applies to the short-story of to-day. The usage of Irving, Poe, and Hawthorne was generally more leisurely than that of present-day masters (though they displayed occasional examples of rapid openings), for the short-story has progressed, in some regards, since the days of its perfecters, and in no respect more than in its introductions. Seldom nowadays does one find the long and irrelevant opening sentences which were tolerated a generation ago. It is true, by this compression the reader loses some finer touches, some detail, some reflective temper, some flights of fantasy, but for these he goes to the novel, and looks to the short-story for those illuminating flashes of word and phrase so rarely found in the longer fictional form. The novelist takes time to be lengthy, the short-story writer takes time to be brief. "Smith," says he, "I want you to know my brother Jack," and the introduction is accomplished, not without thought, not without painstaking, but withal briefly.

Remembering always that several sorts often overlap, therefore not analyzing too minutely, I subdivide the five hundred and forty-nine stories into seven groups, according to the purposes disclosed by their beginnings.

(a) *Two hundred and seven open by giving the setting, often including a glimpse of the characters.*

I have said that the word " setting " includes the surroundings in which the action begins,[7] the mood which dominates the situation, the conditions under which the story opens. It is less concerned with who 's who than with what 's what, and why.

EXTRACT FROM CAPTAIN STORMFIELD'S VISIT TO HEAVEN [8]

TAKEN FROM HIS OWN MS. BY " MARK TWAIN "

Well, when I had been dead about thirty years, I begun to get a little anxious. Mind you, I had been whizzing through space all that time, like a comet. *Like* a comet! Why, Peters, I laid over the lot of them! Of course there warn't any of them going my way, as a steady thing, you know, because they travel in a long circle like the loop of a lasso, whereas I was pointed as straight as a dart for the Hereafter; but I happened on one every now and then that was going my way for an hour or so, and then we had a bit of a brush together. But it was generally pretty one-sided, because I sailed by them the same as if they were standing still. An ordinary comet don't make more than about 200,000 miles a minute. Of course when I came across one of that sort — like Encke's and Halley's comets, for instance — it warn't anything but just a flash and a vanish, you see. You couldn't rightly call it a race. It was as if the comet was a gravel-train, and I was a telegraph dispatch. But after I got outside of our astronomical system, I used to flush a comet occasionally that was something *like*. *We* haven't got any such comets — ours don't begin.

And then follows the first incident of the story.

Of another sort, yet also establishing the setting, are these opening lines of Dr. Watson's story.

[7] It also includes more. See the next chapter.
[8] *Harper's,* Dec., 1907.

A DOCTOR OF THE OLD SCHOOL [9]

BY "IAN MACLAREN"

I

A GENERAL PRACTITIONER

Drumtochty was accustomed to break every law of health, except wholesome food and fresh air, and yet had reduced the psalmist's furthest limit to an average life-rate. Our men made no difference in their clothes for summer or winter, Drumsheugh and one of the larger farmers condescending to a top-coat on Sabbath as a penalty of their position, and without regard to temperature. They wore their blacks at a funeral, refusing to cover them with anything, out of respect to the deceased, and standing longest in the kirkyard when the north wind was blowing across a hundred miles of snow. If the rain was pouring at the junction, then Drumtochty stood two minutes longer through sheer native dourness till each man had a cascade from the tail of his coat, and hazarded the suggestion, half-way to Kildrummie, that it had been "a bit scrowie," a "scrowie" being as far short of a "shoor" as a "shoor" fell below "weet."

Here is another variety of the same general sort.

THE PHILOSOPHER IN THE APPLE ORCHARD [10]

BY "ANTHONY HOPE"

It was a charmingly mild and balmy day. The sun shone beyond the orchard and the shade was cool inside. A light breeze stirred the boughs of the old apple tree under which the philosopher sat. None of these things did the philosopher notice, unless it might be when the wind blew about the leaves of the large volume on his knees, and he had to find his place again. Then he would exclaim against the wind, shuffle the leaves till he got the right page, and settle to his reading. The book was a treatise on ontology; it was written by another

[9] From *Beside the Bonnie Briar Bush.*
[10] See p. 377, No. 20.

philosopher, a friend of this philosopher's; it bristled with fallacies, and this philosopher was discovering them all, and noting them on the fly-leaf at the end. He was not going to review the book (as some might have thought from his behaviour), or even to answer it in a work of his own. It was just that he found a pleasure in stripping any poor fallacy naked and crucifying it.

Then comes the girl and, with her, the story.

A few lines suffice for some writers to fill in the bold outlines of the setting, the rest comes as the story goes on.

AT THE NEGATIVE POLE [11]

BY VAN TASSEL SUTPHEN

Thursday being the first of November and All Saints' day, Miss Belden had attended the vesper services at S. Saviour's. On her way home across the Park she encountered Innsley. She stopped and shook hands cordially, for it had been several months since they had met.

(b) *One hundred thirty-eight open with character delineation, often adding a suggestion of the setting.* Of these a large number begin with the pronoun " He," or " She."

It is not difficult to discern why so many writers should elect to begin their narratives by painting in the setting, and why character-drawing should come first with only a slightly smaller number. Setting and characters are the picturesque elements in fiction, and it is inevitable that the two — one or the other predominating, or both standing on a level — should be present first and last in the author's vision. It is this selfsame vision

[11] *Harper's.* July, 1908.

that the reader must be made to see, and what way so clear and so direct as the opening words of the story.

In the following introduction (in the whimsical style of Irving, but not up to that standard) we have a typical example of the character opening.

AN INSPIRED LOBBYIST [12]

BY J. W. DE FOREST

A certain fallen angel (politeness toward his numerous and influential friends forbids me to mention his name abruptly) lately entered into the body of Mr. Ananias Pullwool, of Washington, D. C.

As the said body was a capacious one, having been greatly enlarged circumferentially since it acquired its full longitude, there was accommodation in it for both the soul of Pullwool himself (it was a very little one) and for his distinguished visitant. Indeed, there was so much room in it that they never crowded each other, and that Pullwool hardly knew, if he so much as mistrusted, that there was a chap in with him. But other people must have been aware of this double tenantry, or at least must have been shrewdly suspicious of it, for it soon became quite common to hear fellows say, " Pullwool has got the Devil in him."

Compare the triteness of the following introduction — always Dr. Doyle's difficult spot — with the freshness of Mr. Hewlett's opening paragraph, the next specimen.

THE MYSTERY OF SASASSA VALLEY [18]

BY A. CONAN DOYLE

Do I know why Tom Donahue is called " Lucky Tom "? Yes, I do; and that is more than one in ten of those who call

[12] *Atlantic*, Dec., 1872.
[18] See p. 377, No. 20.

him so can say. I have knocked about a deal in my time, and seen some strange sights, but none stranger than the way in which Tom gained that sobriquet, and his fortune with it. For I was with him at the time. Tell it? Oh, certainly; but it is a longish story and a very strange one; so fill up your glass again, and light another cigar while I reel it off. Yes, a very strange one; beats some fairy stories I have heard; but it's true, sir, every word of it.

THE JUDGMENT OF BORSO [14]

BY MAURICE HEWLETT

It is happily as unnecessary as it would be unwise to inquire into the ancestry of Bellaroba, a meek-eyed Girl of Venice, with whom I have some concern. Her mother was La Fragiletta, of the Old Ghetto, and her father may have been of the Council of Ten, or possibly a Doge. No one could deny it, for no one knew his name. It is certain that his daughter was not christened as she was called, equally certain that the nickname fitted her. *Bella roba,* a pretty thing, she always had been for her mother's many friends; *bella roba* in truth she looked, as La Fragiletta fastened her dark red dress, stuck a bunch of carnations in the bosom of it, and pulled up the laces around her slim neck, on a certain May morning in or about the year 1469. "The shape you are, child," said that industrious woman, "I can do nothing for you in Venice. It is as timid as a nun's. Ferrara is the place of all the world for you. I look forward to your speedy establishment in a city where a girl may be like a flagstaff and yet not be thought amiss."

(c) *Seventy-six open directly with incident.* No preliminary intaking of the breath, no pause to tighten the belt, not even a "here we go," but just a swift rush ahead. That is typical short-story form, toward which usage is markedly tending and in which writers are

[14] From *Little Novels of Italy.*

showing increasing skill. It follows the dictum of Horace, to plunge at once into the action.

What become of both setting and character delineation? Subtly interwoven as the story moves rapidly on — portraiture in one sure stroke, background in another, atmosphere in a third. Not all stories can be told in this fashion, but those that are, and told well, lay hold of the attention with a nervous grip. The difficulty lies in making the narrative keep the hold. But, difficulty or no difficulty, there is no phase of the story-teller's art which so richly repays labor as does the rapid introduction. The beginner loves his phrases. They grew in sweat and pain. But he must learn the drastic art of amputation and learn it by practising on his own stories. Perhaps the editor does not appreciate how heroic is the author who carves and slices and pares until only the compact, firm, flesh-and-blood story appears on the well-typed page, but at all events he rejoices when he meets that kind of manuscript.

DOYLE'S DEBUT [15]

BY PORTER EMERSON BROWNE

Leading the girl to a corner of the crowded little parlor where a three-legged sofa leaned weakly against the wall, Doyle seated himself tentatively upon it and motioned with spread palm at the vacancy beside him.

"Si' down, Maggie," he invited; and the tall, slender-waisted, high-pompadoured girl before him did so.

"Aw, say, Maggie," continued Doyle, as he endeavored, unsuccessfully, to hold her hand beneath a fold of skirt, "why

[15] *Everybody's,* Dec., 1907.

don' yuh marry me and cut out sellin' stockin's to a bunch o'
fussy dames that don' know what they wants, an' wouldn' buy
it if they did? I'm gittin' eighteen seventy-five now; an' two
can live on that. . . . Wha' d' yuh wan' tuh be worryin'
yuhself with a job fer?"

Alphonse Daudet is a master of all sorts of introductions. A study of *Letters From My Mill* and *Monday
Tales* will be a profit and a delight. The following is
from the latter volume.

THE LITTLE PIES

That morning, which was a Sunday, Sureau, the pastry-cook
on Rue Turenne, called his apprentice and said to him:
"Here are Monsieur Bonnicar's little pies; go and take them
to him and come back at once. It seems that the Versaillais
have entered Paris."
The little fellow, who understood nothing about politics, put
the smoking hot pies in the dish, the dish in a white napkin, and
balancing the whole upon his cap, started off on a run for Ile
St. Louis, where M. Bonnicar lived.

Then follows that charming blending of atmosphere
and incident so characteristic of the author.

LITTLE SOLDIER [16]
BY GUY DE MAUPASSANT

Every Sunday, as soon as they were at liberty, the two little
soldiers would set forth.
They would turn to the right on leaving the barracks, march
rapidly through Courbevoie as if they were out for drill; then,
as soon as they had left the houses behind, they would follow
at a more quiet pace the bare and dusty high-road that leads to
Bezons.

[16] See p. 376, No. 10.

Here we have in sixty-four words the first step in the incident, the characters introduced, and the atmosphere.

(d) *Fifty-five open with the facts, events, or motives, which lead up to the story proper.* These are real, old-fashioned introductions, modified by the new short-story spirit of brevity.

The how-I-came-to-tell-this-story beginning belongs to this class—a device which rarely interests the reader, because it is so palpable an attempt to storm his confidence. Yet the masters use this opening now and then with singular effectiveness. One class of errors, however, they uniformly avoid: introductions containing many or complex facts, events, or motives.

Occasionally a popular writer seems to be so sure of his audience that he ventures upon a start which would not be tolerated in a beginner's manuscript, unless the latter told his story as skilfully as the former. Compare this labored commencement of a really good yarn, with Daudet's ingenious use of an old device.

THE FOUR-FIFTEEN EXPRESS [17]

BY AMELIA B. EDWARDS

The events which I am about to relate took place between nine and ten years ago. Sebastopol had fallen in the early spring, the peace of Paris had been concluded since March, our commercial relations with the Russian empire were but recently renewed; and I, returning home after my first northward journey since the war, was well pleased with the prospect of spending the

[17] See p. 377, No. 20.

month of December under the hospitable and thoroughly English roof of my excellent friend, Johnathan Jelf, Esq., of Dumbleton Manor, Clayborough, East Anglia.

With more of the same unnecessary sort.

THE CURÉ OF CUCUGNAN [18]

BY ALPHONSE DAUDET

Every year, at Candlemas, the Provençal poets publish at Avignon a merry little book filled to the covers with fine verses and pretty tales. Last year's has just reached me, and I find in it a delicious fabliau, which I am going to try to translate for you, shortening it a little. Hold out your sacks, Parisians. It is the very cream of Provençal flour that I am going to serve you this time.

Here is another from the same fascinating Mill.

THE POPE'S MULE

Of all the clever sayings, proverbs, or saws with which our Provence peasants embellish their discourse, I know of none more picturesque or more peculiar than this. Within a radius of fifteen leagues of my mill, when anybody mentions a spiteful, vindictive man, he will say: "Look out for that man! he is like the Pope's mule, that keeps her kick for seven years."

I tried for a long time to find out the source of that proverb, what that Papal mule might be, and that kick kept for seven years. No one here was able to give me any information on that subject, not even Francet Mamai, my fife-player, who, however, has the whole legendary history of Provence at his fingerends. Francet agrees with me that there is probably some old tradition of Provence behind it; but he has never heard it mentioned except in the proverb.

[18] From *Letters From My Mill.*

"You won't find that anywhere except in the Grasshoppers' Library," said the old fifer, with a laugh.

I thought the suggestion a good one, and as the Grasshoppers' Library is right at my door, I shut myself up there for a week.

Notice how this introduction infallibly hints the mood of the story. Nervous or placid, gay or pathetic, grotesque or gloomy, the genuine beginning will suggest the spirit of the narrative.

(e) *Thirty-four open with some general truth which is illustrated in the story.* When the truth is well put no beginning could be more pleasing.

THE GOAT OF MONSIEUR SEGUIN [19]

BY ALPHONSE DAUDET

To M. Pierre Gringoire, Lyrical Poet, at Paris.

You will always be the same, my poor Gringoire!

Think of it! you are offered the place of reporter on a respectable Paris newspaper, and you have the assurance to refuse! Why, look at yourself, unhappy youth! Look at that worn-out doublet, those dilapidated breeches, that gaunt face, which cries aloud that it is hungry. And this is where your passion for rhyme has brought you! this is the result of your ten years of loyal service among the pages of my lord Apollo! Aren't you ashamed, finally?

Be a reporter, you idiot; be a reporter! You will earn honest crowns, you will have your special seat at Brebant's, and you will be able to appear every first night with a new feather in your cap.

No? You will not? You propose to remain perfectly free to the end? Well! just listen to the story of Monsieur Seguin's goat. You will see what one gains by attempting to remain free.

[19] *Letters From My Mill.*

Lucretia P. Hale begins her fantastic sketch, " The Spider's Eye," [20] by enlarging upon the fact that whispering galleries exist.   The chief character finds a spot in a theatre where all sounds, down to the slightest whisper, converge, and the strange things thus overheard make up the narrative.

" The Tale of a Goblin Horse," [21] by Charles C. Nott, begins with a generalization.   " Horses are like babies — chiefly interesting to their owners.   Occasionally they emerge from the enclosure of home life, and become interesting to other people.   One in a million may find his way into print, but most rare are the horses whose *characters* are worthy of record."

Sometimes these observations show a fine insight into human nature:

" Boys who are born in a small town are born free and equal," are the opening words of William Allen White's " The King of Boyville." [22]

(f) *Eighteen open with expressions chiefly designed to attract attention.*   Here are three examples:

" The distinguishing trait of Grubbins was his unexpectedness.   Grubbins was Dikkon's dog." [23]

" No man will ever know the exact truth of this story; though women may sometimes whisper it to one another after a dance, when they are putting up their hair for the night and comparing lists of victims." [24]

[20] *Putnam's Magazine,* July, 1856.   Also see p. 377, No. 19
[21] *Stories of the Army,* see p. 377, No. 23.
[22] See p. 377, No. 27.
[23] *Dikkon's Dog,* by Dorothy Lundt; see p. 377, No. 27.
[24] *False Dawn,* Rudyard Kipling, *Under the Deodars.*

" This is the history of a Failure; but the woman who
failed said it might be an instructive tale to put into print
for the benefit of the younger generation.   The younger
generation does not want instruction.   It is perfectly willing to instruct if any one will listen to it.   None the less,
here begins the story where every right-minded story
should begin, that is to say, at Simla, where all things
begin and many come to an evil end." [25]

(g) *Fifteen open with words about the character who
afterwards tells the story in the first person.*   It takes
either unusual ability or an unusual story to carry the
weight of so timeworn a device.   More " horrible examples " are herded into this corral than into any other.
Kipling does this sort of opening better than his contemporaries, standing almost alone in excellence [26]— but
occasionally even he comes to grief.

In " Long Odds," one of Rider Haggard's Allan Quat-
ermain stories,[27] two-thirds of the seven-hundred-word
introduction is wasted in irrelevancies.   One wonders
how even Daudet makes a success of this old device in
" Master Cornille's Secret," [28] but he does, and imparts
an air of truth, to boot.   Would an editor to-day pass
the following introduction?

" Francet Mamai, an old fifer, who comes sometimes to pass
the evening with me and drink mulled wine, told me the other
evening of a little village drama which my mill witnessed some
twenty years ago.   The good man's story impressed me, and I
propose to try to tell it to you as I heard it.

[25] *The Education of Otis Yeere,* Kipling.
[26] See his Mulvaney stories in *Soldiers Three,* etc.
[27] See p. 377, No. 20.
[28] *Letters From My Mill.*

"Imagine for a moment, dear readers, that you are seated before a jar of perfumed wine, and that it is an old fifer who is speaking."

Instances of this sort rebuke the critic, and show how futile it is to call all things bad which conform to a given type. This introduction is good in spite of its form, not because of it — if we must now and again have recourse to a reason which is not altogether a reason.

There yet remain to be accounted for six stories of the six hundred. This one per cent. I have labeled " unclassified," because their openings show marks of such varied character. One is a prologue of unwarranted length.[29] Another a preface.[30] A third, which shall be nameless, is a hodge-podge of every possible sort, introducing by name no less than fifteen characters in the first paragraph! In the fourth, Kipling[31] makes a native tell a story in the first person and the reader finds it out from the mere manner of the telling. The openings of the last two are quite nondescript.

II. BAD USAGE.

I shall not refer again to the forms which invite disaster, as just noted. In opening your story:

Don't be pert.

Don't be lengthy.

Don't be general.

---

[29] *A Terribly Strange Bed,* Wilkie Collins. See p. 377, No. 20.
[30] *The Legend of the Man with the Golden Brain,* Alphonse Daudet, *Letters From My Mill.*
[31] *In Black and White.*

Don't be garrulous.

Don't be roundabout.

Don't describe when you can suggest.

Don't be heavy, pompous, or too serious.

Don't tell the reader what he can imagine.

Don't be content with a commonplace opening.

Don't think that sincere simplicity is commonplace.

Don't let the introduction weight down or overshadow the story.

Don't strike one note in the introduction and another in the body of the story.

Don't touch anything which is not a live wire leading direct to the real centre of the story.

OUTLINE SUMMARY
THE OPENING OF THE STORY

I. THE BEST USAGE (SIX HUNDRED STORIES EXAMINED).

  1. *Fifty-one Open With Dialogue*

    (a) Twenty-six Use Dialogue to Give the Setting

    (b) Twelve to Delineate Characters

    (c) Nine to Suggest the Spirit of the Story

    (d) Two to Supply Preliminary Explanations

    (e) Two to Win the Reader's Attention

  2. *Five Hundred Forty-nine Open Without Dialogue*

    (a) Two Hundred seven Open With the Setting

    (b) One Hundred Thirty-eight With Character Delineation

    (c) Seventy-six With Incident

    (d) Fifty-five With Introductory Facts

    (e) Thirty-four With General Truths Illustrated by the Stories

(f) Eighteen With Expressions Designed to Win Attention
(g) Fifteen With Words About the Secondary Narrator
(h) Six Miscellaneous

II. BAD USAGE

QUESTIONS AND EXERCISES FOR CLASS OR INDIVIDUAL STUDY

NOTE: Select any plots you please from Appendix C as bases for the following work. The instructor may vary these assignments indefinitely.

1. Write merely the introduction to a story, beginning with dialogue to give the setting.

2. Another, opening with dialogue to delineate a character.

3. Another, using dialogue to lead up to the story proper by fact or explanation.

4. Another, beginning without dialogue, giving the setting.

5. Another, introducing a character.

6. Another, opening directly with incident.

7. Another, with facts or explanations which lead up to the story proper.

8. Rewrite one of the dialogue introductions given in this chapter, without the use of introductory dialogue.

9. Rewrite another of the introductions, recasting it in dialogue form.

10. Do the same with your own writings, as assigned above.

CHAPTER VIII

THE SETTING OF THE STORY

Marble, paint, and language, the pen, the needle, and the brush, all have their grossnesses, their ineffable impotences, their hours, if I may so express myself, of insubordination. It is the work and it is a great part of the delight of any artist to contend with these unruly tools, and now by brute energy, now by witty expedient, to drive and coax them to effect his will.— STEVENSON, *A Note on Realism.*

It is the habit of my imagination to strive after as full a vision of the medium in which a character moves as of the character itself. The psychological causes which prompted me to give such details of Florentine life and history as I have given [in *Romola*] are precisely the same as those which determined me in giving the details of English village life in *Silas Marner* or the "Dodson" life, out of which were developed the destinies of poor Tom and Maggie.— GEORGE ELIOT, quoted in her *Life* by J. W. CROSS.

Setting consists of the circumstances, material and immaterial, in which the characters are seen to move in the story. Its elements are time, place, occupations, and (I lack a more expressive word) conditions. Each of these we must briefly examine, together with the literary devices by which setting is established. First, however, a general view.

149

I. SETTING IN GENERAL

The setting of a short-story no more exists for its own sake than the setting of a diamond. The story — the diamond — is the chief thing. If the setting, by its ornate style, its beauty, its imperfections, its very bulk, should overshadow and obscure the gem, it would be worse than useless. But when story and setting are in harmony, the effect is as of one jewel — each part indeed not indistinguishable from the other, but so integrated that the highest enjoyment arises from considering them as a whole. Hold all things in true perspective.

As the setting exists to glorify the short-story, so the story governs the *tone* of the setting. Do the characters need contrast to silhouette them boldly, the setting must be accommodated to this requirement; and a like adaptation is required if harmony, instead of contrast, be the tone needed for their effective presentation.

In the sketch, setting may rise to the eminent place and become practically the story itself; in the character-study it sinks to a subdued position.

Certain story-tellers delight to create a setting and then let the characters work out their destinies in this fixed environment. There is no objection to this method for those who can employ it successfully, but in either case setting and characters must be harmonized or contrasted artistically, and, as before, setting is for the sake of the story. Its influence is powerful. As in real life environment strongly influences character, so in fiction we may see the power of surroundings working upon the emotions, the moods, the actions, even the destinies of the characters.[1] Zola goes so far as to say that the environment " determines and completes the man." [2]

Setting is first of all a preparation. We have seen in the preceding chapter that its lines are often laid in the very opening paragraphs of the story. But it may also be progressive, and move, like the shadow of the traveler, everywhere the characters go, until at length, with the story's close, it lingers in the mind as an integral part of the picture.

Setting is sometimes prophetic, forecasting, while it assists in creating, the mood of the story.

Upon the reader, setting lays the impression of reality, or of unreality, in the picture. Without its realistic pictorial help the story would be as bare as was the early drama unassisted by special costume and scenery.

When the characters live, move, and have their being in the setting, the result is atmosphere. Atmosphere is thus an effect. It is felt, not seen. *Through* its medium the reader must see all the action, yes, all the details of the story. Atmosphere gives value to the tones of fiction as in real life it does to landscape. The hills are actually the same in cloud and in sunshine, but the eye sees them as different through the mediate atmosphere. And so setting and characters, perfectly adjusted, make the reader, that is to say the beholder, see the story in the very tones the literary artist desires. A story of the sea has an atmosphere of its own, but the atmosphere

---

[1] As in Hardy's *Tess of the D'Urbervilles*.
[2] *Le Roman Expérimental.* Compare Howells, quoted on p. 94.

does not consist merely of the accurately colored picture of sea and strand and sailor and ship and sky. The whole story is informed with the *spirit* of the sea — its tang clings to the garments, its winds breathe through every passage, its wonderful lights and glooms tone the whole story. Without it the story would be a poor thing, bloodless and inert.

Before taking up the elements of setting, it will be well to examine the literary means by which it is effected.

II. DESCRIPTION AS A DEVICE TO ESTABLISH SETTING

Rhetoricians recognize, and it is their function to discuss, at least four forms of discourse: Description, Narration, Exposition, and Argumentation.

This book is not a system of rhetoric; [3] the rhetorical principles and usages it takes up are discussed solely with a view to throwing light upon the structure of the short-story. The fiction-writer has to do with all the forms of discourse, but especially with narration and description. The principles and methods of narration, as applied to the short-story, are distributed throughout this volume, as is evident; but description, as an element of setting, requires a few simple words.

To describe is to picture. In talking of description we naturally speak of portraying, delineating, coloring,

[3] For the use of fiction writers, good general treatments of these subjects are to be found in *English Composition,* Barrett Wendell, and *Talks on Writing English,* Arlo Bates. An excellent formal treatise is *The Working Principles of Rhetoric,* Genung.

and all the devices of the picture painter. To describe is to visualize, hence we must look at description as a pictorial process, whether the writer deals with material, or with spiritual objects.

If you were asked to describe a rapid-fire gun you might go about it in either of two ways: give a technical account of its appearance and nature, in whole and in detail, or else describe it as a terrible engine of slaughter, dwelling upon its effects rather than upon its structure.

With the former kind of description, which is really *exposition* — the precise setting forth of what a thing truly is — the short-story of to-day has but little to do. The form is too short to admit of the circumstantial exposition which is permitted to the novel, but which was employed in short-stories now and then by Poe and Hawthorne. True, minute expository description is occasionally needed in the short-story, and the observation which lies fundamental to all description must be close and painstaking; but it must be brief, for the important result to be attained is a vivid picture, an effect, an impression, of the person or thing described. These " little miracles of observation," to adopt Mr. Howells' clever phrase, need not be dry and lifeless, but may give the meaning of things and subdue the details. Perhaps this may be abusing the distinguished realist's epithet, but at all events it expresses the method of the typical short-story to-day. Some details make an object different from others of its class, while other details identify it with its class. You must learn to decide when and how to use the one and reject the other. It is difficult to make this whole distinction clear, and, after all, nothing but training, or experience, or your own common sense, can teach you that which is vital in a picture and that which is dependent.

Again, this literary, this significant, this selective sort of description is of two kinds: that which has to do with the persons of the story, and that which deals with impersonal objects. Naturally, these two provinces are not always sharply separated, and here and there may intimately overlap. The chapter on " Character and Characterization " takes up the former, while the latter we are now to consider. However, most of the principles laid down for the one will apply also to the other.

In so brief a literary form as the short-story

1. *Description Should be Mainly Suggestive*

It is only the trained observer who notes all the details of a scene. Even familiar landscapes, houses, and rooms, usually leave upon us only general impressions; but take away one of the salient features and the scene at once strikes us as different, yet somehow the same; it may require a friend to tell us just what is missing, but a single feature lacking makes all the change. Now it is the picturing of the striking characteristics in a scene which constitutes suggestive description. Gray, in a letter to West, spoke of minute describing as " an ill habit that will wear off "; and Disraeli said description was " always a bore both to the describer and the de-

scribee "; while Stevenson averred that " no human being ever spoke of scenery for above two minutes at a
time, which makes one suspect we hear too much of it
in literature." [4]

To catalogue all the details is to weary the mind. How
much better to bring out just those points which enable
the reader to supply the rest.   You have seen those ingenious black-and-white sketches which are " so simple "
— until you undertake to do one from life.   A few black
strokes and the figure is complete.   Not an outline, nor
even actual likeness to the features which are suggested.
Those marks are not really in the form of lips and eyes
and nose, yet somehow the face stands out complete —
memory, association, and imagination have filled in the
details.

Coleridge's *Ancient Mariner* is full of this strongly
sketched suggestion.   Of the poet's method in this masterpiece, as contrasted with expository description, Lowell says:

" And how picturesque it is in the proper sense of the
word.   I know nothing like it.   There is not a description in it.   It is all picture.   Descriptive poets generally
confuse us with multiplicity of detail; we cannot see
their forest for the trees; but Coleridge never errs in this
way.   With instinctive tact he touches the right chord
of association, and is satisfied, as we also are." [5]

Note these suggestive lines about Avignon, from Daudet's " The Pope's Mule ": " Ah! the happy days! the

[4] Quoted in *How to Write a Novel,* p. 67.
[5] Prose works, Vol. VI, p. 74.

happy city! Halberds that did not wound, state prisons where they put wine to cool. No famine; no wars."

2. *Brief Description May Be by Epithet*

"Ever-mindful," "blue-eyed," "white-armed," "laughter-loving," are now conventional compounds, but fresh enough when Homer first conjoined them. The centuries have not yet improved upon "Wheels round, brazen, eight-spoked," or "Shields smooth, beautiful, brazen, well-hammered," [6] though they may be thought too heroic for ordinary prose. Observe the effective use of epithet in Will Levington Comfort's "The Fighting Death":

"That 'Come on, fellows!' changed the aspect of affairs in the minds of several of the men — a quick and business-like utterance. In it there was neither rank nor nerves, which are not needed in the Silang gorges. It pulled a cheer from the waiting van, leeched against the cliff; an instant later a raw, high-pitched yell and a drumming of guns came from the heights. Down the steep bank scrambled the little party, the Cumberer limping in the lead. Glawm's trick to occupy the attention of the rebels was pure logic. The Thirteenth had entered the impregnated zone. One was down.

"Birdie turned, unfolded his command, lifted the fallen and chucked the body easily up the trail out of range, rejoining his men in a twinkling. The staff muttered acclaim. Down, down toward the little ribbon of river that boiled with wasted shots, trotted this plaything of the enemy." [7]

[6] *Talks on Writing English*, Bates, p. 197.
[7] *Lippincott's*, March, 1907.

3. *Description May Be by Simple Hint*

Lowell notes a happy instance of this sort of picturing by intimation when he says of Chaucer:

" Sometimes he describes amply by the merest hint, as where the Friar, before setting himself down, drives away the cat.   We know without need of more words that he has chosen the snuggest corner." [8]

4. *Description May be Direct*

This statement is plain enough without exposition. Use your own judgment as to whether in picturing a given scene you had better proceed from a general view to the details, or first give the details and thus build up the general picture.   In the short-story direct description should be very brief indeed.

5. *Description May Depict a Thing by Its Effects*

" When the spectator's eye is dazzled, and he shades it, we form the idea of a splendid object; when his face turns pale, of a horrible one; from his quick wonder and admiration we form the idea of great beauty; from his silent awe, of great majesty." [9]

6. *Description Often Employs Figures of Speech*

(a) *Simile:*

" Harrow-on-the-Hill, with its pointed spire, rises blue in the distance; and distant ridges, like the receding waves, rise into

[8] Quoted in *Talks On Writing English.*
[9] Mozley's *Essays.*

blueness, one after the other, out of the low-lying mist; the last ridge bluely melting into space. In the midst of it all, gleams the Welsh Harp Lake, like a piece of sky that has become unstuck and tumbled into the landscape with its shining side up." [10]

(b) *Metaphor:*

"Before us lies a sea of fern, gone a russet-brown from decay, in which are isles of dark green gorse—" [11]

(c) *Personification:*

"—— and little trees with scarlet and orange and lemon-colored leaflets fluttering down, and running after each other on the bright grass, under the brisk west wind which makes the willows rustle and turn up the whites of their leaves in pious resignation to the coming change." [12]

(d) *Hyperbole:*

" 'Just, so,' said the notary, pulling out his watch, which was two inches thick and looked like a Dutch man-of-war." [13]

7. *Description is Strongly Influenced by Point of View*

Any of three methods may be adopted: The single viewpoint may be maintained throughout the description, as though one would take his stand at the most advantageous point and describe only what could be seen from that single position. *Re-read* IMPORTANT NOTE, p. 124.

Or the viewpoint may shift progressively, as when the reader is being conducted along a highroad.

[10] *Peter Ibbetson,* Du Maurier.
[11] *Ibid.*
[12] *Ibid.*
[13] Quoted in Genung's *Rhetoric,* from Balzac.

Or the viewpoint may remain stationary while the object moves, as when a vessel approaches the beholder.

Oftener than not, description will make use of a number of the foregoing methods instead of confining itself to any one type to delineate a given scene.

8. *The Seven Steps in Description*

A very little consideration will show us that in preparing a careful description we more or less consciously take the following steps: OBSERVATION, READING, IMAGINATION, COMPARISON, SELECTION, COORDINATION, and COMPRESSION.

All of these have to do with first collecting and then arranging the *facts* of the proposed setting for use in building up a description, however simply the scene is to be depicted. The last decade has intensified the discussion as to whether the novelist shall devote his power of faithful delineation to studies in local color, as Mary Wilkins Freeman, or, like Balzac, choose a universal scope. This argument does not directly affect the short-story writer, and may be dismissed with the remark that to what "school" soever an author may incline he will find ample use for his ability to grasp the essentials of a scene.

Later usage has developed more and more the spirit of historical and physical accuracy in the writer's attempt to describe setting. This tends toward realism, and as this spirit grows we may expect to see romance and imagination increasingly subordinated. Even now little really imaginative fiction is being produced; instead, we see much fine work in accurate delineation. The same careful study of historical periods, costuming and local color, which makes the stage so pictorial and the painter so faithful in his portrayals, has inspired the writer of short-stories. But be on your guard lest you lose the spirit of the story in what Frank Norris used to call its " clothes," and so turn a virtue into a folly.

III. THE ELEMENTS OF SETTING

As we now consider the four elements of setting — Time, Place, Occupations and Conditions — remember that two or more of these will produce what is loosely called *background;* that is, that part of the setting which is introduced for the purpose of "bringing out" the characters, whether by means of harmony or of contrast. It is this background, bold or obscure, clear-cut or subtly suggested, that is so potent to charm the reader when it is worked in with a deft and well-considered touch. No other phase of the story-teller's art is so alluring and fascinating as that which causes the characters to play in activity, or reveal their intricate yet sharply defined motives, upon the chosen background. Here is the fairest field for observation. You remember that Flaubert counseled his pupil Maupassant to look at an object until he saw in it all that every one else saw, and then continue to look until he saw what no one else saw. This applies not only to analytical observation but to constructive observation as well.

Lessing inquires: "How do we obtain a clear idea of a thing in space? First we observe its separate parts, then the union of these parts, and finally the whole. Our senses perform these various operations with such amazing rapidity as to make them seem but one. This rapidity is absolutely essential to our obtaining an idea of the whole, which is nothing more than the result of the conception of the parts and of their connection with each other." [14]

So we must regard each of these elements as only a part of the greater fact — the entire setting.

1. *Time*

Here we have an idea broad and effective, more or less openly influencing every story. The author may flatly announce the two elements of time — the period of his story, and its duration; or he may ignore both; or he may merely suggest these conditions; or he may gradually make both period and duration plain as the story proceeds.

(a) *The general period* will be future, present-day, or past. The whole range of history lies before you for choice, and woe to you if you set twentieth-century people to performing against a Roman background, in Greek costumes, while speaking in Medieval phrases! Choose no period that you do not know or cannot master, unless you do not fear the rejection slip. Even a year makes a revolutionary difference in setting when that year is

[14] *Laocoön*, p. 102.

1534 in England, 1861 in America, or 1870 in France.
For another example, it is worth while, if your swash-
bucklers engage in sword-play, to know in what period
duellists held poniards in their left hands, and in what
period cloaks.   Mannerisms of speech, of dress, of sport,
of gaming — a whole world of detail — rest upon time
in the setting, for time influences place, occupation, and
conditions.

(b) *Season,* too, must not be forgotten, with its
pageantry of color and its peculiar chain of limitations.
Either keep birds and flowers out of your picture or have
them sing and bloom in season.   Do not be a " nature
faker " in fiction.

(c) *Day and night* offer pitfalls for the unwary.
Goethe once complained that in describing Ivanhoe's entrance into Cedric's great dining hall, Scott was too minute in recording details, for he showed even Ivanhoe's
shoes, which could not really be noticed by night in the
gloom of that vast apartment.   " If Sidney Lanier [15] had
ever noted carefully the time setting of the climax in
Silas Marner, he could not have written of ' a ray of
sunshine striking through the window and illuminating
the little one's head.' " [16]
What simplicity and sublimity mingle in the setting
established by the opening lines of Tappan's exquisite
hymn, in which spirit and background harmonize so perfectly :

[15] *The English Novel,* p. 28.
[16] *The Study of a Novel,* Whitcomb, p. 78.

> 'Tis midnight; and on Olive's brow
> The star is dimmed that lately shone:
> 'Tis midnight; in the garden, now,
> The suffering Saviour prays alone.

(d) *Duration of time* is not less important, though less prominent, than period. Many an unwary author has slipped on the simple matter of forgetting that it takes time to travel here, there, and back again; that people normally grow older with the lapse of years; and that events must be consistent with the procession of the seasons. Even the many-eyed proofreader overlooks some glaring inconsistencies of time duration in stories. In "Ouida's" idyllic pastoral, "A Leaf in the Storm," [17] Reine Allix is in her ninety-third year before her grandson Bernadou proposes to Margot, and the aged dame is still ninety-three after Bernadou is accepted, is married, and has become the father of a boy then more than a year old!

2. *Place*

Since Julius Cæsar has reminded us that certain tribes "differ among themselves in languages, customs, and laws," we must observe how important a part place plays in the setting. The author may propose to locate his story "nowhere in particular"—and then that is what his setting will resemble. Not that he need announce the name of country, section, and town, but he himself must know it, or mentally construct it, and be faithful to its

[17] See p. 377, No. 20.

local color. How many stories come to the manuscript-reader's desk (they seldom reach the editor-in-chief) the settings of which bring to mind Artemus Ward's naïve confession as to one of the figures on his panorama: " I can conceal it from you no longer—it is a horse!" Their Parisians should be labeled, for their surroundings might equally well be those of Madrid or of Petrograd. A cowboy must be such in more than name to be convincing. Paolo Veronese dressed the people in his painting *The Marriage at Cana,* in the clothes of his day. It was a *tour de force,* and what did he gain?

Local color cannot be dreamed out. If you have not visited and studied the locality of which you write, at least consult a book or a friend, and even then you are liable to go wrong. No African traveler would ever recognize the background of Johnson's *Rasselas.*

A meritorious instance in point is found in the following introduction to Harold MacGrath's novelette, *The Princess Elopes.* The atmosphere, the names, the customs, the color, are Teutonic, yet the grand-duchy and the principality are imaginary. The setting conforms not to unchecked imagination but to the imagined reality.

"It is rather difficult in these days for a man who takes such scant interest in foreign affairs—trust a whilom diplomat for that!—to follow the continual geographical disturbances of European surfaces. Thus, I cannot distinctly recall the exact location of the Grand Duchy of Barscheit, or of the neighboring principality of Doppelkinn. It meets my needs and purposes however, to say that Berlin and Vienna were easily accessible, and that a three-hours' journey would bring you under the shadow of the Carpathian Range, where, in my diplomatic days, I used often hunt the 'bear that walks like a man.'"

Manifestly, it is much easier to write of a specific locality than of a general place — if there be such a thing.   For example, set your scene in North America; now contract the setting to the United States, to the East, to Pennsylvania, to eastern Pennsylvania, to the anthracite coal regions, to Pittston, to the foreign quarter — and as you narrow down the place your pictures increase in vividness and in suggestiveness both to you and to your reader.

In passing, let me say that the same idea applies to the use of specific words for painting in the local color of a community.   Which of these two pictures is the clearer?   " The man was lying on a rock near the large frame house;" " The gardener sprawled on a granite boulder a few yards to the left of the rambling, clapboarded house "?   Generality in the former sentence has been individualized in the latter.   Local color demands precise words.   Not that description is a matter of mere words.   It is not.   It consists rather of calling things by their most precise and simple names, and noting their individualities, that they may be distinguished from all generally similar objects.   It is not words, primarily, but ideas with words exactly fitted to them, that make delineation vivid.

Once or twice I have used here an expression which is current among those who speak and write of fiction — " local color."   What does it connote in the language of criticism?

Mr. James Lane Allen says:

"A friend of mine — a painter — had just finished reading some little thing that I had succeeded in having published in the *Century*. 'What do you think of it?' I asked him. 'Tell me frankly what you like and what you don't like.'

"'It's interestingly told, dramatic, polished, and all that, Allen,' was his reply, 'but why in the world did you neglect such an opportunity to drop in some color here, and at this point, and there?'

"It came over me like that," said the Kentuckian, snapping his fingers, "that words indicating colors can be manipulated by the writer just as pigments are by the painter. I never forgot the lesson. And now when I describe a landscape, or a house, or a costume, I try to put it in such words that an artist can paint the scene from my words." [18]

This is local color. [19]

Local color must be presented pervasively, not in chunks. It must touch everything in the story that would naturally be influenced by local conditions — language, customs, costumes, and all the rest, and it must keep on coloring them, never for a moment allowing the people to speak out of "character," act out of consistency, or break away from the requisite environment.

In "Ouida's" "A Leaf in the Storm," the author gives the local setting thus progressively. The picture of the quaint Normandy village, Berceau de Dieu, grows

[18] *Steps in Journalism,* Shuman, p. 201.
[19] In *The Art of Writing Fiction,* p. 40, Mr. S. Baring Gould **is** quoted as giving similar testimony.

clearer as the story moves on. It is nearly half told
when we see Reine Allix —

"A tall and strong woman, very withered and very bent and
very brown, yet with sweet, dark, flashing eyes that had still
light (*sic*) in them, and a face that was still noble, though
nearly a century had bronzed it with its harvest suns and blown
on it with its wintry winds" [sitting at night by her window in the roof and meditating on the wedding of her grandson Bernadou, just accomplished.] "From her lattice in the
eaves she saw straight up the village street; saw the dwellings
of her lifelong neighbors, the slopes of the rich fields, the gleam
of the broad, gray water, the whiteness of the crucifix against
the darkened skies."

The ability to reproduce the temper and tone of a wide
locality has built up a school of present-day writers
whose very names suggest to the magazine reader their
chosen sections. Will N. Harben has spoken for northern Georgia, "Charles Egbert Craddock" for the Tennessee mountains, Hamlin Garland for the northwestern
farm-country, Mary Wilkins Freeman for humble life
in New England, James Lane Allen for Kentucky, Elsie
Singmaster for the Pennsylvania Germans, George W.
Cable for Louisiana, Thomas Nelson Page for Virginia,
and — not to extend further a list to which many other
excellent names at home and abroad might be added of
those whose work rivals the best — each of these has
found in his characteristic local conditions an appealing
quality that has enriched the American short-story.

A useful device for helping the author to visualize his
locale is to prepare a topographical map of the entire
physical setting, something after the fashion of the au-

thors of *Treasure Island, The Forest Lovers,* and *Quincy Adams Sawyer.* Not all writers would wish to publish the map, but an exact sketch would at least help to keep the movements of the characters in the place consistent and realistic.

3. *Occupations*

The setting not only influences the characters in what they are, but in what they do. Contrariwise, what the characters are doing in a story will govern the setting. The two must be consistent. A football game argues the "gridiron," with eleven men on each team and not nine, as a writer had it in a recent story. A whole vocabulary of technical terms must be at the pen's point — terms of business, of sport, of social life, and of endless other special occupations — in order to a faithful presentment of local color. I know of no fault so prevalent, and so hopeless, as the efforts of the tyro to describe occupations with which he has not made himself familiar.

4. *Conditions*

I have said that this is not a satisfactory word. No more is "environments." By it I mean all the conditions — moral, mental, spiritual, emotional, physical, social — *all* the conditions which are conceived of by the author as limiting the actors in their working out of the story. Some have called it the "mood" of the story, but it is something more than mood. And these surrounding, all-pervading, penetrating conditions must be so sketched in that the reader may be able to measure all the handicaps which work for and against the characters before they start, and while they are doing or becoming.

When " place " and " conditions " are handled carefully together some fine harmonies and contrasts result. The gloomy setting prepares for the catastrophe, as in Poe's " The Fall of the House of Usher; " or the calm after the storm fits in with the mood of self-renunciation after years of struggle. In *The Last Days of Pompeii* the eruption of Vesuvius is in harmony with the mood of the story, as is the case with the burning of Rome in *Quo Vadis,* its weaker successor. See the perfect concord of mood and setting in this passage from James Lane Allen's *The Choir Invisible*:

> The next morning the parson, standing a white cold shepherd before his chilly wilderness flock, preached a sermon from the text: "I shall go softly all my years." While the heads of the rest were bowed during the last moments of prayer, she rose and slipped out. "Yes," she said to herself, gathering her veil closely about her face as she alighted at the door of her house and the withered leaves of November were whirled fiercely about her feet, "I shall go softly all my years."

But the conditions may strongly contrast with the mood of the action. To quote again from " Ouida's " " A Leaf in the Storm ":

> One evening in this gracious and golden time the people sat out as usual when the day was done, talking from door to door, the old women knitting or spinning, the younger ones mending their husbands' or brothers' blouses or the little blue shirts of their infants, the children playing with the dogs on the sward that edged the stones of the street, and above all the great calm heavens and the glow of the sun that had set.

Reine Allix, like the others, sat before the door, for once doing nothing, but with folded hands and bended head dreamily taking pleasure in the coolness that had come with evening —

Suddenly there came along the road between the trees an old man and a mule; it was Mathurin the miller — He paused before the cottage of Reine Allix; he was dusty, travel-stained, and sad. Margot ceased laughing among her flowers as she saw her old master. None of them knew why, yet the sight of him made the air seem cold and the night seem near.

"There is terrible news," he said, drawing a sheet of printed words from his coat-pocket —"terrible news! We are to go to war."

5. *The Setting Entire*

In the ardent effort to secure individual effects, do not overlook the unity of the whole setting. Keep ever in mind Poe's dictum regarding unity of impression. Let the setting constitute a complete scene, a unified picture, clean-cut or hazy, as you please, but nevertheless as effectively set forth as are "good deeds in a naughty world." Setting, in proper harmony or contrast with the plot, will produce convincing work. Then the characters will march toward their destinies with an air of fitness as admirable as it is rare. The storm breaks when the hero's moral tension is at its height. The grisly night prompts the trembling weakling to forswear his evil purposes. The breaking clouds seem to clear up the doubts of the beleaguered soul. Does not all the environment goad Macbeth steadily on to his crime and its doom, just as her surroundings happily conduct Portia to her joy? Hawthorne hedges Donatello about with a setting — conditions past and present — which makes his crime inevitable, and all his after life shares in the same tragic sequence. The skilful dramatist shows the soul in its hour of crisis poised ready for either course. And all the circumstance of music and form and color and air and word combine to move the will to its resolve. Then, when once that resolve is taken, and the deed is accomplished, the setting falls quietly into its new grooves to fit the man in his new mood.

OUTLINE SUMMARY

I. SETTING IN GENERAL

II. DESCRIPTION AS USED TO ESTABLISH SETTING
1. *Should be Mainly Suggestive*
2. *May be by Epithet*
3. *May be by Simple Hint*
4. *May be Direct*
5. *May Depict a Thing by Its Effects*
6. *Often Employs Figures of Speech*
7. *Is Strongly Influenced by Point of View*
8. *Seven Steps in Description*

III. THE ELEMENTS OF SETTING
1. *Time*
   (*a*) General Period
   (*b*) Season
   (*c*) Day and Night
   (*d*) Duration
2. *Place*
   Local Color
3. *Occupations*
4. *Conditions*
5. *The Setting Entire*

QUESTIONS AND EXERCISES FOR CLASS AND INDIVIDUAL STUDY

1. Select from any sources short-stories whose settings are established by (a) direct description, (b) suggestion, (c) epithet, (d) hint, (e) figures of speech.

2. Rewrite the opening setting of one of your old stories from one of these points of view: (a) a distant point, (b) the centre of the scene, (c) a fixed point while the objects move.

3. Which one of the "seven steps in description" seems to you to be most important? Which next?

4. In about two hundred words write the opening setting of a story set (a) in any previous century whose history you have recently studied; (b) in the present; (c) in the future.

5. Describe a night scene (a) at a fire; (b) on the ocean; (c) during a riot; (d) at a college dance; (e) at a secret "spread"; (f) after an athletic victory; (g) in a graveyard; (h) in the desert.

6. Write the opening setting of a local-color story set near your own home.

7. Outline a setting showing an occupation with which you are familiar, as some branch of manufacture, commerce, mining, or farming.

8. Outline settings that will (a) harmonize, (b) contrast, with the characters.

9. Construct a plot in which setting influences the destinies of the characters, as it does in *The Outcasts of Poker Flat*, Harte.

10. Select from Hardy's *Tess of the D'Urbervilles* passages in which nature sympathizes with the action of the story and the moods of the characters.

11. Briefly describe, or suggestively present the picture of, (a) a city street-crossing in winter; (b) the entrance to a place of amusement; (c) a police court; (d) a country fair; (e) a rain-storm in a lonely village.

12. Vary the foregoing by assuming successively (in as many cases as may be assigned) the view-point of a tramp, a cynical old man, a boy, a comical foreigner, an unlucky man, etc.

13. Outline a scene and suggest an incident in surprising contrast to the atmosphere.

14. Suggest an incident in harmony with the same scene.

CHAPTER IX

THE BODY OF THE STORY

We accomplish less by rule than by observation and imitation.— CRAMER, *Talks to Students on The Art of Study.*

. . . the one rule is to be infinitely various; to interest, to disappoint, to surprise, and yet still to gratify; to be ever changing, as it were, the stitch, and yet still to give the effect of an ingenious neatness.— STEVENSON, *On Some Technical Elements of Style in Literature.*

From this chapter heading let no one infer that all, or even most, good short-stories exhibit clearly marked divisions of introduction, body, and conclusion. Quite on the contrary, so free is the form that all sorts of material may now and then be found in all sorts of places in the story. However, the body, or the story proper, is the natural place to look for the essential elements of the story — the really characteristic things which make a story individual. So, too, in general, the body of the story will display the qualities which go to make the short-story a distinct literary species — though no one story is likely to contain them all in a perfect degree. The body of the story, then, is what we wait for, with it the true plot begins and ends, whether the writer prefaces some explanatory words or whether he plunges into his yarn without introduction.

Just about every element of prose composition, as expounded by rhetoricians, may be found in the short-story. To some of them I have already referred, especially in the chapters on " Plot," " Introduction," and " Setting," while to others I shall advert in succeeding sections. There are, however, seven points which particularly bear upon the body of the story, as containing the plot and much of the setting: Incident, Emotion, Crisis, Suspense, Climax, Denouement, and Conclusion.[1]

1. *Incident*

It must be reiterated that the short-story differs from the sketch essentially in that it " cannot consist simply of a fixed picture, a description of a man in repose. It must show him acting and acted upon. . . . The man can only move as he is swayed internally by his emotions; and the movement can only be seen externally in its effect on his surroundings, his background."[2]

Not everyone will go the full length with Stevenson in subordinating characters to incident, but few will dis-

---

[1] It will be observed that nowhere in this treatise have I attempted to name in order all the essential parts of the short-story. In *The Technique of the Novel* Dr. Horne regards the essentials of that literary form as being: Plot, Motive (purpose) and Verisimilitude, Character-Study, Emotional Excitement, Background, and Style. It has not seemed wise to treat the short-story under so rigid a classification, for the reason that some of the subordinate elements — Dialogue, for example — may touch all the parts with equal intimacy: while Emotion may show itself in every phase of the story. The truth is, too close an analysis may cause us to lose sight of the delicate blending of the parts of the story. Its characteristics often pervade the whole rather than stand out as entities.

[2] *The Technique of the Novel.* Horne, p. 23.

pute the dictum that in the short-story the interest becomes attenuated when we are fed upon mere character-
analysis without illustration by incident of how the characters work out their inner spirit. But Stevenson may
speak for himself:

" In character-studies the pleasure we take is critical;
we watch, we approve, we smile at incongruities, we are
moved to sudden heats of sympathy with courage, suffering, or virtue. But the characters are still themselves, they are not us; the more clearly they are depicted, the more widely do they stand away from us, the
more imperiously do they thrust us back into our place
as a spectator. . . . It is not character but incident
that woos us out of our reserve. Something happens as
we desire it to happen to ourselves; some situation, that
we have long dallied with in fancy, is realized in the story
with enticing and appropriate details. Then we forget
the characters; then we push the hero aside; then we
plunge into the tale in our own person and bathe in fresh
experience; and then, and then only, do we say that we
have been reading a romance." [3]

The extreme realists demand, in the words of Paul
Bourget, " mediocrity of heroes, systematic diminution of
plot, and almost total suppression of dramatic action." [4]
In the following quotation substitute " short-story " for
" novel," and you have the golden middle ground.

[3] *A Gossip on Romance.*
[4] *Le Roman Experimental.*

" The sacrifice of action to some extent to psychological evolution in modern fiction may be an advance in
the art as an intellectual entertainment, if the writer does
not make that evolution his end, and does not forget that
the indispensable thing in a novel is the story. The
novel of mere adventure or mere plot, it need not be
urged, is of a lower order than that in which the evolution of the characters and their interaction make the
story. The highest fiction is that which embodies both;
that is, the story in which action is the result of mental
and spiritual forces in play." [5]

However the balance may tilt between pure character-
interest and incident, one thing is sure: in the typical
short-story — let it be repeated — something happens.
The sketch is content with mere pictures of static life,
but the short-story is dynamic. These dynamic happenings we call incidents—*incidents related to plot.*
The whole of the story may comprise just a single
incident, or a main incident may be fed and built up by
one or more minor incidents, related vitally to the forward movement of the plot. In " The Reformation of
Calliope " [6] the main incident is the mistake of Calliope's
mother in thinking that he is city marshal. The contributory incident is Calliope's fight with the real city
marshal. The resulting incident is Calliope's masquerade
as marshal. These are all essential to the plot.
But not all incidents in the average short-story are of

[5] *Modern Fiction,* Charles Dudley Warner.
[6] See p. 73.

equal value to the plot.   Here are some discriminating words from Charity Dye on this point.[7]

" In a well-appointed story, not only must everything that happens seem to grow naturally out of the situation, but it must seem to be the only thing that could happen under the circumstances.   This gives rise to the classification of incidents, according to their importance, into *plot incident* proper and *developing incidents,* each having an especial office of its own.   The author knows his plot before he writes, but he frequently improvises means for its unfolding as the lines flow from his pen. These means for unfolding are called developing incidents."

But some developing incidents serve rather as illustrations than as indispensable elements of the plot.   It is easy to recall a simple example.   In Maupassant's " Moonlight "[8] the entire situation is this: A woman-hating abbé has always warned his niece against earthly love; but coming upon her one moonlight night with her lover, he suddenly concludes that " Perhaps God has made such nights, in order to throw a veil of idealism over the loves of men."   Now, to show how remarkable was this complete reversal of sentiment, the author must first picture the abbé's bitter scorn of womanhood.   " He would shake his cassock when he went out of the door of the convent, and would stride swiftly away as if he

[7] *The Story-Teller's Art,* p. 34.
[8] See p. 376, No. 10.

were flying from some danger." This is merely a developing incident. Another equally expressive action might have been chosen without in the slightest degree affecting the plot. But when the time comes for the author to prepare the reader for the change about to be wrought in the austere priest, the ascetic is looking out into his garden, " profoundly moved by the grand yet tranquil beauty of the pallid night.

" In his little garden, bathed with soft light, his fruit-trees, set in rows, cast the shadow of their slender limbs, scarce clothed with verdure, on the gravelled paths; while the giant honey-suckle clinging to the wall of his house exhaled a fragrant, as it were a sweetened breath, so that a sort of perfumed soul seemed to hover about in the warm, clear evening.

" He began to breathe deep, drinking the air as drunkards drink their wine and he walked slowly, enchanted, wonder-struck, his niece almost forgotten."

This is a vital plot incident. We can feel the crisis approaching. Change this materially and you have changed the entire story. All that follows is built upon the one formative incident — the moonlight has wrought its magic in the priest. Thus, plot-incidents are essential to the plot; developing — or contributory — incidents build up but do not "make" the plot, and must always be secondary in importance to plot-incidents.

So all sorts of problems arise with the handling of happenings in the story. The writer is tempted to insert an incident that peculiarly pleases him, even though it does not contribute to the progress of the plot either vitally or by illustration. He had better cut it out, though I confess that imperfections of this irrelevant sort constitute about all the charm some stories possess. The real remedy would be to build a new story with the attractive though irrelevant incident as a plot-germ.

Again, the writer may be tempted to elaborate an interesting developing incident and allow it to overshadow the plot incidents — a fatal mistake. A word here is enough.

It is not profitable to split hairs as to whether developing or contributory incidents, when closely related to the main happening, are not simply phases of the one real incident. Certainly this is often the case, but the great question is how to keep the plot full of life and yet not overburden it with incident. We have all lost our breath attempting to follow the lively actions of an indefatigable character who keeps busy enough in a story of five thousand words to fit out a yarn of sixty thousand, while perhaps the very next story taken up consumes ten thousand words in developing a single microscopic happening that should have had few words — or none — devoted to its telling.

Naturally, the nature of the story will control the amount of incident that may be introduced. The theme of adventurous action, at the one extreme, and the study of character, at the other, are far apart. Even in the latter kind the writer may elect to reveal character by conduct, and not chiefly by dialogue and exposition so that plenty of incident need not stand for lively action though usually it does.

To be convincing an incident must have verisimilitude — a big word with much in it.[9] To seem true a thing need not be true, but it must be of such a sort as would naturally cause the result, or flow as a result from a previous cause.[10] Here again I must emphasize the importance of intelligent observation. In describing how a man got out of a London four-wheeler Mr. Zangwill did not take into account that there are no handles on the insides of the doors. Another writer might have noted this slight point and yet missed a much more important matter. The value of observation depends upon the observer, and not merely upon the length of time a thing may be observed. An owl has been known to stare fixedly at an object for a long time without at all improving his owlish mind, and a man once patiently observed a great orchestra with the sole result of a wondering admiration for " the coincidence of the fiddlers' elbows." Do better than that, and make your incidents convincingly faithful to reality and yet full of fancy.

A word of warning is needed here. In seeking to make incident seem real do not make the mistake [11] of attempting to be too exact. You are not writing a scientific treatise, but fiction, and short fiction at that.

[9] See chapter on *Fact in Fiction*.

[10] " Our art is occupied, and bound to be occupied, not so much in making stories true as in making them typical."— STEVENSON, *A Humble Remonstrance*.

[11] Referred to in chapter on *Fact in Fiction*.

When Darwin wanted to decide which of two plants produced the more seed he was not certain of his ground until he had counted twenty thousand seeds.   Such methods would kill all healthy inspiration if applied to fiction-writing.   Better have it said of you, as Frank Norris said (not too exactly) of Scott, that though his archæology was about a thousand years " out," he had made his characters and incidents live.

2. *Emotion*

Emotion is a broad word loosely used to embrace all the tones of inner feeling, from the palest sentiment depicted by a Jane Austen, to the darkest passion of a Werther.   In a widely inclusive sense I use the term here.

As do kindred literary forms, the short-story offers room for the play of every type and degree of emotional excitement, but any attempt at an exhaustive systemization and exposition of these varied forms would be out of place in this treatise.[12]   It will be enough to call attention to two general groupings, and then glance at those emotions which are oftenest made the themes of short-stories.

An old grouping of the emotions considers them as those affording pleasure, those of unpleasant effect, and those of neutral character.

[12] There is an elaborate chapter on emotion in Albright's *The Short-Story;* Genung's *Working Principles of Rhetoric* fully discusses the rhetorical uses of emotion; all standard text-books of psychology discuss the emotions.   Gordy's *New Psychology* is especially good.

A second classification recognizes the emotions as being benevolent, malevolent, and variable — that is, benevolent, malevolent, or neutral, according to circumstances.

What is known as the James-Lange theory regards emotion as a complex of bodily sensations — that is, arising from bodily feelings and appetites.

The emotions which commonly dominate whole stories, as well as play only here and there in fiction of a less emotional character, are love, anger, jealousy, ambition, fear, revenge, remorse, pathos and mirth. It will be seen that these are very broadly considered as embracing their subordinate forms. Of course the classification is incomplete.

Professor Francis Hovey Stoddard has said:

" A novel is a record of emotion; the story of a human life touched with emotion; the story of two human lives under stress of emotional arousement; the story of domestic life with emotion pervading it; the story of a great historical character in his day of aroused emotional activity; or the story of the romantic adventures of some person in whom we are forced by the author to take an interest. So that the novel of personal life is really the basal form of the novel, and one may say that all novels become novels only when each is the story of some life stirred by some emotion." [13] Again he says: " A novel is a narrative of human life under stress of emotion." [14] And still again: ". . . the novel has

[13] *The Evolution of the Novel*, p. 9.
[14] *Ibid.*, p. 26.

made its way in a large measure by an assertion of the superiority of that which is apparently a weaker and lesser part of life, namely, emotion. For the novel does not stand in literary history as a record of achievement. It stands as a record of emotion." [15]

Now all this is very full, very explicit, and, some will say, very extreme. But in truth nearly every word might also be spoken of the short-story. The big thing — at once the basic and the climacteric thing — in the short-story is human interest, and there can be no sustained human interest without emotion. The whole creation is a field for its display, and since fiction assumes to be a microcosm, fiction, short and long, must deal intimately with emotion, from its gentler to its extreme manifestations.

Looking again at the group of emotional forces which often dominate whole short-stories, we must observe the singular preponderance of unpleasant and even malevolent inner feelings. But this is not to say that the majority, or even any large percentage, of short-stories deal with malevolent and unpleasant emotions. Indeed, I affirm quite the contrary. Love, pathos and mirth, are the three whose faces are pretty sure to be seen peering forth from one character or another in nearly every story. The malevolent is treated only now and then — and printed when the editor feels particularly brave to withstand the senseless clamor for *merely* the pleasant in short-story themes. In one of his novels Balzac has

[15] *Ibid.,* p. 200.

thrown a vivid light on the deadness of that fiction which knows no emotion — even troublous emotion. " Happiness," he says, " has no history, and the story-tellers of all lands have understood this so well that the words, ' They were happy,' are the end of every love tale." [16]

(a) *Love interest* is of incalculable value to the short-story, if handled with delicacy, naturalness, and fidelity to truth. Its scope is life-wide. Often through no other medium than the affections may the nature and development of character be so adequately comprehended. The touch of love moves every other emotion — with a force that uplifts or debases.

The hackneyed, vulgar, prurient and bestial treatment of love and the passions in the short-story cannot be too strongly condemned, particularly when found in a periodical for home circulation. Surely the sincere story-writer must feel a sense of his responsibility and avoid the cheap sentimentalism which, in spite of its undeserved popularity, is as ephemeral as it is inartistic. " All forms of sentimentalism in literature," says Winchester, " result from the endeavor to excite the emotions of pathos or affection without adequate cause. Emotions thus easily aroused or consciously indulged for their own sake, have something hollow about them. The emotion excited by the true artist is grounded upon the deep truths of human life." [17] This is a vital point in motivation.

Balzac, who was the first master to subject the expression of emotional excitement to the facts of life,

---

[16] *Esther Happy,* p. 70.
[17] *Principles of Literary Criticism.*

speaks, in *Père Goriot,* of " the transforming power of an overmastering emotion," and adds : " Sometimes the dullest spirit, under the stimulus of passion, reaches to such eloquence of thought if not of tongue that it seems to breathe in a celestial ether." [18]

The difference between pure sentiment and fustian sentimentality must be sensed by the writer, as it is by the sensitive reader. It is one thing for a writer to understand the psychology of emotion, it is quite another for him to possess a rich emotional nature. The latter more than the former will be his safe guide in dealing with this subtle element. I wish I could write this in letters a foot high.

The self-respecting author will want to tell the truth about love, particularly where it arouses other emotions, and he will claim the right to deal frankly with its great facts and problems, but he will also scorn to poison young minds with distorted or with inflaming pictures of these great life-forces. Whatever men may hold as to the novel, the short-story must be pure in spirit; and pure it may be, even when frankest in tone.

O Realism, what infamies have been published in thy name!

(b) *Pathos,* in its essence, begins in a feeling of loss, of lack, of sacrifice, of coming short. It may end anywhere. It is as wide as human need and human tenderness. Poe has said that even " The tone of Beauty is Sadness."

[18] Quoted in *The Technique of the Novel,* Horne, p. 189.

"Mrs. Birkin's Bonnet"[19] is simply the story of a plain old woman who keenly wished for a new bonnet for the wedding of a young friend. After hesitating long she decides to buy a particularly handsome one at a reduced price, but foregoes the joy for the sake of giving a new suit to a lad who could not otherwise attend the wedding. She fixes up her old headgear and is rewarded in this manner:

As the bride reached Mr. Birkin's pew she stopped, slipped her hand from the bridegroom's arm, and turning flung both her own, bouquet and all, round Mrs. Birkin's neck. She kissed the old woman before the whole church and whispered loudly in her ear: "Mrs. Birkin, dear, that's the most beautiful bonnet I ever saw."

In another moment she was gone. The last pair of bridesmaids had passed, and after them, visitors and villagers alike thronged into the sunshine. Mrs. Birkin, her bonnet much awry, owing to the heavy bridal bouquet, strayed out with the rest in a sort of solemn rapture. She had been honored above all other women on that great day.

"Wot did 'er say to you?" asked Mrs. Comley, enviously, when they got outside.

Mrs. Birkin laughed. "Bless 'er sweet face!" she exclaimed triumphantly, "if her didn't go and think 't was a bran' new bonnet. I must 'a' made un over-smartish, that I must!"

A different type of pathos is that of "The Fire Rekindled."[20] On Memorial Day Adam Roth looked over the old zouave uniform of his dead brother Dan, and confessed himself a coward.

He had seen his brother volunteer, imbued with the spirit that creates heroes, but he himself had felt the black hand of

[19] L. Allen Harker, *Century*, Aug., 1908.
[20] Claire Wallace Flynn, *Lippincott's*, June, 1907

fear clutch his heart and strike at the very roots of his life. What use to fight against that name of 'coward'! In truth. he had not fought; he had let it sweep over him, engulf him, ruin him.

Again the rat-a-tat of the drums. The man on the bed lifted his head. Oh, to feel just once Dan's simple love for his flag, the glow of patriotism, the thrill of war that trembled a faint, hallowed echo on this day! To feel, if such were possible, all these things that had been denied him in his youth — just to feel them once before he too went to that dim place where the Stars and Stripes and all the other banners of the world are furled in everlasting peace!

Old and feeble, he donned his brother's uniform and marched with the veterans, experiencing all the thrill and ardor and love-of-flag that Dan had known. He felt himself to be a defender of his country's honor.

The ceremonies were drawing to a close. The silent heroes in blue and gray had had their measure of praise meted out to them, when a bugler stepped forward and played the first bar of the "Star Spangled Banner." There was a shout, a sudden concerted movement of the crowd to get a little nearer the bugler, as the long notes rang out. From his higher place Adam saw the man whom he had been watching push his way to the edge of the crowd, directly facing the flag. His face was darker than ever, with an immeasurable hatred. He sneered as he looked at the Zouaves standing gaunt and rugged about the great monument that had been raised to the memory of their brothers. The people were singing now. The man laughed. Above the voice of palpitating youth and earnest age Adam heard it, and clenched his hand at his side. What did this man mean to do? Such wildness, such enmity, would not go unsatisfied. The man's hand went to his pocket. Adam stood tense, watching his every movement. Again the man looked at the flag — the flag that was almost shot away, the flag that perhaps the man argued had been carried aloft on the battle-field at a frightful and needless cost, while a calm government sat back and said, "Let the slaughter go on." Was that, questioned Adam, what the man was thinking? Adam took a step nearer the standard-bearer, whose dim eyes were ignorant of danger. Adam seemed to feel in some intuitive way what this poor, frantic creature below meant to do. But he must not be allowed to do it—he must not! Those smoky, stained old shreds of silk must not feel a wound from the hand of a disloyal son.

The man's arm shot out. Something gleamed in the sunshine, something sang in the air above the words "in triumph shall wave," and an old Zouave stumbled and fell forward upon the white stones. . . . The commander of the post stooped over the fallen man and lifted his head. The man was a stranger to him. He looked at a Zouave standing near, silently questioning him.

"He pushed in front of Peterson, sir, just as that scoundrel fired. He tried to grasp the flag, sir. I guess he saw what the fellow aimed at."

Still the commander looked at the speaker, the man who had marched all the way beside Adam.

"Who is he?" continued the officer. "And what is he doing here? He is not one of my men."

The old Zouave took his ragged cap from his head.

"He was Dan Roth's brother. We have all heard of him— he was the boy who wouldn't join in '61. But to-day he—he—"

The old man knelt down beside Adam. Just below the dim stain on the shoulder of Dan's jacket, the stain which marked that day at Alexandria, there was a new, fresh one. The heart that lay beneath it was at peace.

Then there is the pathos of cheerful, brow-beaten Bob Cratchit and his sweet Tiny Tim, in Dickens' "Christmas Carol." And the grief of the English father for the loss of his half-breed child in tropic India, in Kipling's "Without Benefit of Clergy." And the despair of the poor wretch who watches his own approaching madness, in "The Horla," by Maupassant. And the tragic child-sorrow of the little prince when he learns that royalty cannot keep off Death by posting a guard, in Daudet's "The Death of the Dauphin." And Merimée's "Mateo Falcone," who becomes the self-appointed executioner of his dishonored son. The field of pathos has no boundaries.

In conclusion, I can do no better than quote Miss Albright:

"There are many varieties and degrees of pathos. The emotion aroused may be so sweetly sad as to be almost entirely pleasurable; and again, a story of failure, of repression, of denial, may fill the heart with dull, uneasing pain. There is the pathos which degenerates into a sniffle, and there is that which lies 'too deep for tears.' There is the delicate pathos which wavers tremulously into humor every now and then (as in Steele and the Scotch humorists); and there is that which, pushed too far, falls over the verge into the domain of the ludicrous. And there is the poignant, bitter pathos which is so akin to tragedy that it necessarily accompanies it and cannot be distinguished from it." [21]

(c) *Mirth* lies near to pathos, as laughter lies close to tears. I use it as a general term, including wit and humor and all the range between.

The learned Dr. Barrows has distanced all other analysts in his celebrated exposition of mirth.[22]

"Sometimes it lieth in pat allusions to a known story, or in seasonable application of a trivial saying, or in

[21] *The Short-Story,* p. 200.
[22] Quoted in E. P. Whipple's *Literature and Life,* p. 89.

forging an apposite tale; sometimes it playeth in words and phrases, taking advantage from the ambiguity of their sense or the affinity of their sound; sometimes it is wrapped up in a dress of humorous expression; sometimes it lurketh under an odd similitude; sometimes it is lodged in a sly question, in a smart answer, in a quirkish reason, in a shrewd intimation, in cunningly diverting or cleverly retorting an objection; sometimes it is couched in a bold scheme of speech, in a tart irony, in a lusty hyperbole, in a startling metaphor, in a plausible reconciling of contradictions, or in acute nonsense; sometimes a scenical representation of persons or things, a counterfeit speech, a mimical look or gesture, passeth for it; sometimes an affected simplicity, sometimes a presumptuous bluntness, giveth it being; sometimes it riseth only from a lucky hitting upon what is strange; sometimes from a crafty wresting (of) obvious matter to the purpose. Often it consisteth in one hardly knows what, and springeth up one can hardly tell how, being answerable to the numberless rovings of fancy and windings of language."

Thus we see that the field of mirth is life — life and its record, literature. In the former it appeals to us every day, of the latter it is the preservative element. In this brilliant summary by E. P. Whipple we catch a glimpse of the infinite variety of its play:

". . . to Mirth belong the exhaustless fancy and sky-piercing buffooneries of Aristophanes; the matchless irony of Lucian; the stern and terrible satire of Juvenal; the fun-drunken extravagances of Rabelais; the self-pleased chuckle of Montaigne; the farcical caricature of Scarron; the glowing and sparkling verse of Dryden; the genial fun of Addison; the scoffing subtilties of Butler; the aërial merriment of Sterne; the hard brilliancy and stinging emphasis of Pope; the patient glitter of Congreve; the teasing mockery of Voltaire; the polished sharpness of Sheridan; the wise drolleries of Sydney Smith; the sly, shy, elusive, ethereal humor of Lamb; the short, sharp, flashing scorn of Macaulay; the careless gayety of Beranger; the humorous sadness of Hood; and the comic creations, various almost as human nature, which have peopled the imaginations of Europe with everlasting forms of the ludicrous, from the time of Shakespeare and Cervantes to that of Scott and Dickens." [23]

To expound and illustrate all the phases of mirth would require a volume. Let it be enough to contrast some of the phases of wit and humor.

Wit deals with externals, humor seeks out the heart; wit consorts with contempt, scorn and hate; humor abides with friendship, benevolence and love; wit holds folly up to darting ridicule, humor looks with gentle sympathy upon weakness even while inciting to laughter; wit contrasts with swift surprise, humor slyly points out laughable incongruities; wit strikes down with a withering bolt, humor nurtures with enfolding sunshine; wit

[23] *Literature and Life,* p. 87.

punishes by the whip, humor humanely rebukes by a laughing fillip; wit seeks out the joints of the harness, humor strikes a lusty blow frankly on the shield; wit is momentary, humor is lasting. "Fuller's remark, 'that a negro is the image of God cut in ebony,' is humorous; Horace Smith's inversion of it, that the taskmaster is 'the image of the devil cut in ivory,' is witty." [24]

(d) *Emotion in the story* is shown by certain well-defined literary devices which repay study. Make an investigation, for example, of how death-scenes are handled by expert writers, how they connote fear, how all the varying sentiments, feelings, and passions are made real to the reader. But the emotion must be *in the story.*

Diction is an index to emotion and, besides conveying the mere ideas for which the words stand, often suggests a state of mind. But if you would express emotion you must observe how much more emotional are some words than others. When you feel deeply, use a word that is surcharged with all of your own intensity. There is such a word.[25] Seek it out. Discard time-worn adjectives in old relations. Fit new epithets, and specific ones especially, to your ideas. Stevenson tells in a memorable passage in his *Memories and Portraits,* in the section on "A College Magazine," how he did this very thing painstakingly and with persistence. And his use of the notebook wrought magic results.[26]

Figures of Speech are peculiarly suitable for the

[24] *Literature and Life,* p. 92.
[25] See chapter on *Acquiring a Vocabulary.*
[26] Quoted on p. 280.

expression of emotional excitement. Exclamation is of course the most common. Who can forget Cain's dramatic interrogation, " Am I my brother's keeper? " Or Victor Hugo's use of the historical present as he describes the battle of Waterloo in *Les Miserables?* I recall a passage in Marsh's *The Surprising Husband* in which the injured wife turns aside from speaking to her husband and cries out in apostrophe to no one in particular, " Listen to this — person." The exasperation is unmistakable. Hyperbole, irony and sarcasm, as well as the more delicate figures, all abound in emotional coloring.

Gesture and Posture, whether described alone or used in connection with figures of speech, may be made expressive of emotion. In the novel just referred to, the distraught wife "threw out her arms with a gesture which was expressive of contempt of herself and scorn of him, of which language could give no hint."

Study the expressive gestures of orators and actors. See the world of meaning they suggest by the simplest gestures and attitudes — often more eloquent than words. Ernest Renan, speaking of the Old Testament Scriptures, has said:

" Anger is expressed in Hebrew in a throng of ways, each picturesque, and each borrowed from physiological facts. Now the metaphor is taken from the rapid and animated breathing which accompanies the passion, now from heat or from boiling, now from the act of a noisy breaking, now from shivering. Discouragement and despair are expressed by the melting of the heart, fear by the loosening of the reins. Pride is portrayed by the holding high of the head, with the figure straight and stiff. Patience is a long breathing, impatience short breathing, desire is thirst or paleness. Pardon is expressed by a throng of metaphors borrowed from the idea of covering, of hiding, of coating over the fault. In *Job* God sews up his sins in a sack, seals it, then throws it behind him: all to signify that he forgets them. . . . The idea of truth is drawn from solidity, or stability; that of beauty from splendor, that of good from straightness, that of evil from swerving or the curved line, or from stench. To create is primitively to mould, to decide is to cut, to think is to speak. Bone signifies the substance, the essence of a thing, and serves in Hebrew for our pronoun *self*. . . . in each word one still hears the echo of the primitive sensations which determined the choice of the first makers of the language." [27]

Emotions are the same now as they were thousands of years gone by, and the student of the short-story may gain much from an examination of these primitive but unsurpassed attempts to translate emotion into language.

Arrangement of Words is expressive of emotion. Study the impression of short, nervous sentences as compared with long; the panting effect of the frequent use of the dash; the force of inverted order, and so on. But mere emotional words will not make emotional scenes.

[27] Quoted in Gardiner's *The Bible as English Literature,* p. 114.

(e) *Emotion in the author* is after all the source-spring of emotion in the story and, through it, in the reader. It has come to be out-of-fashion to " cry over a mere book," but I am glad to be able to shed a tear now and then as I follow a pathetic story. I doubt, however, if the reader can be made to feel more deeply than the author felt when he wrote the passage — though neither the author nor the reader need feel angry every time a fictional character loses his temper. It requires some preparation to bring about intense emotional stress. Keep your emotions sane and fresh and genuine and tender. Without emotion the author is as dead as his stories. Study your own heart, but do not neglect to look into other hearts as well. Poe has said that " There are chords in the hearts of the most reckless which cannot be touched without emotion " [28]— an ambiguous sentence that is full of meaning any how you take it.

Emotion in the author often leads to the choice of a theme. Interest in, feeling for, a subject cannot be manufactured, try as you will. Dickens once wrote that he was breaking his heart over the writing of *The Old Curiosity Shop* — and all the world has been doing so ever since. " We yield to sympathy," says Burke, " what we refuse to description." [29]

Powerful emotion gives birth to expression. It is related of Crœsus [30] that his only living son was dumb. When Cyrus captured Sardis, a soldier, not recognizing

[28] *The Masque of the Red Death.*
[29] *On the Sublime and Beautiful.*
[30] *Ancient History,* Rollin, Book IV, chap. i.

Crœsus, was about to give the king a blow upon the head. The emotion of fear and love for his father so wrought upon the young prince that he " broke the string of his tongue, and cried out, ' Soldier, spare the life of Crœsus ! ' "

But, finally, the expression of emotional excitement, of whatever kind and degree, demands a certain restraint. Hawthorne is worth studying for this trait. If the rein be inadvertently loosed, pathos may become bathos, sentiment lapse into sentimentality, tragedy into ranting. Adapt to your art Hamlet's advice to the players:

" Speak the speech, I pray you, as I pronounced it to you, trippingly on the tongue: but if you mouth it, as many of our players do, I had as lief the town crier spoke my lines. Nor do not saw the air too much with your hand, thus; but use all gently; for in the very torrent, tempest, and (as I may say) whirlpool of your passion, you must àcquire and beget a temperance, that may give it smoothness. O, it offends me to the soul, to hear a robustious periwig-pated fellow tear a passion to tatters, to very rags, to split the ears of the ground-lings; [31] who, for the most part, are capable of nothing but inexplicable dumb show, and noise. I would have such a fellow whipped for o'er-doing Termagant; it out-herods Herod. Pray you avoid it.

" Be not too tame, neither, but let your discretion be your tutor: suit the action to the word, the word to the action; with this special observance, that you o'erstep

[31] Auditors on the ground floor.

not the modesty of nature; for anything so overdone is from the purpose of playing, whose end, both at the first, and now, was, and is, to hold, as 'twere, the mirror up to Nature." [32]

(The outline summary of this chapter is included in that of the next chapter on page 215.)

QUESTIONS AND EXERCISES FOR CLASS OR INDIVIDUAL STUDY

1. What are the respective effects of very little and very much incident in a short-story?

2. Select the plot-incidents and the developing-incidents in any two plots in Appendix C.

3. What kinds of short-stories are the least unfavorably affected by the inclusion of unimportant incidents?

4. What kind tends to incident?

5. What kind tends to eliminate incident?

6. From Appendix C select an example of each kind.

7. From a current magazine select a story full of incident.

8. Discuss the devices by which the author has secured verisimilitude.

9. Give the dictionary definition of emotion.

10. Make the fullest classification of the emotions that you can, including all inner feelings.

11. Select short-stories, or plots, illustrating at least five of these emotional forms.

12. What love-situations are the most commonplace in short-stories?

13. Suggest an unhackneyed manner of treating the same situations.

14. How may an author's emotional nature be deepened?

15. Can a sense of humor be cultivated?

16. As you observe it, do you find the short-story rising or declining in moral tone?

[32] *Hamlet,* Act III, Scene 2.

17. What causes contribute to the tendency you observe?

18. How do you discriminate between an immoral and a moral short-story? Novel? Are the standards different?

19. Distinguish pathos from bathos.

20. Can the short-story be as emotional as the novel? Why?

21. Give examples from short-stories of how (a) diction, (b) figures of speech, and (c) gesture and posture, are made to express emotion.

22. Write original examples of how (a) diction, (b) figures of speech, and (c) gesture and posture are made to express emotion.

23. Make a list of as many love-themes as you can, whether original or borrowed, always stating where you got the suggestion. Examples: The sacrifice of a father in working while he was ill; the ingenuity of a lover in outwitting an unscrupulous rival; the love of a man for his friend.

24. Describe a unique proposal scene.

25. Outline a humorous plot, with a surprise.

26. From an emotional short-story make a list of all the words especially expressive of emotion.

27. Trace the " line of emotion " (Whitcomb) in an emotional short-story, somewhat thus:

IMPORTANT NOTE: An "incident" is not a mere statement describing a state of mind, a state of being, or a mere fact, but one complete PART of the plot, such as a definite physical action (a struggle with a thief), a dramatic scene (the discovery of a suspect's innocence), a definite mental event (a man suddenly brought face to face with the idea that he is dishonest), or any similar dramatic event. While an incident may require only a few words in a plot-statement, it generally is expanded into a whole scene, in fiction. Over-compression robs the incident of dramatic value. Yet this does not mean that a fictional incident may "spread"—like a scene in a play, which may include several incidents. It should focus all its action on the "punch-point". An "incident" that is vague and general is not an incident.

CHAPTER X

THE BODY OF THE STORY — *(Concluded)*

Keeping the beginning and the end in view, we set out from the right starting-place, and go straight towards the destination; we introduce no event that does not spring from the first cause and tend to the great effect; we make each detail a link joined to the one going before and the one coming after.— DAVID PRYDE.

I have said that the body of the story is the story itself, and that therefore everything directly bearing upon the short-story is germane to the body. In still further considering this phase of the subject, it must be reiterated that I am now taking up only such elements as I have not treated elsewhere under separate chapter-headings. The preceding chapter was devoted to (1) incident and (2) emotion in the short-story. It remains now to examine (3) crisis, (4) suspense, (5) climax, (6) denouement, and (7) conclusion.

3. *Crisis*

Some writers on the short-story have used this term interchangeably with climax. But crisis is not really climax, which may be defined as an increase of interest up to its highest point. Crisis, however, is a point or a period — note the distinction of terms — of opportunity, of decision, of change. The Greek rhetoricians called it the "turn" in the plot. It is the watershed of the story, the crossroads, the critical moment, and every true short-story has one or more such crucial situations, usually shown dramatically by one or more incidents.[1]

Now the climax also may be a place of opportunity, choice, or turning, but usually climax is a *result* of the crisis—of which more later.

As suggested, a single crisis need not be confined to a single point, but may be broken by periods of suspense, and even by the introduction of developing incidents— that is, one incident may furnish the foundation of the crisis while still others contribute upward steps, the full crisis occurring later, usually just before the climax. Or, each minor crisis may be a separate event—not a part of one long-drawn-out crisis, but a unit contributing to the "big" crisis—as the analyzer will see at the close.

The foundation of the crisis is often laid early in the story. If this certain thing had not happened the ending would have been entirely different. From that first critical point onward, one minor crisis after another occurs until the story rises to its highest point and swiftly falls to its close. This preliminary crisis is gener- ally devoid of dramatic quality. It appears without trumpet and drum. Even the hero may not foresee the far-reaching results which flow from his decision, just as in everyday life, but sooner or later its potency must be made plain. The movement increases in rapidity, forces converge, the final crisis develops, the climax is reached, all is explained, and the story is ended.

[1] See the preceding chapter.

The final crisis in the affairs of an individual, or in the career of any subject of fiction — for animals, institutions, and various other objects may constitute the central figures of plot — need not be sensational to be interesting. The taste of the readers to whom you appeal will guide at this point. A moral crisis holds the attention of certain minds when physical danger arouses them not at all. But in any case the crisis must be such as might confront live people, a thing of actual and appreciable value in the working out of the plot. Study Kipling's use of crisis in " Without Benefit of Clergy," [2] and see the emotional forces which the crucial situations unchain, one after another. There is no tempest-in-a-mill-pond here, no straining after effect, no results too big for causes, no expectation disproportionate to the outcome, no false appraisement of the factors of the crisis. Really, I cannot lay too much stress on this point: let but the crisis be sincere, natural, emotional, momentous, decisive, and you have secured one of the most important plot elements for your story. [3]

4. *Suspense*

The story of plot is constructed first of all to excite and enchain interest. For this reason, in this type of story, a period of suspense generally follows after each minor crisis — if any there be — as well as after the

[2] See p. 376, No. 2.
[3] At the close of this chapter are several short-story plots, so annotated as to illustrate how crisis, suspense, climax, denouement, and conclusion are handled by adepts. See also Appendix C.

main crisis. Then see the characters poised for their final destinies in the story. One of two, or even more, courses they must adopt, slip into, or be thrust upon. If interest has been aroused, this is the period of suspense just before the climax. " What will happen " absorbs the reader. In this period of armistice, of letdown, of watchful inaction, he feels rather than sees the gathering of forces preparatory to the decisive conflict: he recognizes that soon the climax and the denouement will be reached.

Not every story demands or even permits this period of suspense. Stories of slight plot glide smoothly to their natural issue, which is none the less interesting because partly foreseen; but in most instances the reader looks for an anticipatory rest before the resolution of the chord. The day is not yet past when the troubles of the hero and heroine call forth tears. Readers still mentally threaten to pummel the author if the suspense is not satisfactorily relieved. Who does not remember his own feverish impatience, his sweet pain of anxiety, to see how a complicated situation would turn out. Indeed, suspense furnishes half the pleasure of the plot of action, the problem plot, and certain intense kinds of character plots. Remember, *danger is the prime source of suspense.*

Now the handling of the suspense element requires delicacy and a nice judgment, but the most skilful literary manipulator cannot successfully work up an artificial suspense without a genuine crisis to excite interest in the outcome. It is easy to drift upon the shoals of sentimentalism here; however, if the crisis be a real one, and the situation of moment to human lives, the reader will not need to be goaded on to suspense. But don't keep it up too long. That means flagging interest. Simplicity, intensity, seriousness, genuineness—these must mark this important transition-period in the serious story.

5. *Climax*

The climax is "the apex of interest and emotion; it is the point of the story." [4] The term has another meaning—that rhetorical order by which a sentence, a paragraph, a whole story, is made to rise in interest and in power to its highest point—but that is a problem of arrangement, and is not the same as the high-water mark of the plot. The one is a process, the other is a point.

The "big crisis" (the final turning-point of character or of action) may so interpenetrate the "big climax scene" as to seem one with it; yet really crisis shows what *may* be, climax reveals *results*. In Poe's "Ligeia" the full crisis occurs when the husband begins to watch the face of his dead wife, but the climax is reserved for the very close when the dead woman's face changes to that of Ligeia.[5] Though in Poe's story the climax is most sensational, the element of surprise is by no means an essential of a good plot. In fact, the beginner is prone to mar the final effect of his story by straining after a striking climax, for he generally succeeds in being merely absurd. The climax must seem inevitable, though perhaps unexpected. The reader will

[4] *Short Story Writing,* Barrett, p. 171.
[5] See p. 212.

almost surely look back and trace the movement of forces in the story which lead from the first causes up to the climax, and he demands that the climax be what its name implies — a ladder; and he is keen to note missing and unsafe rungs. It is important to remember that while one may slide down a ladder he must ascend it step by step. The gradation toward the climax is no small matter.

Often the outcome of the crisis shows how the threatened catastrophe was avoided, or actually came about; just as either death or recovery may follow the crisis in a disease, and either one prove to be the real climax in the history of the patient.

No pitfall is more treacherous than that of the false climax, which introduces a halting element into the plot and sends the story limping to its close. As you plot the body of the story be courageously relentless in self-criticism. See to it that the grand climax does not come too soon, that the lesser event does not detract from the interest of the greater, and that the climax does not leave the reader still in suspense — if you are going to resolve the suspense at all. Let your climax be brief and intense. No time for descriptions or trivialities then. Deal only with vital things, and don't overdo them. Your climax may be quiet and contain no element of surprise, but let it be convincing and satisfy the reader that everything possible has been made out of the situation. In the climax lies the mainspring of that totality of impression for which you have been working, so do not let it get beyond your control.

One difficulty in this connection is that of handling what Professor Perry calls " the tragic moment "— that is, the preparation for the climax. The crisis, let us say, is past and the results of choice are to appear in the climax. Either the reader feels so certain of the climax that he loses interest, or else the interest has been so wrought up that there is a tremendous fascination in watching the progress of a conclusion which is thus foregone, as one would watch the losing fight of a swimmer doomed to go over the falls. This calls for fine handling, to make the action so pulsate with reality that the reader will sit back and watch a character march on to his fate, perhaps without even a hope of a reversal at the end.

Sometimes there is a hint of a possible reversal, as when Macbeth, grasping at the last slender chance, recalls the prophecy that he would not be slain by one of woman born; but even that hope is quickly quenched. Again, the reversal may actually come, by some ingenious device; but such an ending is pretty sure to do violence to nature, and ring untrue. Happy is that writer of plot-stories who is able to save his hero at the last ditch without wresting the situation from the course of truthful seeming.

6. *Denouement*

From the foregoing it will appear how intimately climax is associated with denouement. Just as crisis leads immediately to climax, so climax tends swiftly toward the denouement. As we have seen, the word

means literally an untying, therefore in mystery stories
and in plots where concealment is necessary to support
interest, the untangling of the threads is likely to be a
part of the climax itself.

In disclosing the mystery in novels it is customary to
spend some time in explaining the complications. That
way danger lies for the short-story writer. In the mystery story the author should begin early to set his wires
so that with a single pull the whole house of bafflement
may come tumbling down before our eyes, at a glance disclosing the secret. In the short-story the mystery must
be less complex than in the novel, hence the uncovering
of the secret will require less time. But if I knew perfectly how to hold a breathless mystery up to the last moment and then disclose it all in a trice, I could not —
and perhaps would not if I could — impart it to others.
This is the very incommunicable heart of the plotter's
craft.[6]

The skilful writer lays the foundation of the denouement all through the story, by which I mean that the
denouement is vitally bone and sinew with the rest of the
story. Sometimes there are hints of the outcome scattered here and there with an elaborate cunning — that
may or may not defeat its purpose. But even when these
hints are not given, the effect must be no greater than
its cause, the disclosure must more than live up to the
hint, in the slightest particulai. Expectation is good,
but it imposes the responsibility of " making good."

In concealing his denouement by a well-articulated

[6] See p. 209.

structure the literary architect must have a care not to let the framework stick out. To do so spoils the literary effect, robs the story of its illusion, and " gives away " the secret which he is attempting to hide. An acute reader can sniff from afar the solution of a mystery, so the issue of a complication must be kept from under inquisitive noses until just the proper moment. When you see a reader who has been absorbed in every word of a narrative suddenly begin to slight whole pages you may know he has scented the outcome.

Are there two possible endings to a perfect short-story? Robert Louis Stevenson argues that a story will not allow the fiction-writer to take liberties with the plot, or the destinies of the characters, as Kipling did in making two different endings to *The Light That Failed*. The denouement of the perfect story is inevitable, and the reader feels its inevitability with perfect approval. " Make another end to it? " writes Stevenson to a friend. " Ah, yes, but that's not the way I write; the whole tale is implied; I never use an effect when I can help it, unless it prepares the effects that are to follow; that's what a story consists in. To make another end, that is to make the beginning all wrong. The denouement of a long story is nothing, it is just ' a full close,' which you may approach and accompany as you please — it is a coda, not an essential member in the rhythm; but the body and end of a short-story is bone of the bone and blood of the blood of the beginning." [7]

Often climax and denouement, and even conclusion,

[7] *Vailima Letters,* Vol. I, p. 147.

are identical, as in " The Horla," by Maupassant.[8]   This
is the diary of a man who feels that some power outside himself possesses his soul and controls it, causing
him to do things he would not, and of which he may
be at the time unconscious.   He makes a vigorous struggle against this obsession, now successfully, now only
to fail.   At last (full crisis) he succeeds in shutting the
haunting presence in his house and then sets fire to the
building, watching it burn, hoping to consume his perse-
cutor.   But he suddenly fears that fire can have no such
effect, and he ends his diary thus: " No — no — beyond
any doubt, beyond any doubt, he is not dead.   Then —
then — it will soon be necessary for me to kill myself! "
(climax, denouement and conclusion identical).

Upon the other hand, we have crisis, climax, and conclusion definitely separated in Marion Crawford's " The
Upper Berth," [9] though there is no denouement, because
the mystery is unexplained.   When the narrator finally
grapples with the unseen thing in the upper berth we
have the full crisis; the climax comes when the struggle
results in his downward fall and that of the sea captain
also; the conclusion — which is rather weak — explains
that thereafter the stateroom was kept locked and that
neither the narrator nor the captain would ever sail again
on that ship.

But not every denouement will contain a disclosure.
That has led some critics to assert that denouement is
not an essential of the short-story.   But we must re-

[8] See p. 376, No. 10.
[9] See p. 377, No. 15.

member that the revelation may merely show how the critical moment is met and perhaps hint at the future course. From such simple outcomes, which require no special concealment, it seems a far cry to the untying of the knotted threads of the mystery plot, but both properly come under the same head.

The more obscure the mystery the greater is the necessity for keeping its outcome hidden until the last moment. I know of no way to accomplish this other than by using the utmost ingenuity you possess. " It is only with the denouement constantly in view that we can give a plot its indispensable air of consequence, or causation, by making the incidents and especially the tone at all points tend to the development of the intention." [10]

The reader is normally hopeful. With all his breathless anxiety for the outcome of the story of plot, he feels a certain confidence in the ability of the characters to rise superior to their entanglements, therefore the author may wish to make a way out seem quite hopeless. Let him have a care lest the complication be tied so tight that no plausible way out is possible. Then the Gordian knot must be cut — much to everyone's disgust.

Magazine editors are generally committed to the " happy ending " fetish. You may be certain of this. I think that they misjudge their readers in this respect, at least if we consider the clientele of magazines of the better sort. The average short-story reader demands that a simple love story end happily, though that does not necessarily involve a wedding; but as for the problem

[10] *The Philosophy of Composition,* Poe.

story, the great majority of readers are more eager that their sense of justice should be satisfied than that the chief characters should "live happily ever afterward." To be sure, they want justice to be tempered with mercy, if the transgressor has been made an attractive character, but it is just so in real life, too. And herein no small moral responsibility rests upon the author.[11] It is much more important that a story should end hopefully than with a smile. Optimism is a pretty good philosophy, in fiction as well as in real life.

The discriminating reader objects to having the fate of characters determined unhappily by mere accident, without a sight of the causes which might reasonably bring about such results. The element of fate is used in the denouement of the novel more frequently than in the short-story, and so also is the idea of retribution, both human and divine. Yet fate and retributive justice as themes afford fine opportunities for the exercise of the highest powers of the short-story writer.[12]

7. Conclusion

The modern tendency, as so admirably illustrated by some of Poe's master efforts, is to allow the denouement to serve as the full close of the short-story. Still there are exceptions a-plenty and formal conclusions are still written.

Some writers seem unable to let go, but go ambling on

---

[11] See *The Problem of Endings,* Mary Tracy Earle, *Book Buyer,* Aug., 1898. Also William Allen White, in *Collier's,* Feb. 11, 1905.

[12] See Appendix C, No. 18.

after the manner of Richardson in his *Pamela*. They insist on moralizing, trying to taper off smoothly, seeing the newly engaged couple happily married, and other-wise disposing of minor characters. Others end so ab-ruptly as to leave their characters in mid-air. Either extreme is absurd enough. In certain stories a single paragraph, or at most two, may well be used to bring the narrative to a satisfying close. No one can give helpful counsel here. Use your own judgment. When you are through, stop; but do your best to conclude with words of distinction.

In Maupassant's " A Coward " [13] the conclusion is identical with the denouement, which we discern ap-proaching like the crawling of an insidious reptile. The " coward " fears to display trepidation in an ap-proaching duel, more than he fears death. He fears fear. We see him examining every detail of the duelling pistol, while he speculates on all his possible experiences should he exhibit fear during the contest. " And yet he was really brave, because he wanted to fight! He was brave, because — The thought that grazed his mind was never completed; opening his mouth wide, he sud-denly thrust the barrel of the pistol into the very bottom of his throat and pressed upon the trigger —— (*climax*).

" When his valet ran in, alarmed by the report, he found him on his back, dead. The blood had spattered the white paper on the table, and made a great stain under the four words:

" ' This is my Will ' " (*denouement and conclusion*).

[13] See p. 376, No. 10.

In Poe's "Ligeia," the narrator first minutely describes the remarkably perfect physique, mentality and attainments of Ligeia, his wife. She falls ill (*foundation of crisis*) and after a period of suspense dies (*end of preliminary crisis*). The narrator then takes an old abbey in a remote part of England, and both restores and sumptuously furnishes it in a weirdly unique style. He then marries Lady Rowena Trevanion, though his whole being is still absorbed with memories of Ligeia. Lady Rowena also falls ill (*foundation for final crisis*). She grows better, then worse, and finally takes a glass of wine to revive her. Three red drops of liquid are seen mysteriously to fall into the cup, and presently she dies (*second step of final crisis*). Three times, as the husband looks upon her dead body, each time thinking of his dead and still-loved Ligeia, the Lady Rowena revives (*full crisis*). Twice she sinks back into death, but the last time that she revives the husband realizes that " These are the full, and the black, and the wild-eyes — of my lost love — of the Lady — of the LADY LIGEIA " (*climax, denouement, and conclusion*).

In Ouida's " A Leaf in the Storm," [14] Reine Allix is a venerable French peasant who lives with her grandson, Bernadou. When the youth marries Margot, the bride comes to live with Reine Allix. A child is born, and all is happiness. Suddenly the terrible news of war, France against Prussia, is announced (*foundation of crisis*). Excitement at length yields to a sort of calm, for the

[14] See p. 377, No. 20; also pp. 163, 166, 167, 169.

village hears only indefinitely of the struggle. But
Reine Allix has forebodings and recalls the days of the
Napoleonic wars *(suspense)*. By and by a Prussian spy
is said to have passed among them, and the news of
French defeat is heard *(second stage of crisis, rise
toward climax)*. Again quiet and suspense. At last,
" The Prussians are on us! " rises the cry *(full crisis)*.
The patriot Bernadou is almost alone as he urges a defense. The Prussians sack the town, but the people do
not resist. Bernadou is shot for refusing to guide the
enemy about the countryside. A rearing horse stamps
out the life of Bernadou's babe and Margot falls dead
(climax). The Prussians fire the village but Reine Allix
is alone with her dead, whom she has carried to her cottage — and that too, with its living and dead occupants,
is consumed in the holocaust *(conclusion)*.

" A Tale of Two Burdens," [15] by Irving Bacheller, is
told by Bill Gwinup, woodsman. Being sent for by Calladay, a millionaire camper, he engages with him as
guide. Calladay has angered the squatters by driving
them off his newly-bought preserves, on which they and
their ancestors had hunted and fished for generations
(foundation of crisis). When starting on a day's fishing, Calladay fits the guide out with a new suit, but
himself dresses in old clothes, and carries the pack. A
squatter mistakes Bill for Calladay, and fires at him, narrowly missing his head *(full crisis)*. The squatter
" holds up " the supposed millionaire offender and forces

[15] *Century,* Aug., 1908.

him to sign a release of the squatter's land *(period of suspense)*. Bill, angered by Calladay's plot to put him in danger, continues to play Calladay's part, forces Calladay, by signing Bill's name, to witness the paper, volunteers to give the squatter a thousand dollars, forces the millionaire to carry the squatter's fifty-pound pack, and otherwise rubs in his temporary advantage *(climax)*. When they get to camp, Calladay takes his medicine by signing the promised check, swearing to the deed, and " resigning his job " as make-believe guide *(conclusion)*.

In " An Error of Judgment," [16] by Elliott Flower, a watchman is standing before the doorway of a burned store anxiously waiting to be relieved. He is accosted by a stranger who observes his discontented air. Learning that the watchman is hungry and " broke," the stranger gives him a dollar and offers to take his post while he goes across the street to eat his breakfast. While the watchman is gone the stranger enters the building and investigates. He is an expert insurance adjuster and soon discovers beneath a counter some charred rags which had been saturated with coal oil *(foundation for crisis)*. He goes out, the watchman returns, is relieved from duty, and the owner of the store comes with his lawyer. The adjuster charges the owner with setting fire to his own store and advises him to make no insurance claim. Suit is brought against the owner for arson *(second step of crisis)*. He finds that he must sue the insurance company for payment, or else tacitly admit his guilt. He seeks to settle with the com-

[16] *Putnam's Reader,* Aug., 1908.

pany, knowing that any payment by them, however small, would be proof that they could not really suspect him of firing his own store. The company declines. Suddenly the owner shows increased confidence in his chances *(third step of crisis)*. This perplexes the company and its adjuster. They feel that the owner is guilty but have no proof to show that he or any of his employees were in the store the night of the fire. At length the case comes to trial *(full crisis)*. After proving the facts, the prosecution rests. The defense admits the facts, denies any knowledge of the crime, and calls the watchman to the stand. He testifies that the insurance adjuster was the only man who entered the building between the times when the firemen left and the police came, and relates how the adjuster got him, the watchman, out of the way. The inference is made that the adjuster himself deposited the rags. The owner is acquitted and the full amount of insurance is paid, though the reader is led to believe that the owner really was guilty *(climax and denouement)*. The adjuster is mildly rebuked by his manager, who agrees never again to refer to his employee's " error of judgment " *(conclusion)*.

OUTLINE SUMMARY

(Including Outline of Preceding Chapter)

THE BODY OF THE STORY

1. *Incident*
2. *Emotion*
    (a) Love Interest
    (b) Pathos

(*c*) Mirth
(*d*) Emotion in the Story
(*e*) Emotion in the Author
3. *Crisis*
4. *Suspense*
5. *Climax*
6. *Denouement*
7. *Conclusion*

QUESTIONS AND EXERCISES FOR CLASS OR INDIVIDUAL STUDY

1. Select the main and the minor crises in plots 6 to 10 in Appendix C.

2. What objection is there to having many minor crises in a short-story?

3. Does suspense necessarily involve the mystification of the reader?

4. Select the full climax in each of plots 6 to 10 in Appendix C.

5. Discuss the wisdom of making a plot climax seem inevitable.

6. Discuss the relation of surprise to climax.

7. Select five plots in Appendix C in which climax is identical with denouement.

8. Five in which denouement is identical with conclusion.

9. Write your opinions upon the "happy ending."

10. (a) What is true tragedy? (b) Can it consist with the "happy ending"?

11. Write a story with but one crisis, and a swift climax thereafter.

12. Write out the climax scene in any one of plots 11–15 in Appendix C without reading the original stories.

13. Now add the denouement and conclusion in your own language.

14. Outline stories in which (a) accident, (b) fate, (c) retribution, form either the pivots for the crises, or the denouements.

15. Outline a plot, but write out the conclusion in full.

16. Read a short-story up to the crisis, then supply a crisis of your own devising.

17. Do the same for (a) climax, (b) denouement, (c) conclusion.

18. Let the instructor assign certain short-stories, or merely plots, for plot-analysis somewhat in the manner of the following diagrams. The points of change in the plots should be clearly indicated on the diagrams by filling in sentences or briefly designating the situations:

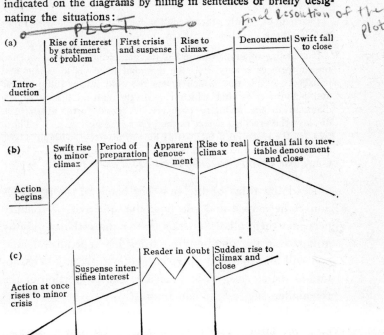

NOTE: Such exercises may be multiplied and varied indefinitely. If accessible, the original stories should later be examined side by side with the student's effort.

CHAPTER XI

CHARACTERS AND CHARACTERIZATION

Learn to see with other people's eyes, and to feel with other people's hearts.— How to Write a Novel, *Anonymous.*

Knowledge of human nature is the gold which is to be worked into a form of beauty, it is the diamond which is to be cut and polished. Art is that which forms the gold into a thing of use and beauty; it is that which reveals the natural beauty of the diamond to the ordinary observer. A good form, a true art, displays the precious object to the best advantage. . . . Those two are the essential principles of human progress, without whose marriage there can be no children of the imagination.— Sherwin Cody, *The World's Greatest Short Stories.*

Read the titles of the first big batch of short-stories you come across and see how the spirit of personality pervades them all. Test this matter more thoroughly by going over the one-hundred titles in Appendix B, and you will find that sixty per cent. refer directly to characters in the stories, while a considerable proportion of the remainder suggest human interest.

Mr. Howells has said that character delineation is at once the largest and best element in the novel; so also is it in the short-story. Length for length, the one gives character-drawing as much prominence as the other. To be sure, notable exceptions exist in both, but generally it is human interest that binds incident into a coherent mass. Certain kinds of short-stories, indeed, can get along with a smaller proportion of character delineation than the novel — as witness many Kipling stories — but that is true largely because rapid play of incident takes so vigorous a part in the shorter fictional form, and we judge the characters by what they say and do rather than by what is said about them.

In *The Evolution of the English Novel* Professor Stoddard has pointed out that, " as in civilization the complete idea of the value of an individual, and even the complete individual name, is slow in development, so in literary expression the complete individual is a very late product." [1] The recent development of the novel and the short-story have therefore quite naturally resulted in a more highly individualized type of character delineation than appeared in the earlier romances and tales. The very term " characters," now more generally used than " persons in the story," suggests individuality. As Mr. Mabie has effectively put it, " Formerly good and evil were indicated by contrasting bands of black and white; to-day they separate from or approach one another through innumerable gradations of gray." [2]

The problem is how to put live characters — I have not said transplant living people — into the short-story. No living being is interesting enough to live bodily, in all his moods and phases, in the short-story. In the biography he is, once in a century; in the novel he may be, though I am not sure; but in the short-story he would

[1] Page 46.
[2] *Stories New and Old,* Introduction.

be too commonplace were he never so individual. " In fiction . . . a character must be exaggerated to appear natural." [3]   He must live, but the course of his life must be unusual while seeming to be usual.   In his essay on *The Really Interesting People,* [4] Colonel Higginson tells how " Sir Robert Walpole, who lived to be nearly eighty, remarked of his coeval Lord Tyrawley, ' Tyrawley and I have been dead for two years, but we don't tell anybody.' "   But when a character in fiction is dead he sits up and shouts it out to everybody — it is the one thing that cannot be hid.   Emotion is the source-spring of character-interest, and emotion a dead character never feels.

Mr. Henry James has given in his *Partial Portraits* an intimate view of how a great Russian fictionist looked upon his character creations.

" Nothing that Turgenieff had to say could be more interesting than his talk about his own work, his manner of writing.   What I have heard him tell of these things was worthy of the beautiful results he produced; of the deep purpose, pervading them all, to show us life itself. The germ of a story, with him, was never an affair of plot — that was the last thing he thought of: it was the representation of certain persons.   The first form in which a tale appeared to him was as the figure of an individual, or a combination of individuals, whom he wished to see in action, being sure that such people must

[3] *Short Story Writing,* Barrett.
[4] *Book and Heart,* p. 191.

do something very special and interesting. They stood before him definite, vivid, and he wished to know, and to show, as much as possible of their nature. The first thing was to make clear to himself what he did not know, to begin with; and to this end, he wrote out a sort of biography of each of his characters, and everything that they had done and that had happened to them up to the opening of the story. He had their *dossier,* as the French say, and as the police have that of every con- spicuous criminal. With this material in his hand he was able to proceed; the story all lay in the question, What shall I make them do? He always made them do things that showed them completely; but, as he said, the defect of his manner and the reproach that was made him was his want of ' architecture,'— in other words, of composition. The great thing, of course, is to have architecture as well as precious material, as Walter Scott had them, as Balzac had them." [5]

I. THE CHARACTERS

1. *Selecting the Characters*

The sources of character-material seem ridiculously plentiful, yet few eyes are trained to discern, and fewer pens to develop them.

(a) *The successful writer must study character* as a preliminary to selecting characters for his stories.

To advise a young writer to look within his own being

[5] *Partial Portraits,* Henry James. Compare this view with Mr. Howells' position, p. 94.

is popular counsel,[6] yet when he does look he is likely
to be confused by the complexities of that inner life.
Self-analysis comes by practice in self-awareness. Question yourself thus: What am I now thinking? What
train of ideas led up to my present thoughts? What
motives influenced my last important act? Were they
simple or complex? Did they involve a conscious struggle? What considerations really formed the decision?
Or was the decision an unconscious one? And did I
awaken to find it ready-made? How did I feel after the
decision was reached?

Questions such as these will light up the chambers,
yes, the caverns, of your inner self, and uncover the
springs of feeling and of motive in other lives too. You
must know the workings of your own mind before you
can read the characters about you.

In practising character-study, remember that many
persons are worth observing who may not be worth
delineating. Skill in reading faces, inferring motive
from conduct, associating habit with essential character,
comes with practice, and you can practise on all comers.
No one ever wrote good stories whose habit it was to
see people only in the mass. What is it, precisely and
intimately what is it, that makes two people different?
Press home that question when next you have a chance
to observe your fellows, remembering always that the
inner man forms the outer, and that each must have its
share of study.

Books, too, will help you. Read the great character

[6] See p. 56.

artists — Dickens, Thackeray, Stevenson, Balzac and Kipling. And don't despise a good text-book on psychology.[7]

(b) *The principles of selection* will arise in your mind quite naturally as your skill in reading character grows. Either your incidents will govern your characters, or *vice versa*. If the former, your selection is limited to the kind of folk who could and would do the things required. If you are writing for a particular class of magazines you will find there another guidepost. *St. Nicholas* and *Harper's* and *Smart Set* welcome characters of different sorts. Some great fiction characters have won a place in the affections of schoolgirl and sage alike, but they are as exceptional as men of genius in actual life.

What characters are worth delineating? A hard question, if one expects a definitive answer. But, speaking generally, the world is in love with the future — in youth and what it will be and do. It wants to read about people who do interesting things in interesting places under interesting conditions; who exhibit strong individuality, whether for good or evil; whose appearance typifies their natures (with exceptions) ; who show the characteristics of a class and yet are individual; whose emotions — love, hate, revenge, greed, humor, ambition, what not — take unexpected though logical courses.

Men are often interested in fictional characters whom

---

[7] Gordy's *New Psychology* is a good one for elementary reading.

they would not care to know in life. It will not do to
exclude a character because he is a prig, or a glutton,
or a thief. Who was it that called d'Artagnan a lovable
rogue and a pestilent good-fellow? Let your character
be but interesting, really known to you, and so human
that he would strike back if you struck him and
your readers will decide as to whether he is a good
fellow or bad. Moral teaching is not a cause, but an
effect.

2. *The Number and Relation of Characters*

	Speaking	Present, but not Speaking.	Mentioned, but not Present	Total
"After the Battle," Joseph A Altsheler (15)	2	0	2	4
"The Piece of String," Guy de Maupassant (28)	3	4	0	7
"The Gold Bug," Edgar Allen Poe (28)	3	2	3	8
"A Yarn Without a Moral," Morgan Robertson (27)	5	0	3	8
"The Ambitious Guest," Nathaniel Hawthorne (works)	8	0	2	10
"How Gavin Birse Put it to Mag Lownie," James M. Barrie (28)	3	0	7	10
"Santa Fé Charlie's Kindergarten," Thomas A. Janvier (Santa Fé's Partner)	5	3	6	14
"Quite So," Thomas Bailey Aldrich (24)	5	0	11	16
"The Man Who Would be King," Rudyard Kipling (28)	5	2	11	18
"The Black Pearl," Victorien Sardou (11)	6	0	14	20
Average	4 to 5	1	6	12 to 13

(The numbers in parentheses refer to Appendix A.)

Following, in part, the method employed by Professor
Selden C. Whitcomb in *The Study of a Novel,* I have

set down a table of those characters actually individualized in ten representative short-stories. Of course, the practice of ten authors could not establish a precedent even if their practices did not vary as widely as they do, but it will be observed that the best writers employ few speaking characters in the short-story, and they rarely equal the number of silent actors.

The relations which the characters are to sustain toward each other will have a strong bearing upon the number to be introduced, as the foregoing table will suggest. In defining the short-story I have limited it to the presentation of one preëminent character; and this is the case even where the study is of two characters each powerfully influencing the other. The usual course is to play the minor characters as contributory to the central figure. But the author cannot always choose which character is to win the spot-light on his stage. Sometimes one character will come to the front in spite of plot and plan. The person making the greatest sacrifice may overtop the one possessing the most pleasing qualities, the foil may unexpectedly outshine the leading light. Some characters naturally belong in the foreground, some in the middle-distance, others in the dim background. Therefore respect their native qualities and treat each with a painter's regard for perspective. To color the one too brightly would be to mar the harmony of the whole as much as to paint the central character in neutral tint.

Character relation must be decided before approach is made to characterization. Plot and counterplot, hero and villain, light and foil, all need careful adjustment, depending considerably upon whether the story is to be one of single character, contrasted character, balanced character, group character, realistic character, idealistic character, romantic character, or no character-story at all, but a narrative of incident.

3. *Character Classes*

Various writers have tried to group the figures of fiction in a few elemental classes. The Explorer, the Defender, and the Dweller; the Wanderer, the Hero, and the Citizen; the Adventurer, the Achiever, the Sufferer, and the Lover — these groupings are sufficiently illustrative. Whether such a classification can or cannot be satisfactorily effected, we must look to great typical figures as heading the classes of characters with which the story-writer deals.

The big word here is TRAITS; that is what we must look for, and when we have grouped a special lot of traits we have found a basis for (a) *typical characters.* The student of character will find this a fascinating study. National traits, sectional traits, class traits, professional traits, sexual traits, personal traits — all furnish bases for types. But, more than this, traits cross and complicate indefinitely. For example, the soldier possesses his class traits, modified by his nationality, his province, and his personality. And this is the fiction-writer's great good fortune, for it offers to his originality the chance of making fresh character combinations every day, either according to the law of character harmony, or, what is still more fascinating, by embodying contradictory traits in the same being.

Professor Bliss Perry [8] has said that we commonly use the word " type " in either of two ways: as meaning the ideal, which combines the essential natures of all of a class; or, as meaning a fair example of one class — an average specimen. This distinction is valid, and bears upon the fiction-writer's treatment of character.

But delineation of types may be pressed too far. Some writers picture for us not a woman, but womanhood; not a suffering man, but suffering. This method is too often purely ideal. While it may exalt our conceptions of truth, or excite our wonder at a general condition, it rarely moves us deeply, for mere types lack flesh and blood.

A second method, equally one-sided, is that of presenting (b) *purely personal characters,* with no attempt to make them also typical of a class. No individual, apart from his typical traits, is likely to be worth delineating in a short-story. He is a mere eccentric, detached from normal humanity, interesting only as a freak. But—better a live freak than a dead type.

(c) *The joint method* is likely to be the most satisfactory. The character may be simple, complex, or inconsistent, still, if a living person is constructed out of a combination of typical and personal traits, a convincing figure will emerge from the background. He will then be more than an American soldier; he will be a Vir-

[8] *A Study of Prose Fiction,* chap. v.

ginian, a reënlisted sergeant, a native wit — and all the rest of his own personality down to his toes. Unless personal traits dominate class traits a character remains a puppet, an abstraction — as, now and then, it may suit an author's purpose to make him. What the reader wants, for the most part, is a Representative Man, with due emphasis laid on each word.

The nuisance of story-telling is the conventional type-character. There are other ways of delineating an Englishman than by forcing him to drop his h's with a dull thud, of picturing a Southern gentleman than by interpolating countless " suh's " into his speech, and of drawing a cow-puncher than by putting on his legs a big pair of sheepskin chaps. Such methods are antiquated and smack of the trashiest photoplay. Goethe has compared Shakespeare's characters to watches in crystal cases, which, while they faithfully point out the hours, disclose to the beholder their inner workings. Some writers seem to think that all personal characteristics are like beauty in the old adage, which lies but skin-deep.

In choosing your type-individuals do not be a slave to fashions in heroes and heroines. Why must your gentleman-adventurer be of the Zenda school, your young woman commit her misdemeanors like Nancy, "dialogue" like Dolly, and look deceptively serious, like a Fisher girl?

4. *The Relation of Characters to Action and Setting*

These three short-story elements are handled in accord with the designer's plan, the one or the other predominating as may suit his purpose and best tell the story. No rule can avail here but the double law of harmony and contrast.[9]   Once your purpose is settled, you will be able to decide which will best bring out your characters.   To select a character that is too big for the setting, to bury character under action, or to emphasize the setting unduly, are equally fatal faults.   The chief purpose of the short-story is to present character as doing, being, or becoming, in an appropriate environment. Hold all in a safe balance.

5. *The Author's Attitude Toward His Characters*

Doubtless many a writer does not suppose that his readers are more or less consciously alert to discover his attitude toward his fictive creatures, yet such is the fact.   Is he content with the present social order, or is he a social reformer? or a social malcontent? or a cynical indifferentist?   His outlook on life, it goes without saying, is likely to transpire in his stories.   In the same manner it will appear whether he views his characters with a cold indifference, as does Maupassant; actual contempt, as disclosed in Flaubert; frank worship, like Scott; or a discriminating sympathy, in the manner of Stevenson.[10]   Perhaps you will agree with me that the last is the only warm-hearted, spirit-kindling attitude to maintain.   It was Sidney Lanier who said that the fiction-writer partakes of the Divine power because it is given to him to look into and mould the inner lives of

[9] Fully discussed in the chapter on *Setting*.
[10] Compare pp. 110 and 175.

his characters. Surely, then, he should feel a temperate sympathy for those whose virtues and vices are the creatures of his art.

II. CHARACTERIZATION

Characterization is the process of setting forth, of depicting, the characters in the story. It is a specialized sort of description, both internal and external in its scope.

1. *Effect To Be Attained*

The result to be sought after is an effect of life-likeness which will make the characters seem to be living beings in whose affairs the readers have a genuine interest. And indeed this end is now and then so fully attained that the characters do become our permanent possession as friends. But such sense of actuality can scarcely be produced upon the reader unless the writer has himself realized his characters. The height of verisimilitude is reached when the author and the reader experience the same emotions as a given character excites in his fellow characters. Then, indeed, there is vital delineation. In *De Finibus* Thackeray describes himself as writing in the gray of the evening and picturing a character so vividly to himself that at length he looks " rather wistfully up from the paper with perhaps ever so little fancy that HE MAY COME IN." [11]

I have said that the author's purpose in characteriza-

[11] Quoted in *The Technique of the Novel,* Horne, p. 185.

tion is to create a life-like impression. But a word, and
only a word, must be added to particularize this general
statement. The literary ideals of the writer will mould
this purpose into one of the following five forms : to depict characters precisely as they are in life *(realism);*
as they ought to be *(idealism);* as they might be under
extraordinary conditions *(romanticism);* as they would
be with their natural characteristics exaggerated to dis-
tortion *(caricature);* or, as they would appear under
conditions which the writer creates for them *(a composite of the other four methods).*

2. *General Methods of Characterization*

The short-story writer must get his people before the
reader at the earliest possible moment, and in doing so
he has choice of three general methods :

(a) *Description* may be applied to the characters in
the story very much as it is to the setting, but it must
be kept in mind that only physical appearance appeals to
the eye, while character centers in some unseen part of
the man.[12]   The outward will interpret the inward and
is often its subtlest expression, so that these two of the
methods of characterization are often used conjointly —
physical description touches upon, suggests and rein-
forces delineation of character.[13]

(1) The direct method of description is often attempted and often fails. The short-story is too short

[12] The reader will of course bear in mind the distinction between the terms *characters* and *character.*
[13] See p. 233; also "Description", pp. 152-100.

to admit of its large use. Of course, an artist in words will succeed where another would not, but the chances are decidedly against successful direct description of the characters.

(2) The indirect method either allows one character to depict another, or develops the delineation gradually as the story proceeds — a very good method indeed.

(3) The suggestive method seizes upon a salient characteristic and makes it stand for the whole, allowing the reader to fill in the details from imagination. This method requires a facile pen and is good — when it is good. It lends itself readily to humor, satire and caricature.

Here is a capital example of direct description from Stevenson's *Treasure Island:*

I remember him as if it were yesterday, as he came plodding to the inn door, his sea-chest following behind him in a handbarrow; a tall, strong, heavy, nut-brown man; his tarry pigtail falling over the shoulders of his soiled blue coat; his hands ragged and scarred, with black, broken nails; and the sabre-cut across one cheek, a dirty, livid white.

The following direct description is from Henry James's " The Tragic Muse."

What Biddy discerned was that this young man was fair and fat and of the middle stature; he had a round face and a short beard, and on his crown a mere reminiscence of hair, as the fact that he carried his hat in his hand permitted it to be observed.

Compare the older with the more modern method, as shown in these direct delineations. The first is from

Irving, the other from " O. Henry," who conveys a suggestion of inner character by picturing the bodily type.

She was a blooming lass of fresh eighteen, plump as a partridge, ripe and melting and rosy-cheeked as one of her father's peaches.

She was a splendidly feminine girl, as wholesome as a November pippin, and no more mysterious than a window-pane.

Dickens's concrete and unified description of Mr. Pecksniff, in *Martin Chuzzlewit,* is a masterpiece. See how the man's bodily appearance inevitably reveals his character :

His very throat was moral. You saw a good deal of it. You looked over a very low fence of white cravat (whereof no man had ever beheld the tie, for he fastened it behind), and there it lay, a valley between two jutting heights of collar, serene and whiskerless before you. It seemed to say, on the part of Mr. Pecksniff, " There is no deception, ladies and gentlemen, all is peace, a holy calm pervades me." So did his hair, just grizzled with an iron gray, which was all brushed off his forehead, and stood bolt upright, or slightly drooped in kindred action with his heavy eyelids. So did his person, which was sleek though free from corpulency. So did his manner, which was soft and oily. In a word, even his plain black suit, and state of widower, and dangling double eye-glass, all tended to the same purpose, and cried aloud, " Behold the moral Pecksniff ! "

Here are three specimens of suggestive physical description, mingled with suggestive delineation of character — taken also from Dickens :

In came Mrs. Fezziwig, one vast substantial smile.[14]

[14] *Christmas Carol.*

Small, shining, neat, methodical, and buxom was Miss Peecher; cherry-cheeked and tuneful of voice. A little pin-cushion, a little housewife, a little book, a little work-box, a little set of tables and weights and measures, and a little woman all in one. She could write a little essay on any subject, exactly a slate long, beginning at the left-hand top of one side and ending at the right-hand bottom of the other, and the essay should be strictly according to rule.[15]

Mrs. Gradgrind, a little, thin, white, pink-eyed bundle of shawls, of surpassing feebleness, mental and bodily; who was always taking physic without any effect, and who, whenever she showed a symptom of coming to life, was invariably stunned by some weighty piece of fact tumbling on her.[16]

This is a more modern specimen of suggestive physical description:

Colonel Marigold was a rosy cherub with a white chinwhisker. He carried his sixty years with a slight soldierly limp, and was forever opening his china-blue eyes in mild astonishment.

(b) *Character analysis* is really a form of description which deals with the unseen, just as description occupies itself more fully with the seen, though the latter also often looks beneath the surface. Naturally, such simple statements as, " Silas Hornberger was a hard-fisted old sinner," can scarcely be regarded as profoundly analytical, yet it requires a direct kind of analysis to arrive at even the simplest and most obvious character. From such elementary though effective characterization we ascend to more indirect delineation, such as the following, which is mingled with dialogue. The two paragraphs are a hundred words apart in the story.

[15] *Our Mutual Friend.*
[16] *Hard Times.*

Angie tipped up the slop-pail. " Yes," she said, without deceit
— she always, by nature of her temperament, spoke her mind
quite plainly —" but I'm a-goin' to git all my hard work done
up t' onct afore I stop."

Angie colored. The change for her raisins went down sharply
on the counter. Her little old chin went up into the air.
" Well," she said, tartly, " I guess ye don't need to come if
ye don't want to ! " [17]

The longer short-stories, like the best of Mr. James's,
afford room for more profound analysis, though now and
then we find an instance of vivisection at once brilliant
and condensed.[18]   Like the compact statement of an intricate problem, the crystalline result does not disclose
the difficult processes involved.

Men as they pass prefer action to analysis, because it
seems more real. What they experience makes a more
immediate appeal to them than what they merely think
about; but when psychological analysis does lay hold,
it fastens its grip firmly, until reflection gradually produces the effect of reality.

(c) *The dramatic method* delineates character by
speech [19] and action — at once the most difficult and most
effective combination of all literary devices. This is the
method of Jesus in the Parables, which never consider
the details of personal appearance except symbolically.
If, as Stevenson has said, " drama is the poetry of conduct," the near approach to the dramatic form in dia-

[17] *The Tea Party,* Muriel Campbell Dyar, *Harper's,* Jan., 1908.
[18] See the opening paragraphs of Maupassant's *The Necklace,*
reproduced in full, Part III, chap. iv.
[19] The next chapter entire is given to a discussion of Dialogue.

logue and action adds life as well as beauty to the short-story. The same authority has said:

"This, then, is the plastic part of literature: to embody character, thought, or emotion in some act or attitude that shall be remarkably striking to the mind's eye. This is the highest and hardest thing to do in words; the thing which, once accomplished, equally delights the schoolboy and the sage, and makes, in its own right, this quality of epics. It is one thing to remark and dissect, with the most cutting logic, the complications of life, and of the human spirit; it is quite another to give them body and blood in the story of Ajax or Hamlet. The first is literature, but the second is something besides, for it is likewise art. . . .

"Readers cannot fail to have remarked that what an author tells us of the beauty or the charm of his creatures goes for naught; that we know instantly better; that the heroine cannot open her mouth but what, all in a moment, the fine phrases of preparation fall from her like the robes of Cinderella, and she stands before us as a poor, ugly, sickly wench, or perhaps a strapping market-woman."[20]

To make characterization, speech, and action harmonize so as to preserve the unity of the character is of no small moment in fiction. Speech and action, each by itself, often disclose too much or too little — as, truly, they will often play us false together in daily life.

[20] *A Gossip on a Novel of Dumas'.*

3. *Specific Means of Characterization*

To enter fully into all the devices employed by literary artists to delineate character would consume a volume. Four, however, require brief mention.

(a) *The naming of characters* is of as great importance in the short-story as in the novel. Names should be fitting. Phyllis ought not to weigh two hundred, nor ought Tommy to commit suicide. Luther must not be a burglar, Maud a washerwoman, nor John spout tepid romance. The wrong surname will handicap a character as surely as the wrong pair of hands. Hardscrabble does not fit the philanthropist any more than Tinker suggests the polished diplomat, or Darnaway the clergyman.

And yet, certain contrasts and side-lights on characters are secured by merely naming them incongruously. If Phyllis *does* weigh two-hundred, and if Maud *is* a washerwoman, it must be for humor's sake, for contrast, or for some such reason as is given by " Mark Twain " in " The $30,000 Bequest " when he argues that the bookkeeper's wife, Electra, and her daughter, Clytemnestra, furnished direct proof of a strain of romance in the family by reason of the names they bore.

There are fashions in names as in flounces and I suppose they must invade fiction as they do drawing-rooms, but Mary will always symbolize steady purity, Nancy a coquettish fly-away, Jerry a worthy solid-head, Walter impeccable virtue, Miriam high-souled idealism, Martha lowly service, and Jasper a prig — all subject to the exceptions of real life, where there is even more misnaming than in fiction.

(b) *Physiological marks,* as hinted in a preceding section, are of emphatic value in character portrayal. Here we see physical description serving the ends of characterization. Darnaway, in Stevenson's *Merry Men,* was "a sour, small, bilious man, with a long face and very dark eyes." The physical everywhere discloses and even limits the mental, moral and spiritual. Darwin has told us that quickened emotions often begin to manifest themselves in quick breathing. We know that, but forget to put the knowledge to use. Learn to interpret the broad face, the small mouth, the deepset eyes, the hiked-up shoulders, the stubby fingers, the high cheek-bones, the bristly hair, and a hundred other physical marks, just as you already read the more commonly understood shambling gait, loose jowl, and low forehead. Study, too, the effect of a combination of physical traits, and learn that one strong point in physiognomy may sometimes quite offset a number of weak ones — and contrariwise.

(c) *Dress and occupations* are also suggestive of character, though there is more room for their description in the novel than in the short-story. When we learn that Rip Van Winkle's children are ragged it impresses us with his easy ways more than to read that he himself is out at elbows. His devotion to hunting while his family is in want confirms the indictment.

Balzac combines several of the foregoing elements in

this description of Monsieur Regnault, the notary, in
" La Grande Brétêche " :

Suddenly I saw a tall slender man, dressed in black, with his
hat in his hand, who entered the room like a ram ready to rush
at his rival, disclosing a retreating forehead, a small pointed
head, and a pale face, not unlike a glass of dirty water. You
would have said that he was the doorkeeper of some minister.
He wore an old coat, threadbare at the seams; but he had a
diamond in his shirt-frill and gold rings in his ears.

(d) *Personality* is the last element to be considered,
but of primary importance, for the persons of the
story often exhibit strong personal characteristics of
mind, morals and heart, in addition to their national, sectional, professional, or other non-individual traits.
There are two main kinds of persons in fiction: those
whose characters do not change, but whose natures are
disclosed by the story (like Lady Macbeth) ; and those
whose characters do undergo a change, whether for better or for worse (like Tess). The former are sometimes
called static characters, and the latter, dynamic. Kipling's Mulvaney is static, Stevenson's Markheim is dynamic.

Outward action is often preceded by struggle of soul,
marking character transformation. Sometimes, as with
Hester Prynne in *The Scarlet Letter,* that struggle is
with the lower nature, striving more and more effectively
to rise above it. Sometimes the battle is with the higher
nature, deterioration being the result, as in Tito Melema,
of *Romola.* Again the war is waged with external
forces, as in Hamlet's bitter problem of how to do justice

in a case which involved his own mother. But somehow, always, character-change must involve, suggest, or disclose, a force big enough to account for the result. It is ridiculous for an author to transform a character by sheer hocus-pocus, or suddenly attribute a momentous deed, good or bad, to a character whose qualities all point the other way.

Critical times in the action fittingly coincide with moral crises in the characters. Remember that some incidents reveal character, while some affect character. Ask these questions: Could such a woman, let us say, being altogether such as she is, do such a deed as you propose to make her do? Next, would she do it? Finally, can no more effective thing be devised? Study " The Outcasts of Poker Flat " and see how character transformation is satisfactorily accounted for. (See Supplemental Chapter, "Making the Story Convincing," for Motivation.)

OUTLINE SUMMARY

I. THE CHARACTERS

   1. *Selecting the Characters*
     (*a*) Character Study
     (*b*) Principles of Selection
   2. *Number and Relation of Characters*
   3. *Character Classes*
     (*a*) Typical
     (*b*) Personal
     (*c*) Composite
   4. *Relation of Characters to Action and Setting*
   5. *Author's Attitude Toward His Characters*

II. CHARACTERIZATION

   1. *Effect to be Attained*

2. *General Methods of Characterization*
   (*a*) Description
      (1) Direct
      (2) Indirect
      (3) Suggestive
   (*b*) Character Analysis
   (*c*) Dramatic Method
3. *Specific Means of Characterization*
   (*a*) Naming of Characters
   (*b*) Physiological Marks
   (*c*) Dress
   (*d*) Personality

QUESTIONS AND EXERCISES FOR CLASS OR INDIVIDUAL STUDY

1. Make a list of characters you have met who are interesting enough to be delineated in short-stories. Give a sentence or two to each to set forth their characteristics.

2. Specifically state how you would modify their everyday characteristics for the purposes of fiction.

3. Make a composite characterization by combining the traits of two or more.

4. Make complete, compressed notes of the life and characteristics of one character in the list (question 1), after the manner of Turgenieff.

5. Follow Turgenieff's method by conceiving a character and building a plot around his personality.

6. After you have decided on a character worth characterizing in a short-story, trace in writing the chain of ideas by which the conception arose and developed in your mind.

7. Select two short-stories in which character-drawing is especially well done, giving reasons for your opinion.

NOTE: The instructor may wish to include character-novels in this assignment.

8. Make a study of several late issues of at least four prominent magazines and say what types of character-stories they publish.

9. In the manner of the schedule on page 224, list the actually individualized characters in four well-known short-stories.

10. Write a character-story with careful attention to the relation of the characters to the foreground, middle-distance, and background.

11. Make a list of such characteristic national (French, etc.), sectional (Northwestern, etc.), class, professional, and local traits as could be embodied in fiction.

12. Write a character-story in the joint typical-individual style.

13. What do you understand by a character that is (a) simple, (b) complex, (c) inconsistent?

14. Make a list of worn-out, conventional characters often seen in fiction.

15. Outline a character and a setting (a) in harmony, (b) in contrast, with each other.

16. Delineate a character by direct description, without the use of dialogue.

17. Delineate the same character by suggestion.

18. Present pictures of the following moods: (a) a girl struggling to retain faith in her college chum; (b) a youth deciding to commit his first crime; (c) an old man just dismissed from a "life-long" position, by the trick of an enemy.

19. Invent at least five other such situations involving character changes.

20. (a) Criticise the names in any short-story you please; (b) select a short-story in which the characters are well-named, and show why.

21. Take the portrait of some person unknown to you and try to read the character from the face, bearing, and dress.

22. Make a list of prominent physical traits (a squint, for one), saying what they mean to you. For example, begin with faces which suggest animals, without necessarily revealing anything bestial.

23. Suggestively describe the dress of ten different characters, differentiating them according to occupations, nationality, class, morals, etc.

24. Describe in your favorite way, but as compactly as possible, the following characters: (a) a romantic blunderer; (b)

two characters in marked contrast; (c) a lover of music who fondly believes he can sing — but can't; (d) a serious man who is always mistaken for a jester; (e) a woman who loves to settle difficulties but who succeeds only in making things worse.

NOTE: In her elementary but suggestive little volume, *The Story-Teller's Art,* p. 43, Miss Charity Dye says that character may be studied:

"1. By its innate tendencies, or its inner promptings independent of any external influence.

"2. By its environment, or surroundings, and the way in which it has overcome them or been overcome by them.

"3. In the light of heredity, or inherited traits.

"4. By its manifestations of willing, thinking, feeling.

"5. By its achievements, or what it has accomplished in the light of its effort and opportunity, and by the development it makes.

"6. By noting all that a character says and does, all that is said and done to him, and all that is said about him.

"7. By noting the dominant motive of his life, whether it be love, hate, revenge, a sense of duty, selfishness, or forgiveness.

"8. A character may be studied by putting one's self in another's place; by being the apple-woman, the newsboy, the bootblack for a time, and looking at life through their eyes. Be a beggar, a millionaire, a master, or a slave, and imagine what you would do in each situation."

From among these methods the instructor may select such as will make satisfactory assignments for (a) character study, (b) character delineation.

CHAPTER XII

DIALOGUE

The use of quotation marks does not convert a passage into dialogue.— ARLO BATES, *Talks on Writing English.*

It is not necessary to say that a woman is a snarling, grumpy person. Bring in the old lady and let her snarl.— ANONYMOUS.

If in the characters is involved the profounder fibre of the story, from the management of the dialogue comes largely its more buoyant and popular effect. Uncritical readers — whose preferences, in fact, ought to be consulted — like a story " with lots of conversation in it." The dialogue serves, as it were, to aërate the movement, which else might grow ponderous and slow. In the give and take of conversation, too, character itself appears, to speak for itself; and many accessory and descriptive elements slip in lightly and unobtrusively in the words that are said. And through it all is traceable the forward movement and the approaching end or crisis.— J. F. GENUNG, *The Working Principles of Rhetoric.*

Conversation belongs to the short-story because it belongs to life. There have been good short-stories without dialogue, as there are brilliant folk who are deprived of speech, but happily both are exceptions. The normal, cheerful mind loves speech, and since the short-story is sought after mainly for diversion, the reader will turn in his lighter moods to the conversational short-story, just as for sheer recreation he will prefer the rapid-fire dialogue of the elder Dumas [1] to the heavier descriptive passages of Scott.

The beginner does not usually put much conversation into his fiction, for conversation is hard to write. He reasons that little dialogue is better than poor dialogue; and so it is. Only, when it comes to that pass, why write at all? Good conversation is a vital element in the story-teller's art, and its mastery often spells success. The *Fifteenth Idyll* of Theocritus depicts the "smart" life of Alexandria in the third century B. C. with such sure and swift conversational strokes that it still lives as a classic. Nowadays it is difficult to sell a story whose long paragraphs of unbroken description and explanation would, the editor feels, surely repel the casual buyer. A page of dialogue attracts the eye, and so gives the author a chance to please the mind.

1. *The Proportion of Dialogue*

It will be interesting to examine the following table of ten more or less famous short-stories, selected quite at random from American, British and French authors, covering a period of about seventy-five years. Some one might profitably compute the proportion of conversation in, say, five hundred representative short-stories, classifying them as to type, and then give us the figures. While no writer would recognize any such result as con-

---

[1] "It [Dumas' Dialogue] can unfold action, character, emotion, description, and stage directions, and it can make all these seem natural even when they are most extravagant, convincing when they are most false."— HORNE, *The Technique of the Novel,* p. 257.

stituting a standard for him, it would at least tell us
something definite as to good usage.

STORY AND AUTHOR.

	CONVERSATION
"The Outcasts of Poker Flat," Bret Harte........	11 per cent
"The Diamond Lens," Fitz-James O'Brien........	13 " "
"The Ambitious Guest," Nathaniel Hawthorne....	30 " "
"Mrs. Protheroe," Booth Tarkington............	38 " "
"A Lodging for the Night," Robert Louis Stevenson	39 " "
"Many Waters," Margaret Deland..............	43 " "
"A Venus of the Fields," "Georg Schock"........	45 " "
"Without Benefit of Clergy," Rudyard Kipling....	54 " "
"La Grande Brétêche," Honoré de Balzac.........	55 " "
"The Gold Bug," Edgar Allan Poe..............	64 " "
Average proportion of conversation..............	39 " "

It has been asserted [2] that present-day usage tends to
the dialogue form more than did the practice of Poe and
Hawthorne. I doubt this conclusion, especially if the
fictions of these masters be compared with those of our
best living story-writers. The lighter the story the
stronger the swing toward the dialogic method, so the
statement may be true of stories of this type; but the
short-story of depth, yesterday, to-day, and always, will
not average fifty per cent. conversation. As an English
expert, Mr. Frederic Wedmore, has pointed out,[3] the
writer is unwise to deny himself the freedom of the pure
dramatic form when he chooses to tell a story wholly
in dialogue. He simply makes his work more difficult
and, at the same time, less effective. Though the drama

[2] Barrett, *Short Story Writing*, p. 107; Albright, *The Short-
Story*, p. 146.
[3] *North American Review*, 43 : 410.

may be studied with much profit by the writer of short-stories, the two types are likely to remain distinct.

2. *The Office of Dialogue*

There is no narrative effect which speech cannot compass, but it must never be introduced for its own sake. Its office is to tell the story, and this it does by several means, one of the chief of which is:

(a) *The revelation of human character.* Just as human interest is the heart of narrative, so human speech is its most vivid expression. In everyday life we do not know a man until we have heard him speak. Then our first impressions are either confirmed, modified, or totally upset. To adapt Dr. Talmage's pun, many a man, in life as in fiction, puts his foot in it as soon as he opens his mouth. The worth of many another is perceived only when he speaks.

The more prominent the character in the story, the more significant must be his every word. Figures in the middle-distance and the background may talk more or less alike, but the leading persons must utter every word " in character." They must be so individual that the only words they could speak are just the ones they do speak. And they must preserve this personality consistently — so consistently that throughout the whole narrative the reader will recognize their language, feelings, thoughts, likes and dislikes, in fact their entire individuality, as being distinct from their fellow characters. Many a story puts the words of men into the mouths of babes, labels women as wise yet makes them spout twaddle, and so hopelessly confuses the reader that he could not, if he cared to try, discover who is speaking. No one ever thus confused the words of Mrs. Gamp with those of any other participant in the dialogue, nor imputed the sentiments of Sam Weller to some one else. They are always delightfully themselves.

The trouble just here is that too many writers thrust their own personalities into their stories. Their characters are simply lay figures, or at best, made-up actors, masquerading as real persons. Their whole business in the story is to declaim their author's views. No error could be more egregious. If its source is ignorance, it should be enlightened; if it is vanity, the rejection-slip may help to puncture it. To be convincing, a fictional character must be somebody, not anybody. His personality and his actions must be of one piece, and his talk cut from the same cloth. But you must know your cloth, its size and its texture. So long as writers persist in choosing their characters from walks of life of which they know little or nothing, so long will their dialogue lack individuality.

The moderns have taken big strides ahead in this respect. Even Poe put uniformly stilted speech into the mouths of his characters, while Hawthorne offended similarly. Dickens was the great modern innovator here, Kipling being the present-day master. "Wee Willie Winkie" *thinks* as a child, and his speech is of a kind with his baby thought. Mulvaney, Ortheris and Learoyd never look at things from quite the same view-point, and so we seldom need a "said Mulvaney" to tell us who says what.

Now, this matter is worth study. The average amateur does not individualize the speech of his characters, and the best story-writers always do. And there you have a tremendous difference.

It is worth while inquiring what things in actual life vividly color a man's manner of speech — I mean, influence his choice and arrangement of words and his manner of utterance. They are five: his antecedents (including habits of speech acquired in childhood), his character (subtly influencing all he says and does), his motives (both general and particular), his present emotion, and his environment (including the influence of the personalities about him). Each of these forces must be weighed by the author when he writes dialogue, as judicially as the judge weighs the conditioning antecedents, character, motives, moods and circumstances of a defendant.

See how utterly Pecksniffian are all the words of that arch bluffer, Mr. Pecksniff.[4] His words and his character coincide.

"Why, the truth is, my dear," said Mr. Pecksniff, smiling upon his assembled kindred, "that I am at a loss for a word. The name of those fabulous animals (pagan, I regret to say) who used to sing in the water, has quite escaped me."

Mr. George Chuzzlewit suggested "Swans."

"No," said Mr. Pecksniff. "Not swans. Very like swans, too. Thank you."

[4] *Martin Chuzzlewit,* Charles Dickens.

The nephew with the outline of a countenance, speaking for the first and last time on that occasion, propounded " Oysters."

" No," said Mr. Pecksniff, with his own peculiar urbanity, " nor oysters. But by no means unlike oysters; a very excellent idea; thank you, my dear sir, very much. Wait! Sirens. Dear me! Sirens, of course."

Dickens has given us another interesting humbug, Mr. Wegg, whose speech could no more be mistaken for that of dear old Mr. Boffin, by whom he was engaged to read aloud of evenings, than it could be confused with the words of the historian he read.

Wegg at length arrives at " Boffin's Bower," and is introduced to Mrs. Boffin. On a table lie the eight volumes of Gibbon in red and gold bindings, with a " purple ribbon in each volume to keep the place where leave off." After indulging in a meat-pie and a swig, Mr. Wegg settles down to his task.

" Hem! " began Wegg. " This, Mr. Boffin and Lady, is the first chapter of the first wollume of the Decline and Fall Off —" here he looked hard at the book and stopped.

" What's the matter, Wegg? "

" Why it comes to my mind, do you know, sir," said Wegg, with an air of insinuating frankness (having first again looked hard at the book), " that you made a little mistake this morning, which I had meant to set you right in, only something put it out of my head. I think you said Rooshan Empire, sir? "

" It is Rooshan; ain't it, Wegg? "

" No, sir. Roman. Roman."

" What's the difference, Wegg? "

" The difference, sir? " Mr. Wegg was faltering and in danger of breaking down, when a bright thought flashed upon him. " The difference, sir? There you place me in a difficulty, Mr. Boffin. Suffice it to observe that the difference is best postponed

to some other occasion when Mrs. Boffin does not honor us
with her company. In Mrs. Boffin's presence, sir, we had better
drop it."

It appears, then, that the sense of reality in dialogue
will be produced if the characters possess individuality
and speak out their true selves. A second consideration is
scarcely less important:

(b) *Dialogue must bring out the incidents,* and this it
must do by harmonizing with them. Will a man make
long speeches in a crisis? Will a time of hurried action
admit of much speech at all? If the one character in the
dialogue would not have time to listen to the other's
windy words, neither will your readers. Ask yourself
what is natural — though not what is commonplace — in
the circumstances, for circumstances alter speeches.

I may merely touch upon two other functions of conversation in fiction, both deserving of fuller treatment.

(c) *Dialogue is used to convey the setting.* See how
in the extracts cited on pp. 128–9 this effect is secured;
and the same device is often used not only in the introduction but throughout the story.

(d) *The entire action,* the incidents, the story itself,
may be told quite as effectively by dialogue as by description, and usually with much more life and interesting effect.

3. *The Subject-matter of Dialogue*

The limits of dialogic subject-matter are, all that is
strictly contributory to the story. No retailing of curious

information, no witty but irrelevant epigrams, no argumentation for its own sake, no pretty talk that leads nowhither, no moral preachment, no impassioned invective, no excursions into inviting by-paths — not one word, in short, that does not urge on the action to its climax.

All these liberties we allow to genius at its best, because the story may be so fascinating that it can carry a load of extraneous comment and still be counted as well-told — like Kipling's Mulvaney stories; or it may be so nearly a sketch that the tone really demands a discursive style — like Hearn's "Chita" and Stevenson's "Will O' the Mill." Such literary privileges, however, are not won by beginners.

On this subject there are some sound words in Anthony Trollope's *Autobiography:*

" The unconscious critical acumen of a reader is both just and severe. When a long dialogue on extraneous matter reaches his mind, he at once feels that he is being cheated into taking something that he did not bargain to accept — he does not at that moment require politics or philosophy, but he wants a story. He will not, perhaps, be able to say in so many words that at some point the dialogue has deviated from the story; but when it does, he will feel it." [5]

4. *The Manner of Dialogue*

Short-story dialogue must be suggestive, not exhaustive. The dialogue of the short-story is not that of the

[5] Vol. II, p. 58.

novel. The former can no more take time fully to reproduce the small talk of a ball-room or of a salon than it can afford space for the minute description of my lady's gown. No, compression, always compression, and a high degree of selection, are what the yarn-spinner must set ever before his mind's eye. What is omitted is quite as important as what is reported. A whole history must be hinted in a sentence, processes of arriving at conclusions struck off in an epigram, the heart of a sentiment packed into a phrase. True, speech will often be idealized — the lofty mood will be symbolized by words more lofty than those of real life; the passionate hour will demand an intensity and compactness of language rarely heard among real folk. But be careful not to overdo this permissible exaggeration.

Conversation is a lost art — except in fiction, and there it is usually more flippant than brilliant. The trouble is that, in book and in life, talk is likely to become stilted the moment the writer or the talker becomes self-conscious. Many a writer suggests Tom Birch, of whom Samuel Johnson said, " He is as brisk as a bee in conversation; but no sooner does he take a pen in his hand than it becomes a torpedo to him, and benumbs all his faculties." Colloquial speech is precisely what dialogue needs — the short, free, unconscious, rapidly shifting speech of everyday life; everyday, that is, in manner, but selected and exceptional in matter. It is well for the literary person to deplore the admitted decadence in the tone and quality of our social converse, for it is painfully evident to the observing, but the short-story must not be turned into a text-book for use in the university conversation course, once proposed half laughingly by Professor A. S. Hill. The meaty talk of *Dr. North and His Friends* [6] needs the desiccation provided by *The Dolly Dialogues* [7] and " The First Hurdle." [8] Let it be repeated: dialogue reports characters in their perfectly representative, typical, characteristic moods. Therefore their speech must show not so much what they say, as what they are.

Of course this brings up the whole question of realism, which I need not again discuss. Much that has been said about its limitations in general [9] may be applied particularly to the speaking character. His words must be truer to ideal truth than to actual talk. To reproduce even the most brilliant conversation just as we have it would result in disappointment. The pivotal and suggestive speeches of your characters are what you must set down so that every word may add some significance to the portrayal. How else should character exhibit individuality? Suppose that all the people in a story were to utter such equally brilliant epigrams as (it is safer to draw these illustrations from novels) they do in parts of Ellen Thorneycroft Fowler's *Concerning Isabel Carnaby,* and in Bulwer's *Parisians;* the effect would be as unconvincing as any other lot of unvaried fireworks. But, really, there is little danger here. There is greater fear of perpetrating the unrelieved dulness of absolute

[6] S. Weir Mitchell.
[7] Anthony Hope.
[8] A short-story by John Reed Scott.
[9] See p. 64.

fidelity to conversational reality. Conversation must be neither too subtle nor too gross, too learned nor too silly, too involved nor too simple. It must idealize the actual speech of men in so far as to discard both the prosings of heavy virtue and the blatancies of flippant vulgarity while typifying both most deftly.

The moulds in which conversation is cast are of forms ɪs various as those of everyday speech, but the manner of reporting them requires some art.

Do not think it necessary to put " he saids " after every remark made by a character. So long as without them the reader understands clearly and easily just who is speaking, such additions hinder rather than help dialogue. But when you do add the explanatory verbs, use some ingenuity in getting away from the conventional forms. Do not discriminate against such good expressions as " he acquiesced," " admitted," " argued," " asked," " assented," " boasted," " called," " cautioned," " chuckled," " corrected," " cried," " croaked," " crowed," " declared," " drawled," " droned," " ejaculated," " emended," " enjoined," " enumerated," " exclaimed," " exploded," " flashed," " frowned," " gasped," " growled," " grumbled," " grunted," " hinted," " inquired," " insinuated," " intimated," " jeered," " jested," " laughed," " leered," " maundered," " mumbled," " nodded," " opined," " pronounced," " puffed," " questioned," " rejoined," " retorted," " returned," " simpered," " snarled," " sneered," " snickered," " stammered," " stipulated," " stormed," " suggested," " urged," " volunteered," " wondered," " yelled,"— and a whole dictionaryful besides,[10] each precisely suited to the shade of mood to be depicted. But do not press novelty too far.

Perhaps it should go without saying that the speeches in dialogue should be brief — yet it doesn't. It will pay to remember that the old man and the boy who " ca'mly drinked and jawed " took sips between remarks.

The baldly " leading question," introduced palpably to help a character to tell some necessary bit of information, is a practice too amateurish to need more than this single word of warning.

A useful conversational device is to make comment both before and at the end of the speech. Either alone is the more common form.

> Nora rose, trembling like a leaf (trite). "Ye bought me Mike's vote, ye say? Ye *bought* it? Oh, Misther Dale, it isn't thrue, is it? Say it isn't. Oh, say it isn't!" The rising wail of a breaking heart spoke in her cry.

Sometimes the author will interrupt the speech of a character to interject an explanation — a dangerous device if the interruption is either long or abrupt. In this example the method is well handled:

> John Gearing was at her side in an instant. "My poor little girl," he murmured, lifting her with all possible gentleness, "are you much hurt?"

The unfinished sentence is often used with good effect:

> "At all events I have not sprained my ankle," said the girl with a faint laugh. "But I slipped once before to-day, and —"

[10] See exercises at the close of this chapter.

The effect of hesitating speech produced by the dash is still another emotional device in dialogue:

"They will search for us — certainly, and find us?"
"If they know — that is, if you — if — I must tell them that I took the spool to — to find you, I could not face them — I could not bear it!"

The " expressive pause " in dialogue is indicated either explicitly, as:

"I really wonder," murmured Betty. Then, after a pause, "I suppose you are right, after all."

Or by the use of the dash:

"I see no other alternative," admitted Buxton. "Either you meet the note on Monday or — The Tombs."

The choice of sentence-forms is an important expedient in dialogue. The short, sharp, rapid sentence fits in with a mood quite different from that suggested by the easy-flowing long sentence. The flippant youth would hardly speak in the periodic sentence, which rises in power by suspending its full meaning until its close.[11] No more would the dignified judge habitually use loose sentences— the balanced form would more clearly suggest the judicial mind. Yet no one would use one form to the exclusion of others. In real life even the educated talk colloquially and use contractions.

Suiting the sound to the sense is a capital conversational expedient. Note these examples:

[11] For sentence-forms see Appendix G.

"Janet!" The loud, jarring voice, etc.

"Um!" he purred, softly stroking the hat in his hand, "we shall see, we shall see!"

The use of dialect in dialogue has aroused a furor of discussion. Some editors hold the dialect story as taboo, others allow a few dialect passages, while a few discriminate against it not at all. All are agreed, however, upon one point: dialect must never be used solely for its own sake.

As local color, the vernacular of the New England villager, the Maine woodsman, the Southern "cracker," the negro, the habitant, the cow-puncher, the Creole, and all the rich and varied types of American life, require the use of dialect in moderation. But when the spelling is altered to no purpose by such nonsensical perversions as "iz," "sur," "sez," "bizness," "peeple," the alleged dialect becomes a nuisance. The short-story that needs a glossary will go down to posterity in manuscript form.

Another abuse of dialect is to over-emphasize characteristics of speech — such as a college man's slang or a broker's technical talk — so as to produce an unintentional caricature.

The language of child-life offers peculiar pitfalls for the fictionist. As an experiment, see in how many different ways you can spell a child's pronunciation of "just the same." In fact, all our common speech is full of softenings and elisions, but it would not do to be faithful to them all in reporting conversation. Each calling, each stratum of society, has its vernacular, much to the detriment, or much to the enrichment, of our English —

according to how you look at it. Just how much of this colloquial, sporting, slang, and " patter " speech you will use in your writing must depend upon your good sense. Four things, however, you will want to avoid: obscurity of meaning, inconsistency of spelling, making the dialect hard to read, and the use of too much dialect.

In writing stories foreign in setting, or in depicting the speech of foreigners when they would naturally use their own language in whole or in part, have a care as to introducing foreign words and expressions. But remember also that certain idioms are especially awkward and strained when done into English. The use of *Monsieur* and *Madame* and *Mademoiselle* is of course desirable, and perhaps the occasional use of *voila, n'est ce pas,* and the like; but, on the whole, it is more effective to salt the speech with a foreign savor by the literal translation of such quaint idioms as are at once characteristic and pleasing, in the manner of the following extract:[12]

Three nights later Gilbert Hannaway sat at dinner in one of the most famous restaurants of Paris. His companion — he had many friends on that side of the channel — touched him on the arm.

"My dear Gilbert," she said, "you ask me to point out to you what I should recognize as the real Parisian type, the absolutely smart woman. Look! I show her to you. There! The girl in the black dress, and the hat with white feathers. Believe me, that is the last thing which Paris can show you. Her shoes, her jewels, her furs, the cut of that long jacket, the little dog she has under her arm, with the gold collar — they are all of the moment, the latest thing. There is your type for you."

[12] *Passers-By,* Anthony Partridge, *Cosmopolitan,* Oct., 1908. Somewhat in contrast is Thackeray's method in *The Ballad of Bouillabaisse.*

A somewhat similar use of idiom as dialect is illustrated by the following passage from "The County Seat," Elsie Singmaster's Pennsylvania German story:[13]

A little farther on he stopped at the opening of a narrow street.

"It is here where we shall live."

"I see where," screamed little Ollie.

Their goods were being unloaded before the door of a tiny frame house.

"I too," echoed Louisa.

Oliver unlocked the door and let them in.

"It is not a nice house," said Louisa.

"It *is* a nice house," reproved her mother sharply. "It is while it is not yet fixed up that it don't look so fine." Then she waved back her husband, who came into the room with a roll of carpet in his arms. "Don't bring it in yet. Did you think I should put down carpet when the house is not yet cleaned?"

"But I must go Mondays to work, and Sundays it is no working, and I can only help to-day and to-morrow."

Susannah looked at him.

"Do you mean I should put down the carpets before it is everything washed up?" she asked.

"No," he answered, meekly. "But you shall wash this room first, and then I can move the things right aways in."

"Begin at the bottom to wash the house!" gasped Susannah. "And go up! I guess not. I begin at the top, like always."

She went upstairs and looked about her. She could not suppress an exclamation of horror. Then she went to the head of the stairway.

"You shall just come up once and see how dirty it is here," she called. "It will be dinner till I make the garret done."

"But the things? Shall they stand all the time out?"

"You can watch them so it don't anybody carry anything off," she replied. "I —" The rest of her sentence was lost in the sound of a stiff scrubbing-brush, pushed swiftly across rough boards.

[13] *Atlantic*, May, 1908

OUTLINE SUMMARY

DIALOGUE

1. *Proportion of Dialogue*
2. *Its Office*
   (*a*) Revelation of Character
   (*b*) To Bring Out the Incidents
   (*c*) To Convey Setting
   (*d*) To Develop the Entire Action
3. *Subject Matter*
4. *Manner*
   Suggestive
   Characteristic
   Diction
   Sentence Forms
   Dialect

QUESTIONS AND EXERCISES FOR CLASS OR INDIVIDUAL STUDY

1. Select from some magazine a short-story containing little dialogue and rewrite it, substituting dialogue wherever possible.

2. Examine the short-stories in a magazine of high quality and make a list of the excellencies and the faults you may discover in the conversations.

3. Take one scene of a play and rewrite it in short-story form.

4. Rewrite in dramatic form one of your previous short-stories, conveying all the facts by dialogue, excepting only stage-directions and outlines of scenes.

5. Write a brief character sketch, or short-story, relying mainly upon conversation to display character.

6. Write a minute report of the most interesting actual conversation you can recall having heard, leaving wide space between the lines.

7. Without rewriting, edit the conversation in the foregoing so that it might be included in a short-story.

8. Criticise the dialect in any available short-story.

9. Write a story told largely by dialogue. After the first few paragraphs, do not say who the speakers are, as " said Tom," etc.

10. Write the opening of a short-story, conveying the setting solely by dialogue.

11. Enlarge as much as possible the list of past participles on page 255.

12. Take about fifty lines of dialogue from any short-story and reconstruct the dialogue by using new explanatory verbs, and by breaking up the dialogue, introducing brief comments at various points in the speeches of the characters.

13. Write a short, exciting dialogue, using crisp, short sentences.

14. Follow this by toning down the same dialogue, forming your sentences in harmony with the changed mood.

15. The appeal of dialect in fiction is to the ear, through the eye. Hence to misspell when the sound is not materially altered is to make the story hard reading just to that extent. Editors dislike that quality, of course. With this fact in mind, criticise, favorably or unfavorably, the dialect of any available story.

16. From the Negro dialect stories of Octavus Roy Cohen, or those of Hugh Wiley, give five examples of how the *order* of the words and unusual expressions convey a convincing sense of dialect without recourse to misspelling.

CHAPTER XIII

THE TITLE

Because of the difference in people's tastes, it is hard to say just why a title pleases or displeases, why it interests or fails to interest. It is probably because of what it does or does not suggest — because of its associations. Some titles are failures in themselves, either in conception or in form; but most poor titles are so because of a deficiency or a falseness of suggestion.— EVELYN MAY ALBRIGHT, *The Short-Story.*

The title of a short-story is its name, and it is with stories as with persons, a unique name suggests an interesting personality; though sometimes, to carry on the comparison, a good name is its possessor's only merit.

Short-story titles seem to reflect the spirit of the times; not so markedly, however, as is the case with novels, which may deal more intimately with the big movements of the day, but still appreciably enough for us to note variations from year to year. Some of these changes in style are as whimsical as the mutations in woman's headgear. Now the fad runs to a fixed order of words. Once nothing but the name of a character would suit the extremist. A little while ago novels and stories were overwhelmed with titles of color — the red this was succeeded by the yellow that, until, with violet t'other the deluge at length subsided.

But all the while a rising appreciation of the value of

effective titles has led authors and editors alike to give them more attention. The result is apparent in every magazine. We now see that there are as many points of difference between the title of a novel and that of a short-story as exist between these two literary forms themselves. What depth of treatment could you expect in a short-story entitled *The Harbor;* or *Danger?*[1] While the broader work would probe character to the heart, the briefer fiction could deal with only one phase of life; and so the significance of such a title would be weakened.

The selection of a title comes about in much the same manner as the choosing of a theme.[2] Indeed, the title may be the first to arise in the mind and from it the whole story develop.

1. *The Functions of a Title*

Miss Albright has well said: "The title has for its main function the advertising of the story to the reading public. Like other advertisements, it may or may not announce the genuine essence of the article. Its first business is to attract the reader's attention by the promise of an interesting story."[3]

But before a title can advertise its wares to the public, it must: (a) *appeal to the editor.*

There is something positively hypnotic in a fetching title. I have seen an editor, jaded by the reading of

[1] Ernest Poole.
[2] See Part II, chap. i.
[3] *The Short-Story,* p. 91.

many manuscripts, freshen like a spent hound at the
sight of water, merely by coming across a promising
title.   First of all it may touch his personal interest, but
in the end he considers that title in relation to other
accepted fiction, to his annual subscribers, to news-
stand sales, to the standing and traditions of his magazine, as well as with regard to its abstract merits.   He
knows that the title of a single story may influence
thousands of readers, pro or con.   So true is this that
I have known several editorial councils and considerable correspondence to be devoted solely to discussing
the wisdom of changing the title of one story.   Authors should give editors the freest possible rein in
the matter of such changes — provided, of course, no
violence be done to appropriateness.   Most magazines —
and throughout this work I include the pictorial weeklies
in the same category — would rather reject a good story
than accept it weighted down with a really bad title.

(b) *The appeal to the public* is quite different.   Here
interest is the primary, almost the sole, consideration.
" A title that piques curiosity or suggests excitement or
emotion . . . has all the advantage of a pretty girl
over a plain one; it is given an instantaneous chance to
prove itself worth while." [4]   Stand some day at a great
railway magazine booth and watch the people as they finger the periodicals.   They vary greatly.   One knows what
he wants, but another will leaf and turn until some title
leaps out from the page and suggests a story of the kind

---

[4] Quoted in Barrett's *Short Story Writing* from *Munsey's,*
May, 1898.

he likes. If the opening sentences are as attractive bait
as the title, the fish is hooked. " I'd like to read that,"
and, " That looks good," have sold many a magazine, because the same influence had been previously at work
upon the manuscript reader.

2. *Good Titles*

A good title should be attractive, short, fitting, specific, fresh, sonorous, literary, and suggestive.

No further word is needed here as to attractiveness,
but young writers do not sufficiently regard brevity. The
average length of the titles of two hundred representative short-stories, specially examined, is a little less than
four words; divided as follows: eight-word titles, 1;
seven, 1; six, 12; five, 30; four, 27; three, 77; two, 39;
and one, 13. Of course, the initial " The " will play
an important part in any such count. Again, the number of syllables in each word is to be considered, as two
long words like " Quarantine Island," by Besant, form
really as long a title as " Ouida's " " A Leaf in the
Storm "— five syllables in each. But be ruled by no such
arbitrary fetish as a passion to have just so many words
and syllables in a title. Let your title be brief, but let it
also be fitting.

The story itself will govern this point. Says Barrett,
in his *Short Story Writing,* "— if you have difficulty
in finding an appropriate title for your story, first examine your plot, and make sure that the cause does not
lie there .   .   .   you may find that your plot lacks the

definiteness of impression required by the short story."

Often the fitting character of the title will appear only as the story progresses, as in " The Window That Monsieur Forgot," Mary Imlay Taylor; " The Liar," Henry James; and " Many Waters," Margaret Deland. But do not rely upon this quality so utterly as to ignore the present interest of the title, as was done in Edward Bellamy's " Lost "— a vague title indeed and unattractive. Remember that titles are intended primarily for those who have not read the story.

Most young writers make the mistake of selecting general instead of specific titles. Narrow down the title to something individual enough to grip the attention. A merely general idea no mind can hold.

That a title should be fresh goes almost without saying, yet every magazine is flooded with stories baptized with titles unconsciously purloined, and such worn-out titles as " A Strange Experience," " My Unusual Dream," and " When We Were Young."

A sonorous title is one that sounds well — is " impressive in sound "; whose words and syllables succeed each other effectively, as well as smoothly and pleasantly. Note the euphonious quality of Poe's " Ligeia," as contrasted with " The Glenmutchkin Railway," by Aytoun. Remember, however, that a title may be so smooth as to be incapable of gripping the attention.

By a literary title I mean one whose words have been chosen with due regard for their shades and beauty of meaning, and arranged in effective rhetorical order. Compare the quality of " A Purple Rhododendron," by

John Fox, Jr., with "A Ride with a Mad Horse in a Freight Car," by W. H. H. Murray.

It is most important that a title should be suggestive. "The Courting of Dinah Shadd," by Kipling, suggests a story of love, humor and unique character, and the reader is not disappointed. A suggestion of love-interest is of no small value.

One province of suggestion is to pique yet baffle curiosity by leading the imagination up to only a certain point, as in the following:

"The Wedding Knell," Hawthorne.
"Terms to be Arranged," Corinne Harris Markey.
"The Last Magazine," Judith Solis-Cohen.
"Shark-Bait," Herman Petersen.
"The Hired Baby," Corelli.
"The Man Who Would Be King," Kipling.
"The Diamond Lens," O'Brien.
"June 6, 2016," George Allan England.

Other suggestive titles more or less fully indicate the theme, as:

"The Fall of the House of Usher," Poe.
"England to America," Margaret Prescott Montague.
"Rosemary for Remembrance," "Harland."
"The Night Run of the 'Overland,'" Peake.
"A Temperance Campaign," Turner.
"The Home-Coming of Colonel Hucks," William Allen White.
"The Trial For Murder," Dickens.

By naming or describing a character the title may suggest a character study:

"Marse Chan," Page.
"The Gingerbread Boy," Laura Rountree Smith.
"Gallegher," Richard Harding Davis.
"The Regulation Guy," Eugene Cunningham.
"Jimmie Jane," Martha King Davis.
"A New England Nun," Mary Wilkins Freeman.
"Rappaccini's Daughter," Hawthorne.
"The Understandy Little Girl," Mabel Dill.

Or the title may suggest a setting:

"The Deserted House," Hoffman.
"The Attack on the Mill," Zola.
"Up the Coulée," Garland.
"Young Strong of 'The Clarion,'" Shinn.
"The Luck of Roaring Camp," Harte.
"The Philosopher in the Apple Orchard," "Hope."

Again, the humorous note may be struck:

"The Transferred Ghost," Stockton.
"William Learns All About Women," Fannie Kilbourne.
"The Battle of Bunkerloo," William Henry Bishop.
"When Knighthood Was in Dutch," Octavus Cohen.

Again, the title may disclose the idea of contrast in the story:

" Too Fat to Fight," Rex Beach.
" The Other Side of the Page," Franklin P. Harry.
" The Unsent Letter," Gouverneur Morris.
" Those Times and These," Irvin Cobb.
" The Mountain Comes to Scattergood," Clarence Buddington Kelland.
" Mendel Marantz—Housewife," David Freedman.
" He Laughed at the Gods," James Oppenheim.
" The Gay Old Dog," Edna Ferber.

Or the title may suggest the basic idea by naming it either directly or indirectly:

" The Avenger," Richard Washburn Child.
" Brides of Wastewater," Kathleen Norris.
" The Derelict," Phyllis Bottome.
" A Wall Street Wooing," Brander Matthews.
" The Profiteer," Albert Kinross.
" Whom God Hath Joined," Bess Streeter Aldrich.
" Bad Ike," Orville Leonard.

3. *Titles to Avoid*

Don't choose a commonplace name for a title. Who would elect to read about "William Lee" when he might know "Pap Overholt"? [5]

Don't choose such general titles as,

"The Organist," Becquer.
" Two Friends," Maupassant.

[5] Alice MacGowan.

" Uncle and Nephew," About.

" The Father," Björnson.

" A Love Story," Webster.

" College Friends," Amicis.

Don't handicap your story with such uninteresting titles as:

" The Sempstress' Story," Droz.

" Father and Son," Rod.

" The Shot," Poushkin.

" Poor Ogla Moga," Lloyd.

" Kittie's Sister Josephine," Elizabeth Jordan.

" A Faithful Retainer," Payn.

" The Village Convict," C. H. White.

Many in the foregoing lists are good stories, but their titles are not encouraging.

Good magazines generally reject such sensational titles as:

" In Love With the Czarina," Jokai.

" Minions of the Moon," F. W. Robinson.

" The Brigand's Bride," Laurence Oliphant.

" A Perilous Amour," Weyman.

" The Revenge of Her Race," Beaumont.

" A Terribly Strange Bed," Wilkie Collins.

" My Wife's Tempter," O'Brien.

Avoid the use of hackneyed words in your titles, as:

" A *Daring* Fiction," Boyesen.

" The *Story* of Two Lives," Schayer.

" A *Struggle* for Life," Aldrich.

" The *Extraordinary* Adventure [6] of a Chief Mate," Clark Russell.

Titles beginning with " How " or " Why " are usually trite and clumsy.

If you use a quotation or a motto for a title, be sure it is not overworked. Two good ones are, " Thou Art the Man," by Poe, and " Such as Walk in Darkness," by Samuel Hopkins Adams. George Ade cleverly modified a quotation in his " To Make a Hoosier Holiday."

Shun titles that " give away " your plot. Of course, there are instances in which the title intentionally discovers the whole plan of the story, as in Poe's " The Premature Burial." In such cases the author either plans no surprise or depends for interest upon a unique handling of a situation, the essentials of which the reader may surmise from the title. In either case it is a bold plan. Even Poe did not carry it off with distinguished success. The saving device was in his beginning the story as though it were a human interest paper — a feature article— and ending by telling the story proper.

Don't indulge freely in sub-titles.

Avoid the *or* and *and* style of double title.

Don't affect baldly alliterative titles. Poe's " The Pit

---

[6] The word "adventure" has been properly used of late in titles of short-stories published in series, such as the Sherlock Holmes stories.

and the Pendulum" is close to the edge, though opinions differ on this point.

Eschew titles that are gloomy, " The Sorrow of an Old Convict," Loti; or old style, " Christian Gellert's Last Christmas," Auerbach; or trite, " The Convict's Return," Harben; or newspapery, " Rescued by a Child "; or highly fantastic, " The Egyptian Fire Eater," [7] Baumbach; or anecdotal, " A Fishing Trip "; or sentimental, " Hope," Bremer; or repellent, " A Memorable Murder," Thaxter.

It must be reiterated that almost all of the short-stories whose titles are here criticised are themselves passable, and a majority of them good, but there can be no doubt that their success would have been augmented had their authors endowed them with attractive, short, fitting, specific, fresh, sonorous, literary, and suggestive titles.

OUTLINE SUMMARY

1. *Functions of the Title*
    (*a*) Appeal to the Editor
    (*b*) Appeal to the Public
2. *Good Titles*
3. *Titles to Avoid*

QUESTIONS AND EXERCISES FOR CLASS OR INDIVIDUAL STUDY

1. Which title do you prefer in each of the following groups, and why?

[7] Changed by translator, from Baumbach's original title. *Freund Lipp.*

"The Light-House Keeper of Aspinwall," Sienkiewicz.
"The Juggler of Notre Dame," France.

"A Ghetto Violet," Kompert.
"A Rose of the Ghetto," Zangwill.
"A Monk of the Ghetto," Wolfenstein.

"The Denver Express," Hayes.
"The Four-Fifteen Express," Edwards.

"The Courting of Dinah Shadd," Kipling.
"The Courting of T'Nowhead's Bell," Barrie.

2. Set down, in a sentence or two devoted to each, the impressions made upon you by five titles from the current magazines, as to what kind of stories they represent.

3. What titles in Appendix B strike you as uninteresting? Why?

4. Criticise fully at least three titles in Appendix C, suggesting improvements of your own devising.

5. (a) Count how many titles in Appendix B begin with "The"; (b) how many with "A"; (c) how many contain the word "of"?

6. Construct two titles of each of the following kinds: (a) sonorous, (b) suggestive, (c) hinting the theme, (d) naming the chief character, (e) suggesting a setting, (f) humorous.

7. Suggest improvements on at least five titles on page 271.

CHAPTER XIV

STYLE

Clear writers, like clear fountains, do not seem so deep as they are.— WALTER SAVAGE LANDOR.

If I am ever obscure in my expression, do not fancy that therefore I am deep. If I were really deep, all the world would understand.— CHARLES KINGSLEY.

If a man has anything to say he will manage to say it; if he has nothing to communicate, there is no reason why he should have a good style, any more than why he should have a good purse without any money, or a good scabbard without any sword.— GEORGE MACDONALD.

Style is a personally characteristic manner of expression. When Buffon declared that style is " the man himself," he as much as said that a writer without individuality of style had not yet attained to individuality in thought. A distinctive Kiplingism is his personal way of saying a thing, just as a British or a French idiom is a national way of saying a thing — individuality in both cases.

Style argues two things: First a personal viewpoint consistently maintained (or at least never flightily departed from); second, habit—and that means more or less conscious practice. By and by the writer of personality betrays his fondness for certain words, sentence-forms, sentence-groups, themes, viewpoints, beliefs and the whole thing. His views of life infuse themselves all through his expressions. Now, when these preferences, these tendencies, become a habit — I do not say a narrow, slavish, one-eyed habit — the habit is his style, as markedly personal as his bow legs, and sometimes just as unlovely.

Here are four paragraphs from as many well-known authors. Are they in any respects alike? Does not each bear the clear impress of a distinct personality? Precisely how they differ not every one could say, but that they do differ every one would declare. Each possesses all of the essential, and some of the special properties of style, as rhetoricians classify them, yet somehow they are as unlike as four descriptions well might be. This unlikeness proceeds from the individualities back of the descriptions.[1]

We know not how to characterize, in any accordant and compatible terms, the Rome that lies before us; its sunless alleys, and streets of palaces; its churches, lined with the gorgeous marbles that were originally polished for the adornment of pagan temples; its thousands of evil smells, mixed up with fragrance of rich incense diffused from as many censers; its little life, deriving feeble nutriment from what has long been dead. Everywhere, some fragment of ruin suggesting the magnificence of a former epoch; everywhere, moreover, a Cross — and nastiness at the foot of it. As the sum of all, there are recollections that kindle the soul, and a gloom and languor that depress it beyond any depth of melancholic sentiment that can be elsewhere known.[2]

[1] It is the function of this treatise not to analyze such differences, but to point them out.

[2] Hawthorne, *Marble Faun,* I, chap. xii. Observe the general concepts set forth in a contemplative mood.

At last I came within sight of the Pope's City [Avignon].
Saints in heaven! What a beautiful town it was! Going right
up two hundred feet above the bank of the river was a bare
rock, steep and straight as though cut with a stonemason's
chisel, on the very top of which was perched a castle with
towers so big and high — twenty, thirty, forty times higher
than the towers of our church — that they seemed to go right
up out of sight into the clouds! It was the Palace built by the
Popes; and around and below it was a piling up of houses —
big, little, long, wide, of every size and shape, and all of cut
stone — covering a space as big, I might say, as half way from
here to Carpentras. When I saw all this I was thunderstruck.
And though I still was far away from the city a strange buzzing
came from it and sounded in my ears — but whether it were
shouts or songs or the roll of drums or the crash of falling
houses or the firing of cannon, I could not tell. Then the words
of the lame old man with the hoe came back to me, and all of
a sudden I felt a heavy weight on my heart. What was I going
to see, what was going to happen to me in the midst of
those revolutionary city folks? What could I do among them —
I, so utterly, utterly alone?[3]

That spring the *mohwa* tree, that Baloo was so fond of, never
flowered. The greeny, cream-colored, waxy blossoms were heat-
killed before they were born, and only a few bad-smelling petals
came down when he stood on his hind legs and shook the tree.
Then, inch by inch, the untempered heat crept into the heart
of the Jungle, turning it yellow, brown, and at last black. The
green growths in the sides of the ravines burned up to broken
wires and curled films of dead stuff; the hidden pools sank
down and caked over, keeping the least footmark on their edges
as if it had been cast in iron; the juicy-stemmed creepers fell
away from the trees they clung to and died at their feet; the
bamboos withered, clanking when the hot winds blew, and the
moss peeled off the rocks deep in the Jungle, till they were as
bare and as hot as the quivering blue boulders in the bed of
the stream.[4]

[3] Félix Gras, *The Reds of the Midi*, p. 69. Specific scene
pictured from the speaking character's personal view-point.
   [4] Kipling, *The Second Jungle-Book*. Note the many epithets,

Noble Mansion! There stoodest thou, in deep Mountain Amphitheatre, on umbrageous lawns, in thy serene solitude; stately, massive, all of granite; glittering in the western sunbeams, like a palace of El Dorado, overlaid with precious metal. Beautiful rose up, in wavy curvature, the slope of thy guardian Hills: of the greenest was their sward, embossed with its dark-brown frets of crag, or spotted by some spreading solitary Tree and its shadow.[5]

Style, then, runs all the gamut of individuality, having graces or crudities as the possessor may have cultivated or neglected himself and his powers of self-expression. A writer's personality will so temper his use of the general qualities of style, will dictate their use in such combinations, as to produce his own style. To be sure, markedly personal development is to be looked for only in exceptional authors, yet it is interesting to note how such individuality begins to show itself in a young writer. A man of petulant nature will naturally adopt a short and crisp manner of expression; he who is easygoing and mild will reflect this temper in his utterances; while the flustry, blustry fellow will lean to a style florid and wordy. It is precisely here that the value of rhetorical training appears, in that it gives the writer command of such variety of expression that he may accomplish his end without either burying his personality or thrusting it into every one's face.

Now, by all this I do not mean that the writer of fiction may make his characters speak and act from his personal view-point. That were absurd. Each character must think, and speak, and act, consistently with his or

[5] Carlyle, *Sartor Resartus.* Apostrophe.

her own personality. Still, all the issue of a single mint-
age may bear a subtle unity of impress, even when the
coins uttered vary from copper to gold. When the
author speaks as the author (Hawthorne, in the preceding examples), he makes no attempt to conceal his individuality; but when the writer puts words into the
mouth of a character (Gras, also quoted in the preceding
specimens), it is the character who speaks. Underneath
it all, the author's personal style will constantly appear
to the trained eye.[6]

It ought now to be plain why it is so futile to study
the great stylists merely with a view to imitation. The
ass in the lion's skin will eventually bray.

What, then! Shall we not study the literary arts of
master story-writers? Has imitation no place in the development of an individual style? Yes, to both queries;
and particularly if imitation be practised consciously as a
study; but note: study the styles of all masters and imitate their sentence forms only so far as to learn (if possible) the devices by which they secured results, to observe
the errors into which they fell, and to master the various
forms in which they cast their thought. You must use
substantially the same tools as they, but the uncut stone
is before you and you need not slavishly follow another's
work if there is an original idea in your brain. Style
implies a certain amount of distinction, and mere imitation is not the mother of invention.

In his essay on "A College Magazine," included in

[6] Compare p. 192.

the volume, *Memories and Portraits,* Stevenson shows how he rose from imitation to originality of style.

" Whenever I read a book or a passage that particularly pleased me, in which a thing was said or an effect rendered with propriety, in which there was either some conspicuous force or some happy distinction in the style I must sit down at once and set myself to ape that quality. I was unsuccessful, and I knew it; and tried again, and was again unsuccessful, and always unsuccessful; but at least in these vain bouts I got some practice in rhythm, in harmony, in construction and co-ordination of parts.

" I have thus played the sedulous ape to Hazlitt, to Lamb, to Wordsworth, to Sir Thomas Browne, to Defoe, to Hawthorne, to Montaigne.

" That, like it or not, is the way to learn to write; whether I have profited or not, that is the way. It was the way Keats learned, and there never was a finer temperament for literature than Keats'.

" It is the great point of these imitations that there still shines beyond the student's reach, his inimitable model. Let him try as he please, he is still sure of failure; and it is an old and very true saying that failure is the only highroad to success. I must have had some disposition to learn; for I clear-sightedly condemned my own performances. I liked doing them indeed; but when they were done, I could see they were rubbish. In consequence I very rarely showed them even to my friends; and such friends as I chose to be my confidants I must have chosen well, for they had the friendliness to be quite plain with me. Thrice I put myself in the way of a more authoritative rebuff, by sending a paper to a magazine. These were returned, and I was not surprised or even pained. If they had not been looked at, as (like all amateurs) I suspected was the case, there was no good in repeating the experiment; if they had been looked at, well then, I had not yet learned to write, and I must keep on learning and living."

Style is characteristic expression, but impression precedes expression. First be, then speak. The full life is not a cistern; it is a fountain, and it *must* overflow. If the stream be big and impulsive it will even wash out new channels for itself, but somehow it will gush forth. Great stylists are no more made by the tricks of rhetoric than rivers are created by watering pots.

The first step toward attaining to an individual style is to put good things, vital, picturesque, significant things, into your life. The second step is to be your best self consistently. The third step is so to master the means of expression that the rules of structure are lost sight of and are become a sensitive literary conscience prompt to warn of error and suggest the good. The final step is to express your own self fearlessly and interpret life sincerely. You will then have established your style —a literary habit precisely as worthy and as individual as your own self. What you write will be marked by personality plus attainment.

QUESTIONS AND EXERCISES FOR CLASS OR
INDIVIDUAL STUDY

1. Select from three great story writers passages which you think are quite characteristic of their style.

2. Comment on each, noting points of similarity and difference.

3. Macaulay observes that Samuel Johnson was not always pompous. In a personal letter Johnson says, "A dirty fellow bounded out of the bed on which one of us was to lie"; but in a book he describes the same incident thus: "Out of one of the beds on which we were to repose, started up, at our entrance, a man black as a Cyclops from the forge." Discuss this difference fully.

NOTE: The instructor may think it wise to assign brief exercises in imitation, such as writing an incident in several different styles, following closely the methods of Kipling, James, "O. Henry," and others.

CHAPTER XV

In fiction you must walk by sight and not by faith.— ANONY-
MOUS.

The smaller your object of artistry, the nicer should be your
touch, the more careful your attention to minutiæ. That, surely,
would seem an axiom. You don't paint a miniature in the broad
strokes that answer for a drop-curtain, nor does the weaver
of a pocket-handkerchief give to that fabric the texture of a
carpet. But the usual writer of fiction, when it occurs to him
to utilize one of his second best ideas in the manufacture of a
short-story, will commonly bring to his undertaking exactly
the same slap-dash methods which he has found to serve in
the construction of his novels. . . . Where he should have
brought a finer method, he has brought a coarser; where he
should have worked goldsmithwise, with tiny chisel, finishing
exquisitely, he has worked blacksmithwise, with sledge-hammer
and anvil; where, because the thing is little, every detail counts,
he has been slovenly in detail.— ANONYMOUS, Quoted in *How
to Write a Novel*.

In the chapter immediately preceding this, style in general and some of its rhetorical qualities receive brief notice. A fuller examination of the general and special
properties of style may profitably be made with the help
of a thorough text-book on rhetoric, for you will find
a knowledge of these formal principles important, if not
essential. How to attain clearness, unity, coherence,
force, ease, and how to master the problems of selection

and arrangement, may best be studied systematically. The same is true of the choice of words, and the laws of description, exposition and narration. But for those who lack either the opportunity or the inclination for such orderly study, one thing at least is indispensable — a careful examination of a few short-story masterpieces. True — as Sir Joshua Reynolds observes in his lectures on art — to compare " your efforts with those of some great master is indeed a severe and mortifying task, to which none will submit but such as have great views, with fortitude sufficient to forego the gratification of present vanity for future honor."

When you have summoned the resolution and the humility to lay your case before so august a tribunal, look for four things in the work of the master, and sedulously mould your own work accordingly:

1. *Harmony of Tone*

The tone of a literary composition is its temper, mood, or spirit. It is gay or grave, satirical or sympathetic, lofty or low — all dependent directly upon the theme and upon the motive, or purpose,[1] of the writer, whether he himself has or has not fully recognized that purpose.

---

[1] I prefer the term *purpose* because there seems to be some confusion of the terms *motive* as applied (a) to the germ idea in the literary material which gives rise to the story (treated as a chapter in Albright's *The Short-Story*); (b) *motive* as the conception in the story-teller's mind of an effect he wishes to produce; (c) *motive* as the actual theme or subject of the story; and, finally (d) the *motive* of the author as applied to his purpose in creating the fiction; whether, for instance, to instruct or amuse (treated very fully in Horne's *The Technique of the Novel*). See Chapter, "Making the Story Convincing."

It is futile to try to limit the purpose, or motive, of the story-writer. Any purpose fitting in life is proper in fiction. The short-story may be the theatre, the rostrum, the school-desk, or the pulpit — doing its work best when its purpose is unconfessed, its art concealed by art.

Since theme and purpose establish the tone, the tone must consistently pervade the whole story. However, that statement needs a word of explanation.

To insist upon congruity of tone is not to forbid variations, even extreme variations, of mood in the story; but through it all must breathe a single spirit. Characters, setting, and plot, may furnish that delightful variety which adds the piquancy of expected surprise. And the unity that arises from this diversity sets the tone of the story.[2] The story of tragedy may contain humor (if you are not a classical purist), but the fun must not rival the tragedy; pathos may mingle with laughter, but the laughter must tremble close to tears. Congruity demands good sense and pure taste.

The purpose of the short-story writer, as determining tone, is colored, I know not how fully, by national spirit as well as by his own individuality. The novel more frequently than the short-story shows the influences of cosmopolitan thought, because the story of pure local color is more likely to be short than to run to novel-

---

[2] In his *Philosophy of Composition* Poe sometimes applies the term *tone* to an effect within the story, as contributing to the totality of impression for which he was working. "Having chosen a novel first, and secondly, a vivid effect, I consider whether it can be best wrought by incident or tone."

length. Mr. Bret Harte, an American Samson whose locks were shorn in London, nevertheless carried with him his native literary gods. In his article on *The Rise of the Short Story* [3] he says:

" The secret of the American short story is the treatment of characteristic American life, with absolute knowledge of its peculiarities and sympathy with its methods; with no fastidious ignoring of its habitual expression, or the inchoate poetry that may be found even hidden in its slang; with no moral determination except that which may be the legitimate outcome of the story itself; with no more elimination than may be necessary for the artistic conception, and never from the fear of the fetich of conventionalism. Of such is the American short story of to-day — the germ of American literature to come."

Is there, then, an American spirit whose tone marks the tone of the American short-story?

In *The Study of the Novel,* [4] Professor Whitcomb has compiled a " comparison of critical estimates of national character " as furnishing " a natural basis for the study of national influence upon fiction. These he finds to be : [5]

English: " Energy with honesty (Matthew Arnold) ; " void of the sentiment of the beautiful — more apt for the sentiment of the true " (Taine).

[3] *The Cornhill Magazine,* July, 1899.
[4] A monument of labor and compressed scholarship, invaluable to all students of fiction for suggestion and reference, but too condensed and analytical to admit of easy reading.
[5] Condensed from the original text.

French: " Lucidity and strong social sense " (Brunetière).

German: " Steadiness with honesty — the idea of science governing all departments of human activity " (Matthew Arnold).

Italian: " What is not refined is not Italian — love of perfect form and artistic finish " (Garnett).

Russian: "— the inability to bring its feelings and its beliefs into harmony " (Waliszewski).

Spanish: " On the one hand empty honor, careless cruelty, besotted superstition, administrative conception, and on the other sobriety, uncomplaining industry and cheerful courage " (Matthews).

Essentially the same ideas are expressed by the most astute of the critics quoted — Matthew Arnold. In his essay on *Equality,*[6] he judges the Hebrew people to have been preëminent in the righteousness of its laws. The Hellenic race stood for " The power of intellect and science, the power of beauty, the power of social life and manners." Four modern nations, he declares, proximately represent these several phases of perfect civilization: the British, conduct; the Italians, beauty; the French, manners and social life; the Germans, the power of knowing a thing scientifically.

But to me it seems that in America a fifth spirit is preeminent, modifying each of the other four as each in larger or smaller measure enters into our national character: it is *the spirit of practicality, the economic fitting of means to ends, together with a tremendous admiration*

[6] *Mixed Essays.*

for things American. This spirit attempts, with rare open-mindedness, to find out what it wants, and then, with characteristic adaptability, goes straight for it — often too directly to consider the just claims of conduct, beauty, manners, and exact science, but still with an increasing understanding of these important elements of civilization, and hence with a growing recognition of their place and value.

We shall find the foregoing national characteristics tonally present in the fiction of the respective European nations, bell-like and distinct, at times, or again just a faint overtone of suggestion. But in the American short-story the dual national notes are quite clearly heard. The briefest examination of our short-stories shows that two kinds are co-eminent: the story of local color, growing out of our frankly naive, youthful wonder at our own infinite variety; and the story of achievement in business, politics, love and war. Other tones there are, of beauty and idealism, but these are present with, rather than dominating the tones of practicality and local pride. It will be most interesting to watch this youthful and, let us be glad to say it, healthful spirit mature and perfect its conceptions side by side with its expression.

2. Proportion

The perfect short-story has balance, proportion. What elaboration could make this more clear? The conscious artist plans the order of events, giving to each just enough stress to lead up to an effective climax. He carefully relates description to narration. Conversation is proportioned to characterization — in a word, he co-ordinates all the parts so as to produce a unified effect.[7]

3. *Simplicity*

The man who puts on airs — has to. "Fine writing" is so plainly the stamp of feebleness that no one but the writer himself takes it seriously. So perhaps there is lit-tle use in attempting to utter a warning against the habit; but at any rate listen to these words from Dr. Bird, an editor of experience:

"When a tale begins, 'The golden orb of day was slowly sinking among the hills, shedding an effulgent glory over the distant landscape,' the discerning reader, whether official or volunteer, is apt to pause right there. He knows exactly what happens when the orb of day finds it time to disappear, and he does not care for your fine language unless it conveys a fact or an idea worth noting."

And even better is this illustration from the pen of Frank Norris:

"Suppose, for instance, the New Testament was all unwritten and one of us were called upon to tell the world that Christ was born, to tell of how we had seen

---

[7] Those who do not wish to make a full study of Æsthetics will find a satisfactory digest in Whitcomb's *The Study of a Novel.*

Him, that this was the Messiah. How the adjectives would marshal upon the page, how the exclamatory phrases would cry out, how we would elaborate and elaborate, and how our rhetoric would flare and blazen till — so we should imagine — the ear would ring and the very eye would be dazzled; and even then we would believe that our words were all so few and feeble. It is beyond words, we should vociferate. So it would be. That is very true — words of ours. Can you not see how we should dramatize it? We would make a point of the transcendent stillness of the hour, of the deep blue of the Judean midnight, of the liplapping of Galilee, the murmur of Jordan, the peacefulness of sleeping Jerusalem. Then the stars, the descent of the angel, the shepherds — all the accessories. And our narrative would be as commensurate with the subject as the flippant smartness of a ' bright ' reporter in the Sistine chapel. We would be striving to cover up our innate incompetence, our impotence to do justice to the mighty theme by elaborateness of design and arabesque intricacy of rhetoric.

" But on the other hand — listen :

" ' The days were accomplished that she should be delivered, and she brought forth her first born son and wrapped him in swaddling clothes and laid him in a manger, because there was no room for them in the inn.'

" Simplicity could go no further." [8]

[8] *Simplicity in Art,* from *The Responsibilities of the Novelist.*

4. *Compression*

The best phrasing of compression as a literary art is to be found in Professor Matthews' encomium of Maupassant's "extraordinary gifts and his marvelous craftsmanship. His Short-stories are masterpieces of the art of story-telling, because he had a Greek sense of form, a Latin power of construction, and a French felicity of style. They are simple, most of them; direct, swift, inevitable, and inexorable in their straightforward movement. If art consists in the suppression of nonessentials, there have been few greater artists in fiction than Maupassant. In his Short-stories there is never a word wasted, and there is never an excursus. Nor is there any feebleness or fumbling. What he wanted to do he did, with the unerring certainty of Leatherstocking, hitting the bull's-eye again and again." [9]

(a) *Compression must apply to single sentences.* Arlo Bates gives us this illustration in his admirable *Talks on Writing English.*

"Water having been brought, Pilate, according to Miss Corelli,[10] thus proceded : —

"'Slowly lowering his hands, he dipped them in the shining bowl, rinsing them over and over again in the clear, cold element, which sparkled in its polished receptacle like an opal against the fire.'"

"The Bible finds it possible to say all of this that is necessary in the words : —

"'Pilate took water, and washed his hands.'"

[9] *Philosophy of the Short-Story,* p. 67.
[10] In *Barabbas.*

(b) *Compression must extend to groups of sentences.*
Here is a capital example from Thomas Hardy:

> The bedroom which she shared with some of the children formed her retreat more continually than ever. Here, under her few yards of thatch, she watched winds, and snows, and rains, gorgeous sunsets, and successive moons at their full. So close kept she that at length almost everybody thought she had gone.[11]

In William Allen White's "The Home-Coming of Colonel Hucks," there is a passage so compact that "to take away a sentence would be to amputate a limb."

> It was thus that young Colonel William Hucks brought his wife to Kansas.
>
> They were young, strong, hearty people, and they conquered the wilderness. A home sprang up in the elbow of the stream. In the fall long rows of corn-shucks trailed what had been the meadow. In the summer the field stood horse-high with corn. From the bluff, as the years flew by, the spectator might see the checker-board of the farm, clean cut, well kept, smiling in the sun. Little children frolicked in the king row, and hurried to school down the green lines of the lanes where the hedges grow. Once a slow procession, headed by a spring wagon with a little black box on it, might have been seen filing between the rows of the half-grown poplar trees, and out across the brown stubble-covered prairie, to the desolate hill and the graveyard. Now neighbors from miles around may be heard coming in the rattling wagons across vale and plain, laden with tin presents; after which the little home is seen ablaze with lights, while the fiddle vies with the mirth of the frolicking party, dancing with the wanton echoes on the bluff across the stream.
>
> There were years when the light in the kitchen burned far into the night, when two heads bent over the table, figuring to

[11] *Tess of the D'Urbervilles*, p. 93.

make ends meet. In these years the girlish figure became bent and the light faded in the woman's eyes, while the lithe figure of the man was gnarled by the rigors of the struggle.

There were days — not years, thank God — when lips forgot their tenderness; and as fate tugged fiercely at the barbed bit, there were times when souls rebelled and cried out in bitterness and despair at the roughness of the path. In this wise went Colonel Hucks and his wife through youth into maturity, and in this wise they faced toward the sunset.

(c) *Compression must pervade the whole plot;* you must draw " everything down to a point." Simplicity, the selection of those salient tones and incidents without which the story would be other than it is, and an eye for the striking in word and deed — these are essentials of your art — and art expresses the man. Build your inner self of compact stuff. How can you write clearly if your thought is hazy, vigorously if your will is flabby, concisely if your mental habit is sprawly!

As for (d) *the length of short-stories,* styles change as they do with coats — sometimes they are worn longer, and again shorter. The average length in the time of Irving, Hawthorne and Poe was little short of ten thousand words. Nowadays, editors would think Poe's limit too long when he declared that, " If any literary work is too long to be read at one sitting, we must be content to dispense with the immensely important effect derivable from unity of impression — for, if two sittings be required, the affairs of the world interfere, and everything like totality is at once destroyed." [12]

The French masterpieces average about 5,000 words,

[12] *Philosophy of Composition.*

with some of the choicest reaching barely 3,000. The British writers affect a limit of 6,000, German and Russian stories run to 8,000, while American writers usually keep within 6,000, with the average reaching no more than 5,000. All in all, from 2,000 to 10,000 words is a fair statement of length, with some few even shorter or longer.

Each magazine has its own length-limits, which you would do well to ascertain. Few periodicals accept short-stories of more than 7,000 words.

The average short-story masterpiece, if we exclude those of Maupassant and Daudet, is longer than the average short-story. The expert often dares a broader canvas, and works in his detail more interestingly, than does the beginner. Even his name seems to warrant a somewhat longer story — just as we listen rapt for an hour to a famous lecturer, and yawn over unadvertised eloquence that flows for more than thirty minutes at a stretch.

"The Insurgent," by Halévy, has 2,000 words; "The Siege of Berlin," Daudet, 2,750 words; "A Passion in the Desert," Balzac, 3,000; "Tennessee's Partner," Harte, 4,000; "Valia," Andreiev, 5,000; "Next to Reading Matter," "O. Henry," 6,000; "The Wind in the Rose Bush," Mary Wilkins Freeman, 6,750; "A Scandal in Bohemia," Doyle, 7,750; "Who Was She?" Bayard Taylor, 8,000; "The Fall of the House of Usher," Poe, 8,000; "The Corpus Delicti," Melville D. Post, 10,750; "Will o' the Mill," Stevenson, 11,500; "The Gentle Boy," Hawthorne, 12,000; "The Gold Bug," Poe, 13,000;

"The Man Who Would Be King," Kipling, 13,750;
"The Liar," Henry James, 20,000.[13]

These figures have little value save to urge the beginner to weigh his words. The story must not be pared down to the skeleton proportions of The Telegrapher's Biography:

> Monday: Hired.
> Tuesday: Wired.
> Wednesday: Tired.
> Thursday: Fired.

OUTLINE SUMMARY
SPECIAL CHARACTERISTICS OF THE SHORT-STORY

1. *Harmony of Tone*
   National Spirit
2. *Proportion*
3. *Simplicity*
4. *Compression*
   (a) In Single Sentences
   (b) In Sentence Groups
   (c) In the Plot
   (d) Length of Short-stories

QUESTIONS AND EXERCISES FOR CLASS OR INDIVIDUAL STUDY

1. Revise one of your earlier stories with a view to congruity of tone.

2. Find a short-story that exhibits the American spirit.

3. From a popular magazine select several sentences which you can compress into clauses; then reduce the clauses into phrases, and, if possible, the phrases into words.

[13] See also the twenty stories synopsized in Appendix C.

4. Try the effect of still further condensing Maupassant's *The Necklace,* on page 326.

5. (a) Compress the story of a college year into a paragraph. (b) Compress the paragraph into a sentence.

Note: The instructor may make other similar assignments.

6. Discuss the effect of over-compression, upon the reader.

7. Take up all your previous short-story attempts and review their defects and merits in the light of what you have learned.

8. Write a final short-story, suiting your own tastes and striving to express your own conception of a good short-story.

Note: In the present author's "Writing for the Magazines" (1916) is recorded the results of an examination of 829 short-stories printed in 120 copies of 40 different magazines. The average length was found to be 4,500 words. Thus it appears that the average length is on the increase. However, it is much easier to sell a shorter story than a longer one; if the writer wishes to stress the factor of salability.

PART III
PREPARATION FOR AUTHORSHIP

The public is composed of numerous groups crying out: Console me, amuse me, sadden me, touch me, make me dream, laugh, shudder, weep, think. But the fine spirit says to the artist: Make something beautiful in the form that suits you, according to your personal temperament.— GUY DE MAUPASSANT, *Pierre et Jean,* Preface.

That story is good which is shot through with the author's personality, which gives us most fully and entirely his perception and emotion and his personal vision of the world. He may perceive a multitude of things, but until he translates the perceptions into himself, impregnates them with individuality and significance, his story amounts to little.— HARPER'S WEEKLY, *Editorial,* May 23, 1908.

PART III

PREPARATION FOR AUTHORSHIP

CHAPTER I

WHAT IS ORIGINALITY [1]

There are two kinds of artists in this world: those that work because the spirit is in them, and they cannot be silent if they would, and those that speak from a conscientious desire to make apparent to others the beauty that has awakened their own admiration.— ANNA KATHERINE GREEN, *The Sword of Damocles*.

Chaucer seems to me to have been one of the most purely original of poets. . . . He is original not in the sense that he thinks and says what nobody ever thought or said before, and what nobody can ever think and say again, but because he is always natural; because if not absolutely new, he is always delightfully fresh; because he sets before us the world as it honestly appeared to Geoffrey Chaucer, and not a world as it seemed proper to certain people that it ought to appear.—JAMES RUSSELL LOWELL.

Samuel Johnson once said of Gray, the author of the *Elegy,* " He was dull in a new way, and that made many people think him great." [2] This savage criticism time has disallowed, but the critic has at least thrown a side-

[1] Adapted from the author's *How to Attract and Hold an Audience* (Noble and Noble, New York).
[2] *Life of Johnson, Boswell,* p. 241.

light upon originality. The great mass of alleged original matter is merely old thought reset in new form. Originality is a relative term.

1. *The Test of Originality*

It is more important to know whether or not your own mind is creative than to determine that fact as to others. Here is a sure test:

How does my mind act when it receives new thought?

Does it take in a thought and then give it out again in exactly or substantially the same words? If credit is given to the author, that is quotation; otherwise it is literary theft.

Upon receiving a thought, does my mind feel stimulated to produce other thoughts, and yet utter the received thought without change? That is expansion.

Does my mind not only receive a stimulus from a new thought but also assimilate it, clarify, transform, and amplify it, so that in uttering that thought I utter it stamped with my own " image and superscription "? That is originality.

Such is the test. It is as high as it is final. An original thought is a new birth — the fruit of a union of truth from without and of thought from within. A fertile intellect, open to new ideas, sensitive to take them in, and ready both to act upon them and to be acted upon by them, is that rarest of all intellectual beings, an original mind.

In *Vawder's Understudy* James Knapp Reeve makes one of his characters remark that an original idea comes to a mind about once in a lifetime, and when it does come it should be entertained. This is too high an estimate for most minds. Ingenuity, novelty, cleverness, they may have, but real originality never. And this is not a disparagement. They are in good company, and have plenty of it. Even an original mind cannot always show its fertility, and many keen, cultured intellects never rise to originality in the high sense just set forth. Furthermore, some thoughts never do more than stimulate even a fertile mind, because they are complete in themselves. To change would be to destroy them. Their function is not to fructify but to stimulate the mind into which they enter. And a large part of our mental output is the result of such stimulating suggestion. This is not originality in the strictest sense, though such it is according to the popular use of the term. It is the only creative spirit that many able writers possess, and second only to pure originality itself. Popularly, we call that man original who stands on his own feet, uses the thoughts of others only to stimulate and supplement his own, and who does his best to color borrowed thought with the hue of his own personality. Such a man, if he be not a creator, is at least a thinker, and a thinker need never be a literary thief. The entrance of any thought that will set the mind to working should be welcome indeed.

2. *The Sources of Originality*

Rare as genuine originality is, the number of those who attain thereto would be largely increased did writers make it the object of serious effort.

A study of the mental habits of original writers reveals several suggestive facts.

(a) *Original minds are observers of nature.* The same perennial source-spring is open to all. Upon every hand are the facts of inanimate and animate nature which spoke so powerfully to others. Human beings are much the same to-day as when their characteristic traits proved suggestive to Balzac and Stevenson. It needs but an alert, receptive mind to take these things and transform them into material for fiction.

(b) *Original minds have learned to think consecutively.* This is an age of second-hand thinking. We ask for our milk malted, our meats peptonized, and our books digested. Reviews, condensations, and reference works, are quite as typical of the intellectual life of the period as labor-saving devices are characteristic of the material world. Short cuts are the mania of the age. One marked result of all this is its effect upon the mental powers. Men are losing both desire and ability to think consecutively on other than business lines. True, education is in part meeting this lack; but only in part, for education cannot cope with the hop-skip-and-jump mental habits fixed by the fragmentary articles which the average man skims over in his daily reading. A book that requires consecutive thought is generally voted dry-as-dust.

Dr. Nicholas Murray Butler proposes five tests of education, in the broadest sense of the term, and among them he places reflection. Here they are:

1. Correctness and precision in the use of the mother tongue.
2. Those refined and gentle manners which are the expression of fixed habits of thought and of action.
3. The power and habit of reflection.
4. The power of intellectual growth.
5. Efficiency, the power to do.

But if the lack of consecutive thinking is so general a failing, all the greater are the rewards offered to the writer who to his powers of observation is willing to add the ability to reflect, and to think systematically.[3] Originality waits for him to crown his desire with gift.

(c) *Original minds cherish the companionship of great thoughts.* How much might here be said! Three sentences must suffice. He who would produce original ideas must fertilize his mind by contact with the epoch-making thoughts of all ages. These he will find preserved to him in a few great books, and animating the minds of living men and women who are worth knowing. If there is anything in a mind, such companionship will call it forth.

[3] *Talks to Students on the Art of Study,* Frank Cramer (The Hoffman-Edwards Co., San Francisco) is full of suggestion for those untrained in thinking. This book is out of print.

(d) *Original minds dare to be themselves.* Dare! The word is not ill-chosen. The penalty for failure is as severe as the meed of success is great. " Insist on yourself — never imitate," said Emerson — himself a most individual man.

The quality of an earnest mind may be tested in this: Am I willing to stand on my own feet now — and so strengthen myself for future walking, even by my very stumbling efforts — rather than use crutches for the sake of more rapid progress in the beginning? The young writer who dares to be himself, casting artificiality to the winds, may begin by writing less brilliant stories than his companions who copy and crib, but his power and invention will increase, and he will end far in advance of his less original rivals. Far better the occasional blunders of an original writer than the inane and icy correctness of a lifeless imitator.

Doubtless natural gifts count for much, but let the young writer patiently observe nature, let him practise consecutive thinking, let him cherish the companionship of great thoughts, let him dare to be himself, and his mind will come to be as original as its native capacity will allow.

OUTLINE SUMMARY

1. *The Test of Originality*
2. *The Sources of Originality*
  (a) Observation of Nature
  (b) Consecutive Thinking
  (c) High Thinking
  (d) Daring to be Oneself

QUESTIONS AND EXERCISES FOR CLASS OR
INDIVIDUAL STUDY

1. Do you recall any book which has especially set you to thinking?

2. In general, did you agree or disagree with it?

3. Which stimulates you more, agreement or disagreement with another thinker?

4. Which stimulates you most: books, observation, or discussion?

5. Do your experiences in this respect vary?

6. What influences work against clear, consecutive thinking?

CHAPTER II

TALENT AND TRAINING

Genius can never despise labor.— ABEL STEVENS, *Life of Madame de Staël.*

I think that most writers, when they have got some particularly good idea into some particularly lucid and effective form of words, often feel that the job is only partly of their doing, and that a good deal of it, and probably the very best of it, came to them by processes more or less independent of their volition. Nobody writes without putting his will into the work and making the indispensable effort; but what comes is partly what is in him, and partly what is given him to say, and which is which he may not know, nor whence came what was given. What we call literary talent, or, in its rarer and more remarkable form, genius, seems to be the gift of having extra-good ideas come into the mind and clothe themselves with extra-good language. Very young writers have sometimes powers of expression which persons less lucky never get. There is an ear for language like the ear for music, and akin to it. Girls of the most limited experience and youths of inadequate education seem now and then to possess by instinct the faculty of expression; of putting their words where they ought to go, and doing the trick that makes literature.— EDWARD S. MARTIN, *Writing, Harper's,* Jan., 1908.

Are short-story writers born or made?

Both. If they are not born, they cannot be made, but those who rely solely upon talent never amount to anything worth talking about. The ideal combination is training added to talent. Superior ability never proves itself until a man sets to work.

John Burroughs has said of style what Emerson once declared of certain methods in mathematics, that it is incommunicable. So is the artistic spirit. All must agree that it is impossible to implant talent, to *inducate* it — to coin a word with a meaning just the opposite of *educate*, which signifies to lead out.

Of course I apply this now to the talent for conceiving and constructing fictions. " This gift of story-telling," writes Professor Matthews, " can exist independently of any other faculty. It may be all that the possessor has. He might be wholly without any of the qualifications of the literator; he might lack education and intelligence; he might have no knowledge of the world, no experience of life, and no insight into character; he might be devoid of style, and even of grammar — all the deficiencies are as nothing if only he have the gift of story-telling. Without that, he may have all the other qualifications and still fail as a writer of fiction." [1]

These words are extreme, but we must recognize their fundamental truth. Genius intuitively knows what lesser minds must needs be taught. The atmosphere in which the genius moves calls forth his creations. " Thus Shakespeare was never taught the principles of dramatic art; Bach had an instinctive appreciation of [the] laws of harmony; and Turner had some insight into the laws of painting—they simply looked—and understood." [2]

[1] *The Gift of Story-Telling,* in *Aspects of Fiction.*
[2] *How to Write a Novel* (published anonymously in London by Grant Richards), p. 4.

But while one writer springs, as did Minerva, full-panoplied from the brow of Jove, a thousand, like Achilles, are born of lowlier parents, trained by demi-gods, and dipped in the Styx to make them invulnerable — and even then one heel is always subject to mortal wounds. Since talent and the artistic spirit and the story-telling gift are incommunicable, what is it that *can* be taught? Why, the knowledge of how master-fiction-ists have told their stories. Though success can never be fully explained, nor guaranteed to those who will fol-low a given course, still you may, by analyzing the results attained by short-story artists, discover two things (and these two things the two important ones to know about the mechanics of any art) — its subject matter, and its form. The rest is a question of ability and application; it remains to put into practice the principles deduced from the work of writers whom men call great, while coloring all with the tone of your own spirit. It is one thing to teach how good short-stories are written; it is quite another to teach one to write a good short-story.

When Mr. William Allen White says that, " Art con-sists in surmounting difficulty to produce beauty," and Mr. Mabie that art is " always and everywhere the best way of doing a thing," we have before us two different views of art. In the one, the short-story artist — and both the authors quoted refer to him — is regarded as attaining an effect which, in so far as it measures up to a standard, is perfect art; in the other, the craft of the literary workman is held in view. The former — that is the artistic result — we may explain and illustrate and analyze. We may help and direct the worker, but no more. As to the latter quotation, " the best way of doing a thing " can be taught in principle and in practice. But after all it is only the *way* to do it, it is not the thing itself. The same distinction holds in teaching art of all kinds.[3]

Mr. Sherwin Cody, in the Introduction to his collection of *The World's Greatest Short Stories,* utters some concise and illuminating words regarding both the nature of literary art and its special relation to the short-story.

" There are two kinds of art, conscious and unconscious. When the knights-errant of genius cry, ' The poet is born, not made,' they by no means intend to imply that form is nothing : they are thinking, ' Genius invents its own forms unconsciously, which are far superior to the forms selected by the conscious artist who is uninspired by genius.' They ignore the conscious artist who *is* inspired by genius, for there is nothing at all incompatible between conscious art and genius. The fact is, however, that the history of nearly every special art is that at first its forms are unconscious, or, let us say, experimental ; and as in its evolution it draws near to perfection and its possibilities are realized to the full, very nearly all its practitioners become conscious artists."

That there is great need for story-writers to make a more careful study of their art is doubtless more apparent to the reader of manuscripts than to the average

---

[3] Mr. Frank Norris presented a different view in his essay, *Novelists to Order,* in *The Responsibilities of the Novelist.*

writer. Men and women who admit the necessity of preparation for doing any other work well, seem to assume that authorship is a gift of the gods — and themselves the recipients of the divine favor!

One of the judges of an important prize short-story contest conducted by *Collier's Weekly* in 1905 was Mr. Walter Page. Of those competing he says:

" So many writers seemed to mistake good materials for good stories that I wonder if this be not a common mistake in our time. Surely it is a fundamental mistake to forget that story-telling is an art, a difficult art, too. A man who has a stirring fact or a thrilling experience has not a story until he has used it in some proper way — has constructed it, has built it." [4]

Another experienced literary worker gives this testimony, which will be seconded by every editor: " There are many writers throughout the country, with good education, with clear brains, and with the ambition to see their work in print, who are failing merely because they are not familiar with the technique of the short-story." [5]

In this connection it is interesting to note that well-known authors themselves differ widely in their estimates of the value of a formal training for authorship as compared with natural ability. But upon one thing they all agree — that constant practice and hard work are at the foundation of success. Not one feels that a native gift,

[4] *Collier's Weekly,* Feb. 11, 1905.
[5] *How to Write a Short Story,* Leslie W. Quirk.

uncultivated, entitles him to a hearing. And all have proved their faith by their works.

Upon the one hand, Thomas Wentworth Higginson says that he came to literature by heredity, for the printer's ink in his blood is three hundred years old. Stedman felt that he inherited from his mother the knack of expression. Lowell thought that " man's style is born with him." Haeckel acknowledged nature " as the first and best mistress " in expression. Miss Corelli professes to " owe nothing to systematic training." Hall Caine says that without a " natural ear for prose " no writer " will ever do great things." " Miss Mulock " believed that " composition is a gift, not an art." General Lew Wallace and Elizabeth Stuart Phelps Ward attribute nothing to method. George Moore says that he was never anything but desultory in his studying. Andrew Lang thinks writing comes by nature. Robert Barr, H. Rider Haggard, Arthur Morrison, and " John Oliver Hobbes " have expressed themselves as doubtful of the value of special training for fiction writing, while George W. Cable " never had a teacher competent to teach the art " of literary construction.

Of course not every littérateur is able to judge of what forces were most effective in contributing to his success. The value of that informal training which a literary worker is constantly giving himself is real, even if unrecognized. The author of genius and the writer of talent both grow as they labor.

Other authors, equally eminent, testify to their regard for training. " The present which is made to some of us at our birth," says Jean Ingelow, " is not that same thing which the others can acquire by study, by thought, and by time. But though what is required is not the same, yet those who have a gift can never make it what it was meant to be until the other has been added." Huxley ascribed his literary ability to the fact that he had learned " to spare no labour upon the process of acquiring clear ideas." Dowden thinks that " Genius is energy quite as much as insight; and insight is as much dependent upon tireless activity as upon Divine gift." Anthony Trollope said that " there is no way of writing well and also of writing easily." Frank Norris declared that in fiction " even a defective training is better than none." George Gissing thought highly of literary training, as also did Wilkie Collins. Renan declared that " Good training of the mind is the only school of good style;" with which Taine agreed, saying that, " The men of my time in France have all received a special training with a view to style," and laying much stress upon classical discipline. George Meredith counsels study, as does Marion Crawford. Grant Allen attached great importance to education, and S. Baring-Gould served an " apprenticeship in literature." William Black and Edward Eggleston recommended incessant practice. Sir Walter Besant believed in studying technique, as did Poe, Balzac, Stevenson and Hawthorne. Ambassador Bryce and John Burroughs advise the study of masterpieces of English. Parkman acknowledged his great debt to training, as does Edward Everett Hale. Oliver

Wendell Holmes and Edgar Fawcett learned how *not* to write, by means of instruction.[6]

In the last analysis, it is a personal problem to discover what course one should pursue in preparing for authorship. The critic hesitates to lay his finger upon any one thing as indispensable, for fear of having some one arise and triumphantly point out that this author and that succeeded without any education, another without having read Shakespeare or even his own contemporaries, another without any knowledge of grammar, rhetoric, and æsthetics—and so on. However, it is surely safe to recommend a secondary-school course and, if possible, a college career as well. Many schools and higher institutions are now giving courses in the short-story, while studies in composition, rhetoric, æsthetics, and the English novel cannot but be helpful. As yet, we have no all-resident schools of authorship, though we do now have that which seems more practicable—schools of journalism.

Then there is no want of admirable books [7] on all these and cognate subjects, with occasional lecture-courses as well. A suggested laboratory method for the study of short-story models is fully outlined in a later chapter. But by all odds the most useful thing is to write. Write persistently, then revise, and then—perhaps destroy, per-

[6] A number of the testimonies cited above are condensed from original statements contributed by the authors named, to *The Art of Authorship,* compiled and edited by George Bainton (Appleton, New York).

[7] See *Appendix* G.

haps preserve, perhaps publish! Be grateful for intelligent criticism whenever you can get it, whether from a teacher or from an active editor. "In my own case," says Mr. Howells, "I noticed that the contributors who could best be left to themselves were those who were most amenable to suggestion and even correction, who took the blue pencil with a smile, and bowed gladly to the rod of the proofreader. Those who were on the alert for offense, who resented a marginal note as a slight, and bumptiously demanded that their work be printed just as they had written it, were commonly not much more desired by the reader than by the editor." [8]

If a chance opens to do newspaper work, you will find it a difficult but profitable school; though it leaves little leisure and less energy for fiction writing; and, as Charles Dudley Warner has pointed out, the newspaper reporter must cultivate compression at the expense of his power to elaborate.[9]

But whatever you do, do not lightly take up literature as a life-work. The way is long, and the rewards are both slight and slow to materialize. To some, literature is a trade, to some an avocation, to some a profession.[10] Succeed in it as an avocation before you venture to adopt fiction as your "visible means of support." But having set professional authorship as your goal, despise not the lightest hint that will make your preparation more thorough and adequate.

[8] *Literature and Life.*
[9] See *Our English*, A. S. Hill, chapter on *English in Newspapers and Novels.*
[10] See *Journalism and Literature*, H. W. Boynton.

Consider these words written by "Mark Twain" to a young friend. They are an allegory, serious and big, for all who would essay the literary life.

"There is an unwritten *law* about human successes, and your sister must bow to that law, she must submit to its requirements. In brief, this law is:
"1. No occupation without an apprenticeship.
"2. No pay to the apprentice.
"This law stands right in the way of the subaltern who wants to be a General before he has smelt powder; and it stands (and should stand) in everybody's way who applies for pay and position before he has served his apprenticeship and *proved* himself."

But even the apprentice must exercise initiative, so do not be afraid to do things your own way —"to be faithful to the coloring of your own spirit," as Walter Pater has put it. In his preface to *Pierre et Jean,* Maupassant finely says: "Each of us . . . forms for himself an illusion of the world, an illusion poetical, sentimental, joyous, melancholy, unclean, or dismal, according to his nature." So the biggest part of your preparation is to cultivate your personality.

To some, rules are fetters which despoil them of freedom; to others, belts which gird the loins for successful effort. "Good judgment lies at the far end of a long and up-hill road. But the well-trained mind comes after awhile to *feel* the right and the wrong of each step." [11]

Finally, I wish that every timorous worker might read and digest "The Magic Story," whose message, in brief, is this:

[11] *Talks to Students on the Art of Study, Cramer.* See p. 303.

" Go, therefore, and do that which is within you to do; take no heed of gestures which beckon you aside; *ask of no man permission to perform.*" [12]

OUTLINE SUMMARY

TALENT AND TRAINING

Talent Incommunicable
Relation of Art to Talent
Relation of Training to Talent
  Education and Study
  Newspaper work
  Apprenticeship

[12] Frederic Van Rensselaer Dey.

CHAPTER III

ACQUIRING A VOCABULARY

The knowledge of words is the gate of scholarship.— WILSON.

The term "vocabulary" has a special as well as a general meaning. All vocabularies are indeed based upon the common everyday words of the language, but each special vocabulary possesses a number of words of peculiar value for its own objects. Such words may be used in other vocabularies also, but the fact that they are suited to a unique order of expression marks them as of special value to a particular craft or calling.[1]

In this respect the short-story writer differs not at all from the poet, the novelist, the scientist, the traveler. To his everyday stock he must add words of value for his special work. The careful study of the diction of a single great story will yield richer results than the hasty reading of a score, be they never so famous. No one truly possesses a word until he knows its exact meaning,

---

[1] Professor Albert E. Hancock says: "An author's vocabulary is of two kinds, latent and dynamic: latent — those words he understands; dynamic — those he can readily use. Every intelligent man *knows* all the words he needs, but he may not have them all ready for active service. The problem of literary diction consists in turning the latent into the dynamic."

understands its relation to other words, and has it ready for use.

How can this be accomplished?

1. *Gather Words from the Stories of Effective Writers.*

Determination and method will do wonders. When you see a familiar word used in an unfamiliar sense, jot it down, look it up, and master it. I have in mind a writer and speaker of superior attainments who acquired his vocabulary by noting all new words he heard or read. These he mastered and put into use. Soon his vocabulary became large, varied, and exact. Use a new word accurately five times and it is yours.

2. *Form the Dictionary Habit*

Do not be content with your general knowledge of a word. Press your inquiry until you have grasped its individual shade of meaning and usage. Fluency may become despicable, but accuracy never. The dictionary contains the crystallized usage of intellectual giants. No one who would write effectively dare despise its definitions and discriminations.

3. *Seek Diligently for the Right Word*

This involves a careful study of synonyms and antonyms. Fortunately, there is no lack of excellent manuals for ready reference.

" I am growing so peevish about my writing," says

Flaubert. "I am like a man whose ear is true, but who plays falsely on the violin: his fingers refuse to reproduce precisely those sounds of which he has the inward sense. Then the tears come rolling down from the poor scraper's eyes and the bow falls from his hand." [2]

The same brilliant Frenchman sent this sound advice to Guy de Maupassant:

"Whatever may be the thing which one wishes to say, there is but one word for expressing it, only one verb to animate it, only one adjective to qualify it. It is essential to search for this word, for this verb, for this adjective, until they are discovered, and to be satisfied with nothing else."

Walter Savage Landor once wrote, "I hate false words, and seek with care, difficulty and moroseness those that fit the thing." So did Sentimental Tommy, as related by James M. Barrie in his admirable novel bearing his hero's name as a title.[3] No wonder T. Sandys became an author and a lion!

Tommy, with another lad, is writing an essay on "A Day in Church," in competition for a university scholarship. He gets on finely until he pauses for lack of a word. For nearly an hour he searches for this elusive thing, until suddenly he is told that the allotted time is up, and he has lost! Barrie may tell the rest:

[2] Quoted in *Appreciations*, Pater, p. 30.
[3] *Sentimental Tommy*, Scribner.

Essay! It was no more an essay than a twig is a tree, for the gowk had stuck in the middle of his second page. Yes, stuck is the right expression, as his chagrined teacher had to admit when the boy was cross-examined. He had not been "up to some of his tricks"; he had stuck, and his explanations, as you will admit, merely emphasized his incapacity.

He had brought himself to public scorn for lack of a word. What word? they asked testily; but even now he could not tell. He had wanted a Scotch word that would signify how many people were in church, and it was on the tip of his tongue, but would come no farther. Puckle was nearly the word, but it did not mean so many people as he meant. The hour had gone by just like winking; he had forgotten all about time while searching his mind for the word.

. . . .

The other five [examiners] were furious. . . . "You little tattie doolie," Cathro roared, "were there not a dozen words to wile from if you had an ill-will to puckle? What ailed you at manzy, or —"

"I thought of manzy," replied Tommy, wofully, for he was ashamed of himself, "but — but a manzy's a swarm. It would mean that the folk in the kirk were buzzing thegither like bees, instead of sitting still."

"Even if it does mean that," said Mr. Duthie, with impatience, "what was the need of being so particular? Surely the art of essay-writing consists in using the first word that comes and hurrying on."

"That's how I did," said the proud McLauchlan [Tommy's successful competitor]. . . .

"I see," interposed Mr. Gloag, "that McLauchlan speaks of there being a mask of people in the church. Mask is a fine Scotch word."

"I thought of mask," whimpered Tommy, "but that would mean the kirk was crammed, and I just meant it to be middling full."

"Flow would have done," suggested Mr. Lorrimer.

"Flow's but a handful," said Tommy.

"Curran, then, you jackanapes!"

"Curran's no enough."

Mr. Lorrimer flung up his hands in despair.

"I wanted something between curran and mask," said Tommy, doggedly, yet almost at the crying.

Mr. Ogilvy, who had been hiding his admiration with difficulty, spread a net for him. "You said you wanted a word that meant middling full. Well, why did you not say middling full — or fell mask?"

"Yes, why not?" demanded the ministers, unconsciously caught in the net.

"I wanted one word," replied Tommy, unconsciously avoiding it.

"You jewel!" muttered Mr. Ogilvy under his breath, but Mr. Cathro would have banged the boy's head had not the ministers interfered.

"It is so easy, too, to find the right word," said Mr. Gloag.

"It's no; it's as difficult as to hit a squirrel," cried Tommy, and again Mr. Ogilvy nodded approval.

.   .   .   .

And then an odd thing happened. As they were preparing to leave the school [Cathro having previously run Tommy out by the neck], the door opened a little and there appeared in the aperture the face of Tommy, tear-stained but excited. "I ken the word now," he cried, "it came to me a' at once; it is hantle!"

Mr. Ogilvy . . . said in an ecstasy to himself, "He *had* to think of it till he got it — and he got it. The laddie is a genius!"

4. *Discuss Words With Those Who Know Them*

Since the short-story closely follows the diction of everyday speech, many useful words may be acquired in conversation with cultivated men. And when such discussion takes the form of disputation as to the meanings and usages of words, it must prove doubly valuable. The development of word-power marches with the growth of individuality.

5. *Do not Overlook the Value of Translating Languages*

6. *Study Word Derivations*

A flood of light may stream over a subject when the origin of a word is disclosed.   A prefix or a suffix may essentially change the force of the stem, as in *master-ful* and *master-ly, contempt-ible* and *contempt-uous, envi-ous* and *envi-able*.   Thus to study words in groups, according to their stems, prefixes and suffixes, is to gain a mastery over their shades of meaning, and introduce us to other related words.

7. *Do not Favor one Set or Kind of Words more than*

Another

" Sixty years and more ago, Lord Brougham, addressing the students of the University of Glasgow, laid down the rule that the native (Anglo-Saxon) part of our vocabulary was to be favored at the expense of that other part which has come from the Latin and Greek.   The rule was an impossible one, and Lord Brougham himself never tried seriously to observe it ; nor, in truth, has any great writer made the attempt.   Not only is our language highly composite, but the component words have, in De Quincey's phrase, ' happily coalesced.'   It is easy to jest at words in *-osity* and *-ation,* as ' dictionary ' words, and the like.   But even Lord Brougham would have found it difficult to dispense with *pomposity* and *imagination*." [4]

[4] *Handbook of English Composition,* Hart, p. 341 (Noble and Noble, New York).

OUTLINE SUMMARY

ACQUIRING A VOCABULARY

1. *Gather Words From Effective Writers*
2. *Form the Dictionary Habit*
3. *Seek Diligently for the Right Word*
4. *Discuss the Meanings of Words*
5. *Translate Foreign Languages*
6. *Study Word Derivations*
7. *Practise Variety*

CHAPTER IV

THE STUDY OF THE SHORT-STORY

A LABORATORY METHOD

The more we study, the more we discover our ignorance.
— SHELLEY, *Scenes from Calderon.*

Let the student take any representative short-story and make a study of the author's method, noting the merits and the defects of the story, with particular reference to its essential parts, after the manner of the dissecting method employed in the following study. First read the story through to gain a general impression; then summarize that impression as briefly as possible. Next write out a short scenario. Read the story a third time, slowly, to make a study of its parts, noting results as in the appended example.

THE NECKLACE

BY GUY DE MAUPASSANT

(1850–1893)

Happy are they whom life satisfies, who can amuse themselves, and be content . . . who have not discovered, with a vast disgust, . . . that all things are a weariness.— GUY DE MAUPASSANT.

324

Maupassant was a Latin of good, clear, solid head, a maker of beautiful sentences shining like gold, pure as the diamond . . . having the good sense, logic, balance, power, and clearness of the old French blood.— ÉMILE ZOLA.

He who destroys the ideal destroys himself. In art and in life Maupassant lived in the lower order of facts, the brutal world of events unrelated to a spiritual order. He drained his senses of the last power of sensation and reaction; he plunged headlong into the sensual life upon which they opened when the luminous heaven above the material world was obliterated. Madness always lies that way as a matter of physiology as well as of morals, and Maupassant went the tragic way of the sensualist since time began.— HAMILTON W. MABIE.

Maupassant saw life with his senses, and he reflected on it in a purely animal revolt, the recoil of the hurt animal. His observation is not, as it has been hastily assumed to be, cold; it is as superficially emotional as that of the average sensual man, and its cynicism is only another, not less superficial, kind of feeling. He saw life in all its details, and his soul was entangled in the details. He saw it without order, without recompense, without pity; he saw it too clearly to be duped by appearances, and too narrowly to distinguish any light beyond what seemed to him the enclosing bounds of darkness.— ARTHUR SYMONS.

Maupassant was the most finished short-story writer of all; but he lacked spiritual power, and so he missed much of the world's beauty. An inflexible realist, he pressed his method farther than did Flaubert, his uncle and preceptor. From life's raw materials he wove incomparably brilliant fiction-fabrics, equally distinguished for plot, characterization, and style. Besides "The Necklace," his ablest short-stories are "The Vendetta," "The Piece of String," "The Horla," "A Coward," "Tallow-ball," "Moonlight," "Little Soldier," "The Confession," and "The Wreck." Thirteen of his stories have been collected in "The Odd Number" (Harper), with an Introduction by Henry James.— J. B. E.

THE NECKLACE

(Published in 1885. Length about three thousand words).

She was one of those pretty and charming girls who, as if by an error of destiny, are born into a family of clerks. She had no dowry, no expectations, no means of being known, understood, loved, wedded, by any rich and distinguished man, and she let herself be married to a minor clerk at the Ministry of Public Instruction.

INTRODUCTION BEGINS
Character-study of central figure.

Pessimistic view of life.
French atmosphere suggested.
Hint of unhappy tone.
Sordid.
Note force of " let."

Note compression of ¶ 1.

2. She dressed plainly since she could not dress well, but she was as unhappy as a woman who has really fallen from her proper station; for women have neither caste nor race; their beauty, grace, and charm act instead of family and birth. Natural fineness, instinct for what is elegant, suppleness of wit, are their sole hierarchy, and make from women of the people the equals of the greatest of great ladies.

Catastrophe strikes the tone.

Author philosophizes.

Author himself a man of good family.

3. She suffered endlessly, feeling herself born for all the delicacies and all the luxuries of life. She suffered on account of the poverty of her dwelling, from the wretched look of the walls, from the dilapidated chairs, from the ugliness of the curtains. All those things of which another woman of her caste would never even have been conscious, tortured her and made her angry. The sight of the little Breton servant who did her humble housework aroused in her despairing regrets and distracted

Key sentence, elaborated throughout ¶ 3.

Maupassant's own love of the refinements of life would dictate this.

Setting by contrast.

dreams. She thought of the silent antechambers hung with Oriental fabrics, lighted by tall bronze candelabra, and with two great footmen in knee-breeches who dozed in the big arm-chairs, made drowsy by the heavy warmth of the stove. She dreamed of the long *salons* fitted up with old silk, of the delicate furniture carrying priceless curiosities, and of the coquettish perfumed boudoirs made for talks at five o'clock with intimate friends, with men famous and sought after, whose notice all women envy and desire.

We feel the contrast just as the heroine does.

Picture.

Throughout, Maupassant proceeds from the general to the particular in his descriptions and analyses.

4. When she sat down to dine before the round table covered with a cloth three days old, opposite her husband, who, as he uncovered the soup-tureen, declared with an enchanted air, "Ah, the good old stew! I don't know anything better than that," she thought of dainty dinners, of gleaming silverware, of tapestry which peopled the walls with ancient personages and with strange birds in the midst of a fairy forest; and she dreamed of delicious dishes served on wondrous plates, and of the whispered gallantries to which you listen with a sphinx-like smile, while eating the pink flesh of a trout or the wing of a fowl.

Discontent still more particularized.

5. She had no fine dresses, no jewels, nothing. And she loved nothing else; she felt that she was made for that. She would so have liked to please, to be envied, to be charming and sought after.

SUMMARY OF INTRODUCTION, WHICH ENDS HERE. FOUNDATION FOR MAIN CRISIS.

6. She had a rich friend, a former schoolmate at the convent, whom she did not like to go and see any more, because she suffered so much when she came home. She wept whole days.

Character description by example.

7. One evening her husband returned home with a conqueror's air, holding a large envelope in his hand.

FIRST PLOT INCIDENT.

8. "There," said he, "is something for you."

9. She tore the paper sharply, and drew out a printed card on which were these words:

Note "sharply."

10. "The Minister of Public Instruction and Mme. Georges Ramponneau ask the honor of M. and Mme. Loisel's company at the palace of the Ministry on Monday evening, January 18th."

Name mentioned for the first time, and then only casually.
Mention of locality here and there fixes the setting as being in Paris.
Winter.

11. Instead of being overjoyed, as her husband hoped, she threw the invitation on the table with disdain, murmuring:

MINOR-CLIMAX.

12. "What do you expect me to do with that?"

13. "Why, my dear, I thought you would be glad. You never go out, and this is a fine opportunity! I had tremendous difficulty in getting it. Every one wants to go; they are greatly sought after, and they are not giving many to clerks. The whole official world will be there."

14. She looked at him with an irritated eye, and said, impatiently:

15. "And what do you expect me to put on my back?"

16. He had not thought of that.

17. "Why," he stammered, "the dress you wear to the theater. It looks very well to me —"

18. He stopped, stupefied, seeing that his wife was weeping. Two great tears ran slowly from the corners of her eyes towards the corners of her mouth.

Just as tears really flow.

19. "What's the matter?" he stuttered. "What's the matter?"

20. But by a violent effort she had conquered her grief, and she replied, in a calm voice, as she wiped her wet cheeks:

Stammering, stuttering, and blank questions show stupefaction.

Most writers would have said "eyes."

21. "Nothing; only I have no dress, and therefore I can't go to this ball. Give your card to some colleague whose wife is better equipped than I."

DEVELOPING INCIDENT.

22. He was in despair. He resumed:

23. "Come, let us see, Mathilde. How much would it cost, a suitable dress which you could use on other occasions; something very simple?"

Contrast her passionate disposition with his practicality throughout.

24. She reflected a few seconds, making her calculations and also wondering what sum she could ask without drawing on herself an immediate refusal and a shocked exclamation from the economical clerk.

Hint at character, which is disclosed without formal description.

25. Finally she replied, hesitatingly:

26. "I don't know exactly, but I think I could manage with four hundred francs."

27. He grew a little pale, for he had laid aside just that amount to

buy a gun and treat himself to a little summer shooting on the plain of Nanterre, with several friends who went to shoot larks down there, on Sundays.

28. But he said:

29. "All right. I will give you four hundred francs. And try to have a pretty dress."

30. The day of the ball drew near, and Mme. Loisel seemed sad, uneasy, anxious. Her dress was ready, however. Her husband said to her one evening:

31. "What is the matter? Come, you've been very queer these last three days."

32. And she replied:

33. "It annoys me to have not a single jewel, not a single stone, nothing to put on. I shall look like distress. I should almost rather not go at all."

34. He rejoined:

35. "You might wear natural flowers. They are very stylish at this time of year. For ten francs you can get two or three magnificent roses."

36. She was not convinced.

37. "No; there's nothing more humiliating than to look poor among other women who are rich."

38. But her husband cried:

39. "How stupid you are! Go hunt up your friend Mme. Forestier, and ask her to lend you some jewels. You're quite thick enough with her to do that."

Local color. Scarcely any in this story.
Thoughtless and dense, but not really selfish.

END OF MINOR CRISIS.
This entire incident not only reveals character but lays the foundation for the main crisis.

FURTHER FOUNDATION FOR MAIN CRISIS.

See ¶ 6.

FURTHER PROGRESS TOWARD MAIN CRISIS.

40. She uttered a cry of joy.

41. "It's true. I never thought of that."

No waste talk.

42. The next day she went to her friend and told of her trouble.

Some might call this the true crisis. SECOND PLOT INCIDENT.

43. Mme. Forestier went to a wardrobe with a glass door, took out a large jewel-case, brought it back to Mme. Loisel, opened it, and said:

Local color.

44. "Choose, my dear."

Note compression throughout.

45. She saw first of all some bracelets, then a pearl necklace, then a Venetian cross, all gold and precious stones, an admirable piece of workmanship. She tried on the ornaments before the glass, hesitated, could not make up her mind to part with them, to give them back. She kept asking:

Character development.

46. "Haven't you any more?"

47. "Why, yes, look. I don't know what may strike your fancy."

See how unconsciously she invites her fate.

48. Suddenly she discovered in a black satin box a superb necklace of diamonds; and her heart began to beat with an immoderate desire. Her hands trembled as she took it up. She fastened it around her throat, outside her high-necked dress, and remained lost in ecstasy at the sight of her own image.

The author has a right to mislead the reader for the sake of a later surprise, but here Maupassant makes a false statement *while speaking as the author*. This is unjustifiable.

49. Then she asked, hesitatingly, in an anguish of suspense:

50. "Can you lend me this, only this?"

51. "Why, yes, certainly."

Contrast with ¶ 49.

52. She sprang upon the neck of her friend, kissed her passionately, then fled with her treasure.

MINOR CLIMAX, AND IMPORTANT ADVANCE TOWARD MAIN CRISIS.

53. The day of the ball arrived. Mme. Loisel made a triumph. She was prettier than them all,— elegant, gracious, smiling, and mad with joy. All the men stared at her, asked her name, endeavored to be introduced. All the attachés of the Cabinet wanted to waltz with her. She was noticed by the Minister himself.

THIRD PLOT INCIDENT.

Contrast. The partial attainment of her desires produces a marked change in atmosphere.

Climax by arrangement.

54. She danced with intoxication, with passion, drunk with pleasure, forgetting all in the triumph of her beauty, in the glory of her success, in a sort of cloud of happiness composed of all that homage, of all that admiration, of all those awakened desires, and of that complete victory which is so sweet to woman's heart.

55. She left about four o'clock in the morning. Her husband had been sleeping since midnight in a little deserted anteroom, with three other gentlemen whose wives were having a very good time.

FOURTH PLOT INCIDENT.
Character contrast, supported by surroundings — blazing ball-room, deserted anteroom. Irony.
A trifle sardonic.

56. He threw over her shoulders the wraps which he had brought — modest garments of everyday life, whose poverty contrasted with the elegance of her ball dress. She felt this, and wanted to escape so as not to be noticed by the other women who were enveloping themselves in costly furs.

Touch of nature.

57. Loisel held her back.

Consistently dense.

58. "Wait a little. You'll catch cold outside. I'll go and call a cab."

PREPARATION FOR MAIN CRISIS WELL HIDDEN.

59. She did not heed him, but rapidly descended the stairs. When they were in the street, they could

not find a disengaged carriage, and began to look for one, shouting after the cabmen whom they saw passing at a distance.

60. They went down towards the Seine, in despair, shivering with cold. At last they found on the quay one of those ancient noctambulant coupés, which, just as if they were ashamed to uncover their misery during the day, are never seen in Paris until after nightfall.

Local color.

61. It took them to their door in the Rue des Martyrs, and once more, now sadly, they climbed up to their apartment. All was ended for her. And as for him, he reflected that he must be at the Ministry by ten o'clock.

First mention of their home " place."
Note fall of spirits in the story.
Still acting " in character."

62. She removed the wraps which covered her shoulders, standing before the glass, so as once more to see herself in all her glory. But suddenly she uttered a cry. The necklace was no longer around her neck!

Contrast.
MAIN CRISIS BEGINS.

63. Her husband, already half undressed, demanded:

64. "What is the matter with you?"

65. She turned madly towards him.
66. "I have — I have — I've lost Mme. Forestier's necklace."

Note emotional expression in these paragraphs.

67. He sprang up, distracted.
68. "What!— how?— Impossible!"
69. And they looked in the folds of the dress, in the folds of the cloak, in all the pockets, everywhere. They did not find it.

70. He asked:

71. "You're sure you had it on when you left the ball?"

72. "Yes, I felt it in the vestibule of the palace."

73. "But, if you had lost it in the street we should have heard it fall. It must be in the cab."

74. "Yes. Probably. Did you take the number?"

75. "No. Didn't you notice it?"

76. "No."

77. Thunderstruck, they looked at one another. At last Loisel put on his clothes.

78. "I shall go back on foot," said he, "over the whole distance we walked, to see if I can't find it."   **Practicality.**

79. And he went out. She sat there on a chair in her ball dress, without strength to go to bed, overwhelmed, without fire, without a thought.   Emotion shown by inaction.

80. Her husband came back about seven o'clock. He had found nothing.   SUSPENSE.

81. He went to Police Headquarters, to the newspaper offices, to offer a reward; he went to the cab companies—everywhere, in fact, whither he was urged by the least suspicion of hope.   Note natural order of his efforts at recovering the jewels.

82. She waited all day, in the same state of mad fear in the face of this terrible calamity.

83. Loisel returned at night with hollow, pale cheeks; he had discovered nothing.

84. "You must write to your friend," said he, "that you have broken the clasp of her necklace, and that you are having it mended. That will give us time to turn around."

The practical mind dominates the emotional temperament in this crisis.
Emotional excitement declines, suspense subdued.

85. She wrote at his dictation.

86. At the end of a week they had lost all hope.

Despair shown by short sentences.

87. And Loisel, who had aged five years, declared:

Description by suggestion.

88. "We must consider how to replace the necklace."

89. The next day they took the box which had contained it, and they went to the jeweler whose name was within. He consulted his books.

FIFTH PLOT INCIDENT.

90. "It was not I, Madame, who sold that necklace; I simply furnished the case."

Forecast of denouement, yet not disclosed.

91. Then they went from jeweler to jeweler, searching for a necklace like the other, consulting their memories, fairly sick, both of them, with chagrin and with anguish.

92. In a shop at the Palais Royal they found a string of diamonds which seemed to them exactly like the one she had lost. It was worth forty thousand francs, but they could have it for thirty-six thousand.

SIXTH PLOT INCIDENT.
Then (1885) the jewelry center of Paris.

93. So they begged the jeweler not to sell it for three days, making a bargain that he should buy it back for thirty-four thousand francs, in case they found the lost necklace before the end of February.

Verisimilitude.

94. Loisel had eighteen thousand francs which his father had left him. He would borrow the rest.

Verisimilitude.

95. He did borrow, asking a thousand francs of one, five hundred of another, five louis here, three louis there. He gave notes, assumed ruinous obligations, dealt with usurers, and all the race of money lenders. He compromised all the rest of his life, risked his signature without even knowing if he would be able to meet it; and, frightened by the pangs yet to come, by the black misery which was about to fall upon him, by the prospect of all the physical privations and of all the moral tortures he was yet to suffer, he went for the new necklace and put down upon the merchant's counter the thirty-six thousand francs.

Climax of sentence arrangement suggests how he drained his borrowing capacity.

MAIN CRISIS ENDS. Henceforward we get results of the crisis.

No details between ¶ 95 and ¶ 96.

SEVENTH PLOT INCIDENT.

96. When Mme. Loisel returned the necklace, Mme. Forestier said, with a chilly manner:

97. "You ought to have returned it sooner. I might have needed it."

98. However, she did not open the case, as her friend had so much dreaded. If she had detected the substitution, what would she have thought, what would she have said? Would she not have taken her for a thief?

Mme. Loisel reasons.

99. Madame Loisel now experienced the horrible existence of the needy. But she took her part, all on a sudden, with real heroism. That dreadful debt must be paid. She would pay it. They dismissed their servant; they changed their lodgings; they rented a garret under the roof.

Character transformation through trouble.

100. She came to know what heavy housework meant and the odious tasks of the kitchen. She washed the dishes, wearing away her rosy nails on the greasy pots and pans. She washed the dirty linen, the shirts and dish cloths, which she dried upon a line; she carried the slops down to the street every morning, and carried up the water, stopping to take breath at every landing. And, dressed like a woman of the people, she went to the fruiterer's, the grocer's, the butcher's, her basket on her arm, bargaining, insulted, defending her pitiful money sou by sou.

101. Each month they had to meet some notes, renew others, beg for more time.

102. Her husband worked evenings straightening out some tradesman's accounts, and late at night he would copy manuscript for five sous a page.

103. And this life lasted ten years.

104. At the end of ten years they had paid everything, everything, with the charges of usurers, and the accumulations of compound interest.

105. Mme. Loisel looked old now. She had become the woman of impoverished households — strong and hard and rough. With frowsy hair, skirts askew, and red hands, she talked loudly while washing the floor with great splashing of water. But sometimes, when her husband was at the office, she sat down near the window, and she thought of that gay

---

Compare this with her comparatively easy former state, ¶'s 2, 3.

Careful detail.

Suspense suggested again.

Note power of this simple climactic statement of result of crisis, also emphasis by repetition.
Intensifies former crisis.

Results of crisis.

Tremendous contrast with ¶ 53.
Whole nature changed through struggle and environment.

evening of long ago, of that ball where she had been so fair and so fêted.

106. What would have happened if she had not lost that necklace? Who knows? Who knows? How strange is life, and how changeful! How little a thing is needed to ruin or to save us!

MORAL OF THE STORY, SUM-
MARY OF FINAL IMPRES-
SION.
This pervades the whole conclusion.
EIGHTH PLOT INCIDENT.

107. But one Sunday, having gone to take a walk in the Champs Élysées to refresh herself after the labors of the week, she suddenly observed a woman who was leading a child. It was Mme. Forestier, still young, still beautiful, still fascinating.

Minor crisis of this meeting prepares for full climax.
Contrast with Mme. Loisel.

108. Mme. Loisel was moved. Should she speak to her? Yes, certainly. And now that she had paid, she was going to tell her all about it. Why not?

109. She approached her.

110. "Good-day, Jeanne."

Note swift rise to climax.
Emotion shown in rapid,
short sentences, crisp and
direct. All details and
comments are suppressed.

111. The other, astonished at being familiarly addressed by this plain goodwife, did not recognize her at all, and stammered:

112. "But — Madame! — I don't know— You must be mistaken."

113. "No, I am Mathilde Loisel."

114. Her friend uttered a cry.

115. "Oh, my poor Mathilde! How you have changed!"

116. "Yes, I have had days hard enough since I last saw you, days wretched enough — and all because of you!"

117. "Because of me! How so?"

118. "You remember that diamond

necklace you lent me to wear at the Ministers' ball?"

119. "Yes. Well?"

120. "Well, I lost it.'

121. "What do you mean? You brought it back."

122. "I brought you another just like it. And we have been ten years paying for it. You may imagine that it was not easy for us — who had nothing. But at last it is ended, and I am very glad."

123. Mme. Forestier stopped.

124. "You say that you bought a diamond necklace to replace mine?"

125. "Yes. You never noticed it, then! They were very like."

126. And she smiled with a joy which was at once proud and naïve.

127. Mme. Forestier, strongly moved, took her two hands.

128. "Oh, my poor Mathilde! Why, my necklace was paste. It was worth at most five hundred francs!"

Climax, denouement, **and** conclusion.

Denouement forecast in ¶ 90.

Naturally, Mme. Forestier returned the jewels, but the ten years could not be returned, nor all they cost and wrought. Maupassant is too wise to tell a word of this.

QUESTIONS AND EXERCISES FOR CLASS OR INDI-
VIDUAL STUDY OF "THE NECKLACE" AND
OTHER SHORT-STORIES.

1. What kind of story is this?
2. Is the title adequate?
3. What is the theme of this story?
4. Write out a brief scenario of the plot.

5. How many characters (a) speak, (b) are present but do not speak, (c) are referred to but are not present?

6. What is the proportion of dialogue to description and comment?

7. What is the author's attitude toward his characters?

8. Are the characters idealized?

9. Do you regard this story as being either realistic or romantic?

10. Is the author's purpose apparent?

11. Do you find any defects in the story in any respect?

12. What is the final impression the story makes upon you?

NOTE: Nine distinct methods for the study of a novel are outlined in the appendix to Whitcomb's *The Study of a Novel*. Some of these may be applied to the short-story.

PART IV
THE MANUSCRIPT AND
ITS MARKET

341

Perhaps the greatest lesson which the lives of literary men teach us is told in a single word: Wait! — LONGFELLOW, *Hyperion.*

There is probably no hell for authors in the next world — they suffer so much from publishers and critics in this.— BOVEE, *Summaries of Thought; Authors.*

PART IV

THE MANUSCRIPT AND ITS MARKET

CHAPTER I

WRITING THE STORY

Write till your ink be dry; and with your tears moist it
again.— SHAKESPEARE, *Two Gentlemen of Verona*.

It is no use to write a book and put it by for nine or even
ninety years; for in the writing you will have partly convinced
yourself; the delay must precede any beginning; and if you
meditate a work of art, you should first long roll the subject
under the tongue to make sure you like the flavor, before you
brew a volume that shall taste of it from end to end.— STEVEN-
SON, *The Morality of the Profession of Letters*.

When shall I begin the actual writing of my story?

No one can tell you that — though plenty will try.
After reading all the rhetorical treatises and books of
advice, excellent as they are, you still must work out
your own problem. The habits of successful authors differ. It will not help you to know that one plunges
headlong into his story as soon as he has selected the
theme, trusting to the heat of inspiration to carry him
through, but it may be encouragement to learn that the
great majority map out their work beforehand, so as-
sembling their material as to have every point well in

hand before actual writing begins. Try both ways and adopt the method that yields the best results. David could not fight in Saul's armor.

1. *The Management of Notes*

I assume that you will at least try the more methodical plan of taking notes. Perhaps you will even write out scraps of description and conversation. The next thing will be to draft the outline of your plot. Test it for balance (proportion), climax, order of the crises, suspense, concealed denouement, and whatever other considerations you wish to observe. Then carefully fashion the introduction, and after you have finished it, write the rest of the story at white heat. Don't bother about rules then. If they have not formed themselves into an unconscious sense of judgment, it will not avail to keep them before you while doing the first writing. Above all, don't follow this, or any other, method of work if it doesn't fit you.

2. *Revision*

I have said the *first* writing because, whatever be your method of writing, revise you must if you intend to produce an artistic piece of work. "The writing of what *not* do is often an indispensable preliminary to the writing of what *will* do." [1] Once in a while it will pay you to employ a literary critic to go over your story. At all events read your work aloud to yourself,

[1] *The Art and Craft of the Author,* Heisch, p. 14.

and if you read it also to others seek their criticism, not their praise. I wish I could show you a certain piece of discarded manuscript of " Mark Twain's." He has recast one sentence six or seven times, and every stroke of his pen has left a record of growing perfection of expression. At first, it is evident, his thought was general and hazy, but with the labor of revising his expression, the thought itself clarifies, until finally the expression is as crystal clear as his perfected thought.

Sometimes you will have to revise until the cutting actually hurts. " I remember, when I was young," says Sir Arthur Helps, " writing some paper — about sanitary matters I think it was — and showing it to an older and much wiser friend. I dare say it was full of the exuberant faults of youthfulness. He said to me, ' My dear fellow, I foresee that this is not the only thing you will write. Let me give you a bit of advice. Whenever you write a sentence that particularly pleases you, *cut it out.*' " [2]

Yes, you must revise. You must recast. You must even rewrite —" seventy times seven," which, being a parable, means unto the measure of perfection. But do not revise the ginger out of your story. Be not, as Cowper put it, " more nice than wise." " If," said William Matthews, " you cannot put fire into your story, you can at least put your story into the fire."

Write at white heat because you can think big thoughts only under stress of emotion ; but revise in a cool mood.

[2] Quoted in Hill's *Principles of Rhetoric,* from Helps' *Social Pressures.*

In the hour of revision, Judgment, not Emotion, sits on the Throne; but Emotion must still stand at his right hand to inspire and guide. Patience and persistence mean much here. Sometimes you will revise until you feel sick of the whole story and ready to burn your last character at the stake. Perhaps you ought to, but perhaps it is better to lay the story aside for a clearer-visioned hour, and then it may grow into the similitude of your dream.

Young writers are apt to despise this plodding progress. They prefer to see the building rise by enchantment. The easy, graceful style of some popular writers deludes them into thinking that the structural work was easy. The scaffolding they cannot see, nor the hewing of stone, nor the cutting of timber. But the magic wand of the builder is the two-foot rule, and his enchanter's ball is the plummet.

I have already referred to Poe's disclosure of his method in writing "The Raven,"[3] besides quoting at length the experiences of Wilkie Collins and Sir Walter Besant. None of these, nor a thousand others worthy of emulation, found that labored composition dulled the edge of inspiration. "I cannot revise," a young writer once said to me, "it takes all the life out of my story." After years of writing she has made no progress. We have testimony enough to show that the practice of the best authors has been to labor long over their manuscripts, revising, as did "Miss Mulock," even up to the

[3] *Philosophy of Composition.*

fourteenth time.[4] Where one strong story is conceived and finished in a few hours, a thousand require all the pains which mark the production of any other work of art. Ruskin has pointed out [5] that composition means to place carefully, designingly, together — not to throw together, as a laborer would toss a pile of stones into a cart. The mosaics of St. Peter's at Rome are only simple bits of stone and glass, but how wonderfully they have been composed!

3. Preparing the Manuscript

Must I typewrite my story?

You need not, but you ought to. Hand-script is difficult to read at best and irritates your very busy judge; the manuscript reader cannot give full attention to your fiction if the act of reading becomes laborious; unconsciously he regards hand-script as the sign manual of inexperience; and, lastly, it is much easier for you and for the editor to gain a complete impression of a typed story than of one which must be read slowly and whose script conveys no suggestion as to its final appearance on the printed page. *Besides, you surely need a carbon copy.*

Neatness counts for as much in a manuscript as clean cuffs on a salesman. If you must revise the typed copy, do it with the same color of ink as that of the typewritten

---

[4] See Erichsen's *Methods of Authors,* Bainton's *The Art of Authorship,* the chapter on *How Authors Work,* in *How to Write a Novel,* and a rich chapter on *The Process of Composition* in Whitcomb's *The Study of a Novel.*

[5] Third letter on *The Elements of Drawing.*

page. Any unabridged dictionary will give you a list of proofreader's marks.

Be sure to use double space in typewriting. You have no idea how appalling it is to face a long story, badly typed, on poor paper, and every line huddled between two others.

Keep your typewriting machine in good order, clean out the types, and see to it that no inadvertent marks are constantly being made on the paper to confuse the editor. Watch the paragraphing, correct the spelling, leave generous margins, and don't use tissue paper.

The short-story is too short to warrant your dividing it into chapters. If breaks are needed, use Roman numerals or simply leave a blank line.

Do editors take such little things into account when selecting stories?

The editor's only tool is his judgment. Anything — from flies in hot weather to cold feet in winter, from a crying baby the night before to a Bohemian repast — may befog this precious asset. You are not responsible for these distractions, but find him — just once in thirty days — in a bad humor, and then hand him a manuscript typed with | a | bar, | marked | by | a | reckless | machine, | after | every | word, and then give him a second story with spasmodic *; punctuation, - marks '... hiccoughing " along every line, and ask yourself whether you, in his place, could judge those stories seriously and with the same fairness with which you would consider the perfectly typed manuscript.

These are both actual cases, and I may add that, notwithstanding their defects, I bought both stories, but it was in spite of the handicaps placed upon them by the careless authors.

Use letter size (8½ x 11) white or cream paper, unglazed, of good quality, neither extremely thin nor unduly heavy. Prepare your first page thus:

Miss Satin Robe,   3,000 words.
  1101 Euclid Ave.,
    Cleveland, Ohio.
Stamped addressed
  envelope enclosed.

THE AFFAIR AT OAKLEY
By Satin Robe

In estimating the number of words, count several lines on the average page in order to average the number of words to the line. Multiply by the number of lines to the page, and then by the number of pages. Count the short lines just as though they were full, except in dialogue; and estimate carefully.

Type or print your name and address, do not write it in script. Some writers use a small, plain rubber stamp with which to record their name and address on the upper left-hand corner of each page of their manuscript, to prevent straying leaves.

Number (folio) your pages consecutively.

Most literary agencies, and a few authors, cover and bind their manuscripts by cutting a piece of heavy paper, dark and not easily torn, to a size 12 x 8½. The entire back of the manuscript is covered, the extra inch folded over the top, and the whole clipped across the top margin. In typing your story be careful to leave enough margin so that the binding edge may not hide any part of the top line, or even make it hard to read. The first page may be kept clean by adding an extra sheet of letter-paper bearing precisely the same wording as you place at the top of the title page.

Some editors prefer loose-leaved manuscripts, but no one seriously objects to bound manuscript if the pages can be handled *with perfect ease and without danger of tearing,* so do not pin your manuscript or use any freak style of binding or stitching that is not substantial, and is likely to cause you extra labor in the end.

In a word, do all you can to make it easy for the publisher's reader to pass upon your story. Of two stories of equal merit he will surely lean toward the one which has unconsciously pleased his eye. I have known it to be actually restful to turn to a neat, plain, clearly-written manuscript after being tortured into a headache by its opposite.

Do not practice false economy by using a badly worn or a faint ribbon. And absolutely never use a "copying" ribbon—the ink easily smudges and stains the hands and the cuffs of the one who reads or edits the manuscript, to the detriment of his disposition.

Finally, keep a carbon copy of your manuscript.

CHAPTER II

> Full many a gem of purest ray serene
> The dark, unfathomed caves of Ocean bear,
> Full many a flower is born to blush unseen,
> And waste its sweetness on the desert air.
> — GRAY, *Elegy in a Country Churchyard.*

When he conceived these lines, had the poet before his mind's eye a vision of unsold manuscript? Doubtless many a disappointed author feels that the allusion is appropriate to his own undiscovered gems and flowers. However, most good stories finally see the light, for editors everywhere are keenly on the lookout for really good " stuff "— as manuscript is called, and not disrespectfully. I estimate that it costs the leading magazine publishers of this country more than one hundred thousand dollars a year to read unsolicited manuscripts. This does not include professional and technical journals, or the countless smaller publications, many of which pay for fiction manuscript. The publisher and the editor do give writers— known or unknown — a fair chance.

What is the best way to sell a short-story manuscript? There are four ways, each having merits of its own.

1. *The Ordered Manuscript*

This is a rare bird, for whose extinction editors are almost unanimously hoping. None but a writer who has shown that he is able to write the kind of story the editor asks for, need ever hope to get an unqualified order for a short-story. Even then most authors freely confess that it is generally harder to do good work on an ordered story than on the manuscript written on speculation.

As the result of competition for the most popular material, a few much-sought-after writers have promised — perhaps to only two or three magazines — all they can write for many months ahead, but they know very well that they are expected to revise any unsatisfactory stories, and even substitute others if they cannot be brought up to editorial requirements.

If such a policy were approved by his publisher, almost any editor would feel reasonably safe in agreeing in advance to accept short-stories from any one of a group of our most brilliant American or British writers, for none of them would dream of foisting upon a magazine a really inferior piece of work, and most good writers feel quite confident of their ability to dispose of their wares in open market.

In arranging an order for a short-story, or for a series, the author generally submits an outline of the field and treatment proposed. If these appeal strongly, the order may be given and in nearly every case the transaction is consummated to the satisfaction of all concerned. But the writer whose work is not greatly in demand must not expect to receive advance orders for his stories, even when he submits a scenario or a partly completed manuscript. It is hard enough to judge a story when it lies complete before you, without attempting to forecast what it will be like when you have seen only a title, or at most an outline.

2. The Literary Agent [1]

Many successful authors sell practically all their manuscripts through agencies, most of which have European branches or connections. The usual arrangement is for the writer to set a modestly low minimum price upon his story, pay a deposit to cover reading and mail charges, allowing to the agent a commission out of the price received from the publisher. Reputable agencies may be relied upon to make prompt settlement with the writer.

The advantages claimed for his system by the agent are, that he keeps in touch with editorial tastes, peculiarities, and needs, and so is able to send just the kinds of manuscripts which are likely to be salable; that he is more likely than the author to know which magazines, syndicates and papers are overstocked, and which may have suddenly developed a special market; that he not only secures for the author better prices, but also saves him the embarrassment of commercial dealings, thus enabling him to pursue his art without the daily fear of confronting a rejection slip.

[1] See chapter in *The Building of a Book,* Hitchcock (Grafton Press, New York)— an excellent symposium covering all branches of the title-theme.

Against all this it is urged, that agents have been known to send out batches of manuscript with obvious disregard for the expressed needs of the magazines; that the writer had better study the magazine field himself, and so save the agent's commission — when he sells his story; and that some agents have even proved to be dishonest.

So there are two sides to the question, and the author must decide — if, indeed, the agent upon his part is willing to undertake the sale of that author's work. There are a few really reliable literary agencies doing business on both sides of the Atlantic, and almost any editor will advise you (stamped addressed envelope enclosed in your letter to him) as to those he has found trustworthy. Authors living or sojourning abroad, those producing a considerable amount of manuscript, and those who prefer not to negotiate the sale of their own stories, will doubtless find a conservative agency a real boon.

3. *Calling on the Editor*

Many writers — chiefly those who are inexperienced — think that a personal interview with an editor will further the interests of their manuscripts. Therefore they use ingenious devices to secure a little — or much — of his time, from the letter of introduction to the plea that " a lady wishes to see the editor upon an important errand."

The practice among editors as to meeting unknown writers is as various as it is with other busy men and women. But, no matter who you are or who introduces you, it is a mistake to suppose that a personal talk will help the chances of your manuscript. It may even prepossess the editor unfavorably. Upon the other hand, the editor may be able to give you valuable hints as to his special needs and likings. After that, it rests with the story.

But, says the novice, how can I be sure that my manuscript will be read by the editor himself unless he promises me to do so?

Really, you cannot be sure; but you may be certain that the editor's assistants, who will read your story first, are as competent as the editor himself to say if your manuscript contains any promise; and that if it is promising, nothing can keep the editor from reading it, so eager is he to find material suitable for his pages.

No editor is too busy to meet for the first time an author whose work he has accepted, or knows from its having appeared in other periodicals; the length of that first call and the question of after visits, good taste alone will dictate. No man ever gained anything by being a bore.

Never expect an editor to read your story while you wait. He must do his work in a methodical fashion in order to get through at all; besides, he prefers to read it when his mind is undisturbed by any outside force. As I have already said, an editor's only stock in trade is his judgment, and naturally he is suspicious of any attempt to force it.

When you leave your manuscript with the editor, do

not insist upon an answer inside of two or three weeks. It may come earlier, but do not demand it. And do not forget to leave postage — not loose postage stamps, but a stamped and carefully addressed envelope of a size to fit your manuscript. You are a salesman trying to dispose of your product in a crowded market, and the easier you make it to handle your manuscript — yes, even to the extent of making it easier to return it — the more cheerfully will your story be examined. It is a simple case of buying and selling.

One word more: A " hard luck story," true and sorrowful though it may be, will not influence the editor to buy your work. How could it? He is employed by a publisher who demands results, and the editor soon learns that it is cheaper, and more honest, to give charity from his private purse — never a fat one — than to allow his judgment to be swerved by sympathy.

4. *Offering the Story by Mail*

By far the greatest number of manuscripts sold are received by ordinary post. If you keep a carbon copy of your story — and you ought to — it is scarcely necessary to register the parcel. However, the publisher is not responsible for the loss of unsolicited manuscript.

Never roll your manuscript. If your paper is letter size — and it should never be so large as foolscap — it will please an editor to have you send it flat, folded once, or folded twice, as suits your envelope. If you use note size, send the manuscript flat, or, at most, folded once. In a word, it will pay you to consider the convenience of the person who is to pass upon your offering.

If your manuscript has been out several times and shows signs of much reading, re-type the soiled pages and supply a new top-sheet.

Manuscripts unaccompanied by proof sheets must carry full letter-postage in the United States. Do not forget to enclose full return postage, always in the form of a stamped and fully addressed envelope of appropriate size; never merely stick the stamps fast to your letter. Do not use flimsy envelopes which may be torn in the mails. Many a manuscript so enclosed is received in bad condition, and sometimes several of its pages are lost in transit. It adds unnecessarily to the cost of mailing and return to pack your manuscript between pasteboards.

Never write long letters to the editor. They hurt rather than help. Recommendations and letters of introduction will not secure an acceptance. Neither will letters addressed to the editor and marked " personal." Except in rare instances, when an emergency justifies the editor's taking up a manuscript out of its regular order of receipt, or before one of his helpers has passed upon it, all manuscripts take the same course. You will hurt your standing with a magazine by constantly asking for special readings. It is enough to send your manuscript with your name affixed, or at most the briefest note, sent under the same cover as your story, in form somewhat like this:

Cleveland, Ohio, Mar. 1, 1909.

Editor of Harper's Magazine,

    Franklin Square,

        New York City.

Dear Sir:

I submit herewith a short-story of three thousand words, entitled, " The Affair at Corson's," offered at your regular rates. Enclosed is a stamped addressed envelope.

        Very truly yours,

          Warren W. Hill,

            2000 Euclid Avenue.

Don't ask for personal criticism of your story. That is the work of a professional critic, who will write you an opinion at regular rates. The editor is paid to do other things. He would like to help all young writers, but he is too busy.

If you have sold enough manuscript to warrant it, you may wish to set a price upon your story, but by doing so you run a risk. No ordinary circumstance will lead an editor to deviate from his regular rate. The fact that you have sold one or two stories at five cents a word to one magazine will not warrant your expecting another to pay you more than its accustomed honorarium. At the same time, if your minimum rate is actually five or three or two cents a word, frankly say so and abide by the consequences. If you offer a manuscript " at regular rates " do not haggle about the price after your story has been accepted. Remember that some magazines pay "on acceptance," others pay "on publication," while others pay not at all.

With what rights do you part when you sell a story?

Customs differ. Many publishers insist upon purchasing "all rights," while others specify only "serial rights." "All rights" include foreign and American rights for book publication, serial or magazine rights, syndicate rights (the right to syndicate for publication in other periodicals, usually included in serial rights), and rights of dramatization and translation. If you wish to specify the kinds of rights you reserve, do so in the letter in which you offer the manuscript. Most magazine publishers are willing to allow the author to retain book and dramatic rights if the request is made when the short-story is sold. See that the receipt you sign specifies the rights you sell.

You may obtain American copyright for your story, though *never before publication,* by having the publisher agree to transfer the copyright to you after publication. The copyright fee for any manuscript is one dollar. Information blanks will be sent you upon application to the Register of Copyrights, Library of Congress, Washington, D. C. Remember that copyright is nothing more than a registry of your claim to authorship or ownership. As to foreign copyright, consult an expert, or your lawyer.

As a rule it is unwise to send more than one story at a time to a magazine. Nor is it ever wise to bombard an editor with manuscript the moment he accepts one of your offerings.

Never offer the same story to more than one magazine at the same time. It is not fair to ask an editor to pass on a manuscript only to learn that it has been accepted elsewhere.

Never send the same story to a second magazine before you have heard from the first periodical to which it has been submitted. If you do not get an answer in three weeks, it *may* be wise to drop a line courteously asking for a decision, but you had better wait the month out. Editors sometimes fall ill, take a holiday, or are otherwise delayed. No reputable magazine wilfully neglects manuscript. It may be that your story is being considered by several advisers, and impatience upon your part will never help your cause.

Never put a string to your offer of a manuscript by telling the editor that you will accept his offer if it is good enough. If he is human, such a request will irritate him and may cause him to reject the story forthwith.

Don't let the printed rejection slip humiliate you. Really great writers get them, constantly. It would take too much time and money for an editorial staff to write personal letters to all who offer unsolicited manuscript.

Never write back sarcastic letters when your offerings are rejected. You may need that editor some day. Although personal pique seldom actuates him, he may be frail enough to be annoyed when his well-meant efforts are assailed.

Don't load up your envelope with printed notices of your privately-published book, your lecture, or any sort of personal advertisement. They will all go to the waste-basket unread. The editor is concerned only with your story. If that is good, he may accept it in spite of your previous literary offenses. There is some excuse for a writer's saying in his letter, "This month's *Scribner's* contains a story of mine, and I send you another in the same vein." The editor likes to know that, for he may prefer an accepted author, under certain conditions, and may have overlooked your story in the other magazine, though usually he glances over "all the periodicals"—and always reads those in his own line.

Don't send a story to a magazine unless you are sure you understand the spirit of that particular periodical.[1] All magazines are not alike. Study *several* copies, *recent* copies, of the magazine to see if you have hit its general tone and favorite length. *I cannot sufficiently emphasize this point.* Remember that stories too similar to those lately published are as likely to prove unavailable as those which are too different in general tone. Err rather upon the side of brevity than of length.

Don't be discouraged if your story comes back. Re-read it, and if you are quite sure it is the best you can do, send it out again, using your best judgment as to the magazine to which it seems suited. If it comes back again, lay it aside for another reading when it will be fresh again. If you see anything wrong then, bravely rectify it and send it out again. Many a story has been

---

[1] *The Writer's Monthly,* Springfield, Mass., contains a very full department listing the needs of publishers.

sold on its tenth, yes, its twentieth trip. But it is a waste of postage and patience and editorial brain to keep on sending inferior material to magazines which are plainly too critical to accept loosely constructed work.

Timeliness is an important element. Every magazine is flooded with Christmas material sent during November. Send all " timely," " seasonable," or " occasional " material from four to six months ahead of the time it is expected to appear. This is important.

Keep a careful record of where, when, and how you send and receive back your short-stories. Here is one simple form for a manuscript book or card index:

Title	Sent to	Date	Returned from	Date	Sold to	Date	Price

Some writers number their manuscripts, but that is more necessary when the writer deals in such small items as jokes, and — as one author puts it — " worse."

CHAPTER III

WHY STORIES ARE REJECTED — A COLLOQUY

The land is full of young writers of promise, whose performance is not yet. They have graduated at high schools and seminaries, and sometimes at colleges for either sex; they have ability — lots of it, but it is ability in the raw, in the rough. Their minds are immature, their experience inadequate to the accurate and satisfactory portrayal of life and society and human nature. One would not be harsh with them, for they may grow to full stature some day and do fine things. As it is, they frequently get into print (in books), and sometimes make a success, for there are many like them among the readers of books. But the doors of magazines must remain mildly but firmly closed against them till they have tarried a sufficient time at Jericho, and learned to understand, to observe, and to depict realities, instead of drawing on their own disordered fancies.— FREDERIC M. BIRD, *Magazine Fiction, Lippincott's,* Nov., 1894.

The Editor had just finished a pile of short-story manuscripts, when his friend the Young Author dropped in.

" Ah, glad ' you came ! " he said. " No, I'm not too busy — I'm about through for to-day, and rather fagged out. A man can't trust his judgment when he's tired or cross. See that first pile of stuff? Half of it I've marked ' re-read ' because I'm uncertain whether it's good or not. To-morrow I'll know in short order. An editor must make allowances for his moods. Some days he can't laugh, and on others he can't cry."

" And what's in that second pile? "

" ' Not available ' stories."

" I thought most of the manuscripts were weeded out for you by your assistant readers."

" So they are, usually; but every now and then I want to read everything that comes in myself, and then have a talk with my staff so as to be sure that we're looking at things from pretty nearly the same view-point."

" You get a pile every day, I suppose."

" Oh, it varies; about two thousand a month, if you count manuscripts of all kinds — articles, stories, verses, epigrams and jokes."

" And every one is read? "

" Certainly! But not necessarily all through. Some-times a glance is enough to show that it is ' impossible.' But everything which on brief examination looks at all hopeful is read, sometimes by five different persons, before it is sent back, or accepted. In this respect all good magazines are alike; every manuscript gets a square deal."

" Now that ' not available ' lot, do you know definitely why you reject each one? "

" Yes; at least, I could formulate a reason if I tried; but mostly I don't try. I sort of know when they won't do. Let's look these over for a moment, in confidence, and I'll explain. Here's a story — a good thing too — of nine thousand words. Entirely too long. We rarely use a short-story of more than five thousand. And look at this one — facts all mixed up, details plainly inaccurate, and yet a good yarn at bottom. That's the trouble with lots of writers — they will not take the trouble to do things well. Then see here: you can't say of *this* story that it's too slender. The fault is all the other way — it has incident enough to stock a novelette. The next is out of date, both in subject-matter and in treatment. It's too late a day for the troubles of a horse-car driver to seem real to our readers. This next story is realism — and nothing more. It isn't a short-story at all, but merely a photograph, very minute and very clear, of an absolutely uninteresting group of people. They talk exactly as ordinary people would talk. It's too obviously true to commonplace life. Here's another. The first ten lines, and a look at the rest, show that the writer has modeled his style after the shilling shocker. And I can't use this other one either, though it's really a good story."

" How's that? "

" Well, a year ago the fellow sold another magazine a story he had deliberately cribbed from an old copy of *The Atlantic*. Editors tell each other such things, you see. This next story I couldn't get interested in, though it's smoothly written and shows no little experience in handling. It's simply dull. I'm sorry, too, for the writer generally sends us first-rate stuff. He must have a careful letter explaining."

" That seems fair."

" Now look at this dainty little sketch. I like that, but I can't accept it. Within two months we've bought more of that kind than can be used in as many years, Sorry, but back it goes."

"This looks like a Memorial Day story."

"It is; and it came in just four months too late. Last November I was down on my knees for something of this kind. Then in December two good ones came in — one we're using this year, and the other will keep till next May. This one isn't quite big and strong enough to hold over for two years, so I'll have to let it go. You see how chance runs? Last November it would have been accepted, almost surely."

"Tough luck!"

"Yes, but there's no help for it when they come in too late. Now, there's another story that's brilliantly written — but it's nasty. Pity! Here's one that's funny, very funny — in spots. The rest of it is too strained to be redeemed by the genuinely humorous parts. Sustained humor is so rare that we jump at it when it comes our way."

"Well, what's the matter with this one?"

"Needlessly horrible. Good plot, climactic interest, very well written, but simply reeking with gore; while here's a would-be tragedy that is so pink-papery that it is ridiculous. The villain fairly lisps while he daintily slaps at the heroine!"

"Here's a bright girl; I've seen several of her things in good magazines lately. What is her story like?"

"Evidently a juvenile effort she's trying to float on the wave of her present popularity. She'd better burn it. If it gets into print it will do her more harm than good.

Not that it's so bad—just childish, you know. By the way, yesterday I laid aside another of her stories which we're going to ask her to change. It can be used if she cuts out three hundred words from the first half. It's probably not conscious padding, but it simply clogs the action without helping the atmosphere. She'll do it, too, and thank me. It's a delight to deal with an author who believes that an editor is genuinely interested in his writers."

"What would you say, now, is the chief defect of stories as they run?"

"They're merely good, that's the trouble. They lack distinction. So many people can write fair English nowadays, and possess some ingenuity in plot construction, that it is easy to write a fairly good short-story. But no magazine can afford to be merely 'fairly good,' so that kind of stuff won't sell. It *must* be unusual in one quality at least, if not in all. Most writers are commonplace imitators. See that file of *Harper's* there? Let me have the January number — 1908. See here: it's by Edwin S. Martin:

"'It is a great advantage to a writer to have sense, but he can get along with a moderate supply of it if he is a good enough writer. It is an advantage to him to have learning, provided he has it under good control and doesn't let it run away with him or dam him up. But the thing he *must* have is ideas. It is hard sledding for a writer to get along without ideas. Somehow, if he is going to be a writer, he must have bubbles in his mind. He can borrow a great many thoughts if he knows where to find them. What is learning but the assimilation of other men's ideas! But while some persons are writers because they are possessed with ideas that demand to be expounded, a good many others attain more or less painfully to the possession of ideas because they are called to be writers and are peremptorily constrained to have something to impart. It isn't quite enough to have language, though if you know enough words and attain to a truly skilful use of them, you can make them go a good ways. You must have some kind of an idea to string them on if you are going to make a tolerable literary job. Sit down with pen, paper, ink, and a dictionary — if you need one. Then we all know what happens. You have got to think. There is no way out of it. Thinking is to the natural man a severe and repugnant exercise, but the natural man is not a writer. Before anybody becomes a writer he must subjugate nature to the extent of partially overcoming his distaste for consecutive thought.' "

" I see. The average short-story is short on ideas."

" Exactly."

" But, apart from that, you must have some definite principle in mind by which you judge fiction. You surely don't sit here and turn down stories simply on account of technical defects."

" That depends on what you mean by the term. Technical defects are not theoretical, but the big faults of structure which rob a story of its grip. Technique has grown up out of the usage of good yarn-spinners, and not contrariwise. Most of the stories we accept are imperfect, but not glaringly so. If they throb with human interest, do not drag, strike a fresh note, vibrate some emotion, and are generally well-done, the minor technical defects are likely to be overlooked, or we may ask the author to correct them. In a word, the story counts more than the manner, though we want both."

" But you haven't answered my question."

"As to a general underlying principle? I'm afraid I couldn't formulate one. An editor tries to keep his tastes sane and fresh and manly, and then select the stories he feels his readers will like. Professor Brander Matthews once said a good thing about writers, and it fits the editor's case too, I suppose. In his essay 'On Pleasing the Taste of the Public,' in *Aspects of Fiction,* he suggests that the only way is, not to attempt a sly survey of the field and then 'give the dear public what it wants,' but to give the public the best you have and depend upon there being enough of similar mind to appreciate what you offer."

"Of course I see what he means, but an editor can't do just as he pleases, can he?"

"Not altogether; he is limited in his choice not only by his own magazine, but by the fact that he is buying magazine material. The broadest magazine must be narrow as compared with a book, for its clientele is more or less fixed. A book the public may take or let alone, but the management must consistently give the man who subscribes for a magazine what he has a right to expect."

"If a chap could run an endowed magazine, with no eye to the box-office!"

"Y-e-s, he might print things 'regardless,' I suppose, but I doubt if the humanizing element of 'a public' is not the very thing needful to keep the editor from becoming a mere visionary. Anyhow, as some one has said, 'the editor is merely a middleman who caters to the wants of his customers'— and isn't always certain as to what they want. If he guesses right more than sixty per cent. of the time he is happy."

"All this sounds pretty hopeless for a young fellow like me. Now look at that quotation from Dr. Bird you have pasted up there on your desk:

"'In one case only, or in one set of cases, the most stringent rules may be relaxed — not broken. It is a case which editors are always hoping for, but which seldom occurs to gladden them. Do something that nobody has done before; let in light on a dark place; make a dull theme attractive, raise the dead to life, invest a trivial topic with dignity, cause the desert to rejoice and blossom, turn old things into new :— before such a key doors open, and hearts, too. What was expected of monkeys and bears and tigers? Yet there is the *Jungle Book*. Huguenot wars were counted stale and threadbare, but *A Gentleman of France* has revived them. The world is still conservative, not ready to welcome its Kiplings and Weymans till they show the stuff that is in them; but that once done, theirs is the right of way everywhere. It was the misfortune or the fault of the magazines if they did not "discover" and first exploit these two; but many a talent has risen from obscurity to fame through the monthlies, and in their pages the stars of the future may now be faintly twinkling and preparing to mount aloft.'"

"Yes, it does sound hopeless, until you consider that this is only one magazine, that there are a thousand other fiction markets not quite as exacting in their requirements, and that a writer may learn to write — if it's in him."

"Of course, that's the point — if it's in him. But how is he to know?"

"Set to work and dig—— just the way a woman goes about finding out if she is a real singer, or a man a merchant genius. They judge from natural tendencies and then try it. The average writer doesn't succeed any earlier than the average lawyer — and, frankly, not so easily, and rarely so largely, if dollars measure success. For ten years Conan Doyle sent manuscripts around, and in no one year did he earn so much as two hundred and fifty dollars. Suddenly his work took hold, and — well, you know how it is now: we all want him. The difference was not in the editors, it was in him. He had served his apprenticeship and had arrived. You see, all these rejected manuscripts are not failures, by a long shot. A lot of them will be sold elsewhere. They simply do not fit in with our plans, or are untimely, or in some other way are unsuitable. Many a good story gets away from us because I haven't sense enough to see its value until some other fellow has published it. Then I'll turn around and discover something that has slipped through his fingers. Odd, isn't it?"

"But how about the rest of these?"

"Well, that one is a good story, but what sense is there in writing a yarn just to say bitter things about a form of religion with which you are not in sympathy? Singularly enough, the very next story is a covert defense of the cult the other woman attacks! Here's a story that gives away its mystery before it is half through. There's one that is so full of technical musical terms that it would require a lexicon to read it. And so on down the list. Many could be remedied if some one could just take the writer aside and explain. But you see how hopeless a job that would be for an editor to take up! As for the rest — they are simply without merit. Their authors never will learn how to write, for they show not the faintest glimmerings of ability. What a pity a fellow can't tell them so frankly!"

"And this last little pile?"

"Ah, they are fine! Only three; and it took our entire staff four days to find them out and decide upon them. But they make up for all the drudgery put on the rest."

And the Young Author went away thinking.

PART V
APPENDICES

Some day, when nobody is about, line yourself up in a corner and find out just what you are capable of doing in this literary game. Point your finger sternly and make yourself surrender your knowledge. Can you depict sentiment, romance, adventure? Have you ever lived or loved? Do you study technical advice, or do you just scan it? Do you practise faithfully? Are you a steady current or an intermittent jumpspark? What can you do? What will you do? What can't you do? After you're robbed of your conceit, and duly ashamed, you'll be able to look your friend Ability in the face without flinching. After that — Well, anyhow, corner yourself and get a view of the situation.— The Editor, *October, 1908.*

"It's too hard," you say, "and you're tired and sick of it all." Why, man, you're a shirker and a coward. Here is a woman who is blind, patiently smiling and writing her way to success. Here's a man whose health gave out and who turned to literature as a last resort, finding it not only a successful profession, but a solace for his affliction. Here's a man in prison, writing with faith untouched. Here's a woman all heart and soul, with a body God could hardly have meant for contact with life: look at her face, read her work, and think of yourself — quite strong, quite capable, quite clever enough to reach the heights. It *is* hard, but that's what makes it worth while. Would it suffice if we all could write — the butcher's boy and the street urchin and you and me? It's the task that makes the reward. If you're weary of it all, your perspective of life is distorted: you shirk and you fear. The prize is worth the struggle — and, remember, the struggle must come first.— Ibid.

PART V

APPENDIX A

COLLECTIONS OF SHORT-STORIES, SKETCHES AND TALES

The figures used in this list are for reference, and correspond to the figures in parentheses in *Appendices B and C*. There has been no attempt to make this list exhaustive, nor to include collections which are not published in America. Volumes made up exclusively of tales and sketches not closely akin to the short-story type, have been excluded. It has not seemed necessary to list the collected short-stories of authors (such as Poe, Dickens and Balzac) whose works commonly appear in complete sets. Since each author is represented by but one volume, the writer of this treatise does not wish to imply that the volume selected necessarily contains the author's most important story or stories. Other representative short-story writers are listed in *Appendices B and C*.

1. *Miscellaneous Collections*

(*Appendix E* contains a list of American publishers with their addresses, and the abbreviations used throughout this volume.)

1. *American Short Stories;* edited, with introductory essay, by Charles S. Baldwin; 1 vol. Longmans.

2. *Book of the Short Story, The;* edited, with introductory essay, notes and full epochal lists of tales and short-stories, by Alexander Jessup and Henry Seidel Canby; 1 vol. Appleton.

3. *Chap Book Stories;* 2 vols. Duffield.

4. *Digit of the Moon, A* (East Indian tales and stories); 1 vol. Putnam.

5. *Great Short Stories;* edited, with biographical notes, by William Patten; 3 vols. Collier.

6. *Harper's Detective Stories;* containing forty-nine stories, by A. Conan Doyle, Maurice Leblanc, Arthur Morrison and Samuel M. Gardenhire; 6 vols. Harper.

7. *Harper's Novelettes* (short-stories by contemporary authors); edited, with brief introductions, by W. D. Howells and H. M. Alden; 7 vols. Harper.

8. *Library of the World's Best Mystery and Detective Stories;* edited, with introduction, by Julian Hawthorne; 6 vols. Review.

9. *Little Classics;* edited, with introduction, by Rossiter Johnson; 18 vols. (several of which are verse and sketches). Houghton.

10. *Little French Masterpieces;* edited, with introductions by various critics, by Alexander Jessup; 6 vols. (Flaubert, Mérimée, Gautier, Balzac, Daudet, Maupassant). Putnam.

11. *Little Masterpieces of Fiction;* edited by Hamilton W. Mabie (who writes the introduction) and Lionel Strachey; 8 vols. Doubleday.

12. *Little Masterpieces of American Wit and Humor;* edited by Thomas L. Masson; 6 vols. (including many sketches and anecdotes). McClure.

13. *Love Tales;* 5 vols. Jacobs.

14. *Modern Ghosts;* 1 vol. Harper.

15. *Short Story Classics,* American; edited, with introduction and biographical notes, by William Patten; 5 vols. Collier.

16. *Short Story Classics,* Foreign; edited, with biographical notes, by William Patten; 5 vols. Collier.

17. *Short-Story, The;* edited, with introduction and notes, by Brander Matthews; 1 vol. American.

18. *Specimens of the Short Story;* edited, with introduction and notes, by George Henry Nettleton; 1 vol. Holt.

19. *Stories by American Authors;* 10 vols. Scribner.[1]

20. *Stories by English Authors;* 10 vols. Scribner.[2]

21. *Stories by Foreign Authors;* 10 vols. Scribner.

22. *Stories from McClure's;* 5 vols. McClure.

23. *Stories from Scribner's;* 6 vols. Scribner.

24. *Stories New and Old, American and English;* edited, with introduction and notes, by Hamilton W. Mabie; 1 vol. Macmillan.

25. *Studying the Short-Story,* Esenwein; 1 vol. Noble.

26. *Tales from McClure's;* 5 vols. McClure.

27. *Tales from Many Sources;* 1 vol. Dodd.

[1] Cheaper edition issued by Success Co., New York, as *Library of American Fiction.*
[2] Cheaper edition issued by Success Co., New York, as *Library of English Fiction.*

28. *World's Greatest Short-Stories, The;* edited, with introduction and notes, by Sherwin Cody; 1 vol. Mc-Clurg. (See also Appendix H.)

2. *Volumes of Stories by One Author*

29. Aldrich, Thomas Bailey; *Marjorie Daw and Other People.* Houghton.

30. Barr, Robert; *Revenge.* Stokes.

31. Barrie, J. M.; *A Window in Thrums.* Scribner.

32. Bell, J. J.; *Wee Macgregor.* Harper.

33. Benson, E. F.; *The Babe, B. A.* Putnam.

34. Bierce, Ambrose; *In the Midst of Life.* Putnam.

35. Björnson, Björnstjerne; *The Fisher Maiden, and Later Stories.* Houghton.

36. Black, William; *The Magic Ink.* Harper.

37. Bourget, Paul; *Monica.* Scribner.

38. Brown, Alice; *Tiverton Tales.* Houghton.

39. Canfield, Dorothy; *Hillsboro People.* Holt.

40. Child, Richard Washburn; *The Velvet Black, and Other Stories.* Dutton.

41. Chesterton, Gilbert K.; *The Club of Queer Trades.* Harper.

42. Cobb, Irvin; *Sundry Accounts.* Doran.

43. Cohen, Octavus Roy; *Polished Ebony.* Dodd.

44. Crockett, S. R.; *The Stickit Minister.* Macmillan.

45. Davis, Richard Harding; *Van Bibber, and Others.* Harper.

46. Deland, Margaret; *Old Chester Tales.* Harper.

47. Field, Eugene; *A Little Book of Profitable Tales.* Scribner.

48. Fox, John, Jr.; *Hell fer Sartain.* Harper.

49. Fraser, W. A.; *Thirteen Men.* Appleton.

50. Freeman, Mary Wilkins; *A Humble Romance.* Harper.

51. Garland, Hamlin; *Main Traveled Roads.* Macmillan.

52. Gerould, Katharine Fullerton; *Vain Oblations.* Scribner.

53. "Gorky, Maxim"; *Twenty-Six and One.* J. F. Taylor & Co.

54. Hale, Edward Everett; *The Man Without a Country and Other Stories.* Little.

55. Halévy, Ludovic; *Parisian Points of View.* Harper.

56. Hardy, Thomas; *Life's Little Ironies.* Harper.

57. Harris, Joel Chandler; *Uncle Remus and His Friends.* Houghton.

58. Harte, Bret; *The Luck of Roaring Camp.* Houghton.

59. "Henry, O."; *Heart of the West.* McClure.

60. Hewlett, Maurice; *Little Novels of Italy.* Macmillan.

61. Hichens, Robert; *The Black Spaniel.* Stokes.

62. Hoffman, E. T. W.; *Weird Tales.* Scribner.

63. "Hope, Anthony"; *Dolly Dialogues.* Harper.

64. Hopper, James; *Caybigan.* McClure.

65. Howells, William Dean; *A Pair of Patient Lovers.* Harper.

66. Jacobs, W. W.; *The Lady of the Barge.* Dodd.

67. James, Henry, Jr.; *The Wheel of Time.* Harper.

68. Johnson, Owen; *Murder in Any Degree.* Century.

69. Kelly, Myra; *Wards of Liberty.* McClure.

70. Lewis, Alfred Henry; *Wolfville.* Stokes.

71. Lincoln, Joseph C.; *The Old Home House.* Barnes.

72. London, Jack; *The Love of Life.* Macmillan.

73. Loomis, Charles Battell; *Cheerful Americans.* Holt.

74. MacGrath, Harold; *Enchantment.* Bobbs.

75. " Maclaren, Ian "; *Beside the Bonnie Briar Bush.*

76. Matthews, Brander; *The Story of a Story, etc.* Harper.

77. Maupassant, Guy de; *The Odd Number.* Harper.

78. Meredith, George; *Short Stories.* Scribner.

79. Moore, George; *The Untilled Field.* Lippincott.

80. Norris, Frank; *A Deal in Wheat.* Doubleday.

81. O'Higgins, Harvey J.; *The Smoke Eaters.* Century.

82. Osbourne, Lloyd; *The Motormaniacs.* Bobbs.

83. " Ouida "; *A Dog of Flanders, etc.* Lippincott.

84. Page, Thomas Nelson; *In Ole Virginia.* Scribner.

85. Phelps, Elizabeth Stuart; *Men, Women and Ghosts.* Houghton.

86. Poe, Edgar Allan; *Monsieur Dupin* (collected detective stories). McClure.

87. Post, Melville Davison; *The Strange Schemes of Randolph Mason.* Putnam.

88. Poushkin, A. S.; *Prose Tales.* Macmillan.

89. Rinehart, Mary Roberts; *Affinities*. Doran.

90. Sienkiewicz, Henryk; *Hania*. Little.

91. Smith, F. Hopkinson; *The Wood Fire in No. 3*. Scribner.

92. Stockton, Frank R.; *The Lady or the Tiger*. Scribner.

93. Stuart, Ruth McEnery; *The Second Wooing of Salina Sue*. Harper.

94. "Thanet, Octave"; *Stories of a Western Town*. Scribner.

95. Turgenieff, Ivan; *The Jew, and Other Stories*. Scribner.

96. "Twain, Mark"; *The $30,000 Bequest*. Harper.

97. White, Stewart Edward; *The Blazed Trail*. Mc-Clure.

98. White, William Allen; *In Our Town*. McClure.

99. Wiggin, Kate Douglas; *The Village Watch Tower*. Houghton.

100. Zangwill, I.; *The Celibates' Club*. Macmillan.

NOTE: See additional reading and reference lists—made in 1923—in "Appendix H," p. 431. See also the additions in "Appendix H" made in 1928.

APPENDIX B

ONE HUNDRED REPRESENTATIVE SHORT-STORIES

This is not an attempt to select "one hundred best short-stories," for the opinions of competent critics would be sure to differ as to the exclusion or inclusion of many writers and stories. Accessibility to the general reader has governed some selections; other stories chosen were thought to be more representative of their authors than better-known examples; while most are widely recognized as typical masterpieces. The fact that certain excellent magazines are not referred to in this list is accounted for by the fact that many short-stories which originally appeared in their pages were later collected in the sets listed in *Appendix A*. The numerals in parentheses refer in every case to the collections listed in *Appendix A* — which, with *Appendix C,* will also largely supplement this list. The names of publishers not in italics, following story titles, indicate that the stories are published in book form under the same titles *Appendix E* gives the full styles and addresses of publishers whose names are abbreviated elsewhere in this volume.

1. Abbott, Eleanor Hallowell; "The Sick-a-Bed Lady." *Collier's,* Oct., 1905.

2. Ade, George; "To Make a Hoosier Holiday." (15)

3. Aldrich, Thomas Bailey; " Marjorie Daw." Houghton.

4. Andrews, Mary R. Shipman; " A Good Samaritan." McClure.

5. Anstey, F.; " The Black Poodle." (20)

6. Atherton, Gertrude; " The Bell in the Fog." Harper.

7. Bacon, Josephine Daskam; " Edgar, the Choir-Boy Uncelestial." *McClure's,* Jan., 1902.

8. Balzac, Honoré de; " The Unknown Masterpiece." (16)

9. Bangs, John Kendrick; " The Utilitarian Mr. Carraway." From *" The Booming of Acre Hill."* Harper.

10. Barbour, Ralph Henry; " The Dub." *Lippincott's,* Nov., 1905.

11. Barrie, James M.; " The Courting of T'Nowhead's Bell." (11)

12. Beach, Rex; "Too Fat to Fight." *Cosmopolitan,* Jan., 1919.

13. Bourget, Paul; "Another Gambler." (21)

14. Brainerd, Eleanor Hoyt; "Concerning Belinda." Doubleday.

15. Brown, Alice; "The Flying Teuton." *Harpers,* Aug., 1917.

16. Bunner, H. C.; "Love in Old Cloathes." (19)

17. Burnett, Frances Hodgson; "Little Saint Elizabeth." From *"Sara Crewe."* Scribner.

18. Butler, Ellis Parker; "Pigs is Pigs." McClure.

19. Cabell, James Branch; "The Wedding Jest." *Century,* Sept., 1919.
20. Cable, George W.; "Posson Jone." *Appleton's,* April 1, 1876.
21. Conrad, Joseph; "The Brute." *McClure's,* Nov., 1907.
22. Cooke, Grace MacGowan; "Their First Formal Call." Harper.
23. "Craddock, Charles Egbert"; "The Mystery of Witch-Face Mountain." Houghton.
24. Crawford, F. Marion; "The Upper Berth." (15)
25. Cutting, Mary Stewart; "The Suburban Whirl." McClure.
26. Daudet, Alphonse; "The Goat of Monsieur Seguin." (10)
27. Davis, Richard Harding; " Van Bibber's Man-Servant. (45)
28. Deland, Margaret; "An Encore." (7)
29. Dobie, Charles C.; "All or Nothing." *Harper's,* June, 1921.
30. Ferber, Edna; "A Gay Old Dog." *Metropolitan,* Oct., 1917.
31. Forman, Justus Miles; "The Dream." *Harper's,* Oct., 1908.
32. France, Anatole; "The Juggler of Notre Dame." (21)
33. Frederic, Harold; "Brother Sebastian's Friendship." (15)
34. Futrelle, Jacques; " The Gray Ghost." *Everybody's,* Aug., 1903.
35. Garland, Hamlin; " Up the Coulée." (51)
36. Gautier, Théophile; " The Dead Leman." (10)

37. Harben, Will N.; "The Whipping of Uncle Henry."
   From *Northern Georgia Sketches.* Harper.
38. Hardy, Thomas; "On the Western Circuit." (56)
39. Harte, Bret; "The Outcasts of Poker Flat." (11)
40. Hawthorne, Nathaniel; "Ethan Brand." (24)
41. Henry, O."; "Cupid a là Carte." (59)
42. Hewlett, Maurice; "Madonna of the Peach-Tree."
   (60)
43. Heyse, Paul; "Andrea Delfin." (8)
44. Hibbard, George; "The Governor." Scribner.
45. Holloway, Edward Stratton; "The Master."
   Reader, Nov., 1905.
46. "Hope, Anthony"; "The Sin of the Bishop of
   Modenstein." From *The Heart of the Princess
   Osra.* Stokes.
47. Hopper, James; "Caybigan." McClure.
48. Hurst, Fannie; "Humoresque." *Cosmopolitan,*
   Mar., 1919.
49. Howells, W. D.; "Editha." (7)
50. Irving, Washington; "Rip Van Winkle." (3)
51. James, Henry; "Owen Wingrave." (67)
52. Jewett, Sarah Orne; "Marsh Rosemary." *Atlantic,*
   57:590.
53. Johnson, Owen; "The Hero of an Hour." *Saturday Evening Post,* Aug. 29, 1908.
54. Jokai, Maurice; "In Love With the Czarina." (21)
55. Kipling, Rudyard; "The Man Who Was." (17)
56. Knapp, George; "Blood o' Innocence." *Lippincott's,* Nov., 1907.

57. Lewis, Will; "Mike Grady's Safety." *Everybody's,* Oct., 1905.

58. Linn, J. W.; "The Girl at Duke's." *McClure's,* Aug., 1903.

59. Long, John Luther; "The Siren." *Century,* July, 1903.

60. "Maartens, Maarten;" "The Little Christian." *Lippincott's,* March, 1900.

61. McCutcheon, George Barr; "The Day of the Dog." Bobbs.

62. MacGowan, Alice; "A Doll." (7)

63. MacGrath, Harold; "The Blind Madonna." (74)

64. "Maclaren, Ian;" "A Doctor of the Old School." (75)

65. Maeterlinck, Maurice; "The Massacre of the Innocents." (21)

66. Martin, Helen; "The Betrothal of Elypholate Yingst." *Cosmopolitan,* June, 1903.

67. Maupassant, Guy de; "Vain Beauty." (10)

68. Mérimée, Prosper; "The Venus of Ille." (6)

69. Mitchell, S. Weir; "A Draft on the Bank of Spain." From "Hepzibah Guinness." Century.

70. Morris, Gouverneur; "Simon L'Ouvrier." *Collier's,* Aug. 25, 1906.

71. Norris, Frank; "The Passing of Cock-eye Blacklock." *Century,* July, 1902.

72. "Ouida" (Mlle. Louise de la Ramée); "A Leaf in the Storm." (20)

73. Page, Thomas Nelson; "Marse Chan." (19)

74. Phelps, Elizabeth Stuart; "His Soul to Keep." *Harper's,* Sept., 1908.

75. Phillips, Henry Wallace; "Red Saunders at Big Bend." *McClure's,* Jan., 1904.

76. Poe, Edgar Allan; "The Pit and the Pendulum." (24)

77. Poushkin, Alexander; "The Shot." (21)

78. Reade, Charles; "The Box Tunnel." (18)

79. Singmaster, Elsie; "The County Seat." *Atlantic,* May, 1908.

80. Scott, John Reed; "The First Hurdle." *Lippincott's,* Nov., 1907.

81. Spearman, Frank H.; "A Million-Dollar Freight Train." (22)

82. Stevenson, Robert Louis; "Markheim." (3)

83. Stockton, Frank R.; "The Lady or the Tiger." Scribner.

84. Stuart, Ruth McEnery; "A Note of Scarlet." *Century,* May and June, 1899.

85. Sudermann, Hermann; "The New-Year's Eve Confession." (16)

86. Tarkington, Booth; "Monsieur Beaucaire." McClure.

87. Taylor, Bayard; "Who Was She?" (19)

88. Taylor, Mary Imlay; "The Window That Monsieur Forgot." *Booklovers,* Jan., 1904.

89. Tolstoi, Lyof; "An Old Acquaintance." (21)

90. Turganev, Ivan; "Mumu." (21)

91. "Twain, Mark"; "The £1,000,000 Bank Note." From "*The American Claimant.*" Harper.

92. Van Vorst, Marie; "Bulstrode in Loco Parentis." *Scribner's,* Nov., 1906.

93. Watson, H. B. Marriott; "A Delicate Story." *Ainslee's,* June, 1907.

94. Weyman, Stanley J.; "A Perilous Amour." (20)

95. Wharton, Edith; "The Duchess at Prayer." From *"Crucial Instances."* Scribner.

96. White, Stewart Edward; "Life of the Winds of Heaven." *McClure's,* Aug., 1902.

97. White, William Allen; "The King of Boyville." (27)

98. Wiggin, Kate Douglas; "The Bird's Christmas Carol." Houghton.

99. Wister, Owen; "The Game and the Nation." (24)

100. Zola, Emile; "The Death of Olivier Bécaille." (11)

APPENDIX C

THE PLOTS OF TWENTY SHORT-STORIES

The numbers in parentheses refer to the collections of short-stories listed in *Appendix A*.

1. MARKHEIM, by Robert Louis Stevenson (1850–1894) ; about 7,000 words; written in 1884. A psychological character study of intense emotional force (25).

Markheim enters the shop of a dealer in antiques, ostensibly to buy a Christmas present for a lady. He stabs the old dealer with a long skewer-like dagger, and then is stricken with terror as " the whole room was filled with noiseless bustle . . . the tall shadows nodding, the gross blots of darkness swelling and dwindling as with respiration, the faces of the portraits and the china gods changing and wavering like images in water." The striking of clocks, the reflections of mirrors, the sound of his own steps, a score of other matters, all stagger him with fright. " On every side he was haunted and begirt with presences." At length he brings himself to go upstairs, still beset by fearful fancies. Suddenly a step is heard upon the stair, a face peers in the doorway. A Visitant enters and shows Markheim that He knows all. He offers the murderer immunity in exchange for a service, but Markheim fears such a bargain might cost him his soul. He seeks to disclose all his motives, to uncover his very heart to the Tempter — whose face suddenly takes on an almost angelic smile as Markheim decides to place himself beyond the possibility of doing more evil. The Visitant fades away, and Markheim descends the stair, saying to the maidservant whom he confronts on the threshold, " You had better go for the police : I have killed your master."

2. THE MAN WHO WAS, Rudyard Kipling (1865–   ) ; about 6,500 words ; written in 1889. A human-interest story, with strong emphasis laid upon the setting. The middle-distance characters stand out clearly (16).

" Dirkovitch was . . . an officer in a Cossack regiment, and corresponding for a Russian newspaper." In India he visited one troop after another and, by order of the Indian government, was civilly treated. Finally he became the guest of the White Hussars. During a gala dinner the mess was disturbed by the capture, outside, of a wretch in native rags who had apparently been one of a band of desperate carbine thieves. The miserable fellow seemed a lunatic, but as he wept an Indian officer noticed that he cried like an Englishman. A Hussar heard him moaning, " My God ! " in English. They set him at table and gave him a stimulant. He reached out to a piece of silver plate on the table and touched a spring known only to the Hussars. Then in a child-like way he inspected the room and thickly asked for a certain picture of a famous old regimental drum horse, which used to hang above the mantel. Had he once belonged to their regiment? They tested him with their own peculiar toast to the Queen, and he responded as only an officer of the White Hussars could. Then Dirkovitch addressed him in Russian, and the man groveled. It gradually transpired that he was Lieutenant Austin Limmason, recorded as missing before Sebastopol thirty years prior. Captured by the Russians, he had insulted their Colonel, was knouted horribly, and after years of suffering, his mind now a blank, he had stumbled home to his regiment — he was not a carbine thief. The care of his comrades came too late, however, for three days later he died and was buried with an officer's honors. As Dirkovitch ended his visit he predicted a clash in the East between Britain and Russia.

3. A DERELICT, by Richard Harding Davis (1864-1917); about 11,500 words; from "Ranson's Folly," 1902. A character study of crisis and denouement (15)

James Keating, reporter, is sent by the Consolidated News to Santiago Harbor, wherein Cervera's fleet is bottled up. In Jamaica he runs across Charlie Channing, a newspaper man of rare genius, but of dissolute habits. The latter is unattached, and when his hoped-for assignment does not come, he is reduced to leading the life of a "beach-comber." The Syndicate reporter, Keating, offers Channing a job as stoker on the press boat — the only one there at the time. Channing at first refuses, then decides to accept. When he goes on board he finds

Keating drunk, and he is still drunk the following day, when the Spanish fleet makes its dash to escape. Though sick with fever, Channing writes a great story — braced up with quinine — and orders the captain to steam to Port Antonio and get the story on the wire. Because he knows that Keating's future is imperilled by his debauch, and that he has a young wife, Channing generously signs Keating's name to the dispatches. Then he succumbs to the fever, and when he gets on his feet again, six weeks later, the war is over. The Fruit Company at Port Antonio sends him north in one of its steamers. When he reaches New York he goes to a Bohemian restaurant, and there meets acquaintances who tell him that they are giving Keating a farewell banquet on this the eve of his departure for Paris, where he is to cover the Peace negotiations, and then become the Syndicate's Washington correspondent. Keating, he learns, owes his good fortune to the remarkable news-beat he (Channing) sent in about the destruction of the Spanish fleet. Channing looks in and sees Keating at the head of the long, crowded table, then he draws back. "You say 'good-by' to him for me," he says. "And, Norris — tell him — tell him — that I asked you to say to him, 'It's all right,' that's all, just that, 'It's all right.' He'll understand." As he moves away from the only place where he was sure of food and a welcome that night, the revelers break into the chorus, "For he's a jolly good fellow!" But it was for Keating that the chorus rang out.

4. THE PIECE OF STRING, by Guy de Maupassant (1850–1893); about 2,500 words; written about 1885. A psychological story of compact plot and swift, pathetic denouement (25).

Old Master Hauchecorne had just come from the country to market when he saw a bit of string lying in the roadway. Being economical, he picked it up, and was about to thrust it into his blouse when he realized that the Harness Maker, an old enemy, was looking at him. Ashamed of his niggardly act, he fumbled about, pretended to be looking for something else, concealed the string, and then painfully hobbled on. Later in the day peasants and citizens were summoned by drumbeat to the market square and told that a wallet containing five hundred francs had been lost. Presently Master Hauchecorne was sent for by the mayor, who told him that the Harness Maker had seen him pick up the wallet that morning on the road. Hauchecorne explained that it was merely a bit of string that he had picked up. The mayor was incredulous, the old man protested, was confronted by his accuser, and at last temporarily discharged. Everywhere he went he repeated his story and everywhere he was not believed. The next day the wallet was found and restored. Hauchecorne again started out, triumphant, and buttonholed every one with his story, but people laughed and were still unconvinced. They thought he had tossed the wallet where it would be found. He was dumfounded at their incredulity. Thereupon he again made his rounds, still explaining.

" ' Those are a liar's reasons,' people said behind his back.

" He realized it; he gnawed his nails, and exhausted himself in vain.

" He grew perceptibly thinner.

" Now the jokers asked him to tell the story of *The Piece of String* for their amusement, as a soldier who has seen service is asked to tell about his battles. His mind, attacked at its source, grew feebler.

" Late in December he took to his bed.

" In the first days of January he died and in the delirium of the death-agony he protested his innocence, repeating:

" ' A little piece of string — a little piece of string — see, here it is, m'sieu' mayor.' "

5. THE GREAT STONE FACE, by Nathaniel Hawthorne (1804–1864) ; about 8,500 words; published in 1850. An allegorical, idealistic, didactic story (27).

The Great Stone Face " was a work of Nature in her mood of majestic playfulness, formed on the perpendicular side of a mountain by some immense rocks." " Its features were noble, and the expression was at once grand and sweet, as if it were the glow of a vast, warm heart, that embraced all mankind in its affections, and had room for more." There was a tradition in the populous valley that there would some day appear a noble man with the very countenance of the Great Stone Face. As little Ernest sat with his mother he wished that such a man might indeed appear. The boy, who grew up under the benignant inspiration of the Face, one day heard it said that Mr. Gathergold had returned to his native place after having become very rich. With ceremony the citizens acclaimed him as the man of prophecy, but as Ernest saw him give out merely coppers in charity, he knew that it was not he. Later another son of the valley returned full of glory — Old Blood-and-Thunder they called this military hero — and thought they had found in him the desired likeness. But in the " warworn and weather-beaten countenance, full of energy, and expressive of an iron will," Ernest could see no similarity to " the gentle wisdom, the deep, broad, tender sympathies " of the Great Stone Face. Next a great statesman returned to his native valley, and because the people thought he looked like the Face, they called him Old Stony Phiz, but Ernest knew that he too was lacking.

At length a Poet visited the home of Ernest, now an old man. The two conversed profoundly, and in his visitor Ernest sought to find the expected Man, but the poet suddenly, " by an irresistible impulse, threw his arms aloft, and shouted — ' Behold! Behold! Ernest is himself the likeness of the Great Stone Face!'

" Then all the people looked, and saw that what the deep-sighted poet said was true. The prophecy was fulfilled. But Ernest, having finished what he had to say, took the poet's arm, and walked slowly homeward, still hoping that some wiser and better man than himself would by and by appear, bearing a resemblance to the Great Stone Face."

6. "Next to Reading Matter," by "O. Henry" (Sidney Porter), (1865-1910); about 6,000 words; *Everybody's Magazine,* Dec., 1907. A humorous surprise story, ingenious in diction.

The narrator is accosted on the street in New York by Judson Tate, the homeliest man imaginable. "His ugliness was less repellent than startling — arising from a sort of Lincolnian ruggedness and irregularity of feature that spellbound you with wonder and dismay." The two men struck up a hasty acquaintance and Tate tells his story. As a "gentleman adventurer" he had become a great man and the real power behind the president of a South American republic, all through his wonderful gift of speech. At an early age he had perceived that what he lacked in looks he must make up in eloquence, and now no one could stand before him. Judson Tate had a friend, Fergus McMahan, who was as handsome as Tate was ugly, but "his conversation was about as edifying as listening to a leak dropping in a tin dish-pan at the head of the bed when you want to go to sleep." McMahan falls in love with "Señorita Anabela Zamora, the beautiful daughter of the Alcalde of Aratama," and arranges with Tate to visit her window by night and woo her — for McMahan — by his eloquence. The ruse succeeds, but when Tate finally sees her beauty he himself falls in love and warns his friend that he will marry the young lady. McMahan only laughs, but Tate's eloquent words actually charm her away from his handsome rival and she engages to marry the homely Tate.

Suddenly, while calling upon the Señorita, the charmer loses his voice — and with it his hold upon his fiancé. In six days she runs away with McMahan. But Tate, after hurrying to the apothecary and getting some throat medicine, overtakes the eloping couple. The medicine has worked a miracle, his voice is as potent as ever, and the young lady once more succumbs to the eloquence of Judson Tate. They were married, and are now, he tells the narrator, living in Jersey City. He is now devoting himself to the sale of " Tate's Magic Chuchula Bronchial Lozenges," which did so much for him — but the listener at this point tears himself away.

After some reflection, the narrator decides that he has as much right to turn Tate's advertising dodge into a story as other fiction-writers have to puff a favorite make of automobile — and so he does. But he warns the reader that he " can't buy the *chuchula* plant in the drug stores."

7. THE MONKEY'S PAW, by W. W. Jacobs (1863–) ; about 3,500 words; *Harper's Magazine,* 105 ;634. A story of ingenious plot and surprising denouement, dealing with the supernatural. (25).

While visiting an elderly couple and their grown son in an English village, a British soldier, who has just returned from India, shows them a dried monkey's paw, upon which, he declares, an Indian fakir once cast a spell, so that by means of it each of three men could have three wishes granted him. He tells them that the previous owner had three wishes, the last being for death; and that he himself had three also, but he refuses to explain what the wishes were. He seems to fear the gruesome object and finally throws it on the fire, from which it is rescued by the son. The soldier finally consents to the old man's keeping it, though he warns him that no good will come of it. The visitor then leaves and the old man takes the paw in his hand and wishes for two hundred pounds to clear their home of its mortgage. The next day a stranger comes and tells them that their son has been mangled to death by being caught in some machinery, and on behalf of the mill-owners offers them two hundred pounds. Ten days later the old woman again thinks of the monkey's paw, and insists that her husband wish their boy alive again. Under protest he does as she wishes. In the night they are aroused by a familiar rapping on their door. Expecting to see her boy, the woman runs to open the door, despite the entreaties of her husband, who remembers the awful condition of their son's body. While she is struggling with the door fastenings, the husband hurriedly finds the monkey's paw, and utters his third and last wish. Immediately the knocking ceases, and when the woman gets the door open, the street lamp flickering opposite is shining on a quiet and deserted road. His third wish has been granted.

8. THE SUBSTITUTE, by François Coppée (1842-1908); about 3,500 words; written about 1883. A pathetic story of unexpected moral heroism (25).

Jean François Leturc "was scarcely ten years old when he was arrested for the first time for vagabondage." With a man's cynicism he tells the judge of his checkered life of vagrancy. "Nobody claiming him, they sent him to a reform school." When at seventeen he was set free, he fell among his old reformatory associates and followed their criminal courses. One arrest followed another until he had a bad name with the police and at length served five awful years at Toulon. When he was released he broke bounds and slipped back to Paris. Moved by the recollections of early teaching in the Brothers' school, he reforms thoroughly and finds a friend. "Jean François and Savinien scarcely ever left each other. For a while they both throve and expanded under this friendship, but Savinien is infected with the gay life of Paris, spends too much for his income, commits a theft, and the gold is found in his trunk.

"'Listen,' said Jean François, who came to take his (Savinien's) hands. 'I understand you stole the three gold pieces to buy some trifles for a girl. That would have been worth six months of prison for you. But you do not get out of that except to go back again; . . . I have done seven years in the reform school, one at Sainte-Pelagie, three at Poissy, and five at Toulon. Now, do not get scared. It is all settled. I have taken it on my shoulders.'

"'Poor fellow,' cried Savinien; but hope was coming back to his cowardly heart."

Jean François ended up a life-prisoner at Cayenne, registered as incorrigible.

9. THE CASK OF AMONTILLADO, by Edgar Allan Poe
(1809-1849) ; about 2,500 words; *Godey's Lady's Book*,
Nov., 1846. A sombre and characteristic Poe story, told
partly by suggestion; it is compact, swift and climactic.
The plot is slight, but the manner perfect (2).

" The thousand injuries of Fortunato I had borne as
I best could; but when he ventured on insult, I vowed
revenge. . . . A wrong is unredressed when retribution overtakes its redresser. It is equally unredressed
when the avenger fails to make himself felt as such to
him who has done the wrong." Fortunato is a connois-
seur in wines, so Montresor, the narrator, professes to
have a cask of alleged Amontillado which he wishes to
have judged. Fortunato is in carnival dress, but he desires to go at once to test the wine. Montresor craftily
leads him on while professing that Fortunato ought not
to enter the damp vaults. When they reach Montresor's
palace the servants are all gone to the carnival, so the
two at once enter the catacombs which form the wine-
cellar. Montresor first makes Fortunato drunk, and
then suddenly chains him to the wall in a dark and remote niche beneath the river bed. From beneath a pile
of ancient bones Montresor draws some stone and mortar
and, despite Fortunato's cries and pleadings, walls him
up in his tomb.[1]

10. MRS. KNOLLYS, by F. J. Stimson (" J. S. of
Dale "), (1855-   ) ; about 6,000 words; *Century Maga-*

[1] Compare Balzac's *La Grande Bretêche* and Edith Wharton's
The Duchess at Prayer. See note on page 88.

zine, Nov., 1883. A delicate, poetic story, centering about a single novel idea (15).

The story deals with the steady movement of the great Pasterzen glacier, which " rises in Western Austria and flows into Carinthia, and is fourteen or seventeen miles long, as you measure it from its birth in the snow field, or from where it begins to move from the higher snows and its active course is marked by the first wrinkle."

Charles Knollys was a young English government clerk who was spending an ideal honeymoon in the Alps, when one day he " slipped into a crevasse and vanished utterly from the earth." For many days the eighteen-year-old bride would not leave the place but sat and watched the crevasse while they made hopeless efforts to recover the body. One day a German scientist explained to her the character and the movement of the glacier, thus blunderingly crushing her hopes. A year later, in England, she received a letter from the great scientist saying that the loss of her husband had caused him to make a more exact study of the glacier, and assuring her that the body would be preserved in that icy world and move down with the slow-moving glacier. It might be recovered, he said, in forty-five years. And this pathetic hope made her willing to live. " There were but two events in her life — that which was past and that which was to come." And so she waited until at length the five and forty years had passed, and, true to the scientist's prediction, the glacier delivered out of its mouth the perfectly preserved husband of twenty-one to the bride of sixty-three.

11. THE INSURGENT, by Ludovic Halévy (1834-1908) ; about 2,000 words; written in 1872. A compressed human-interest story (16).

Martin, a Parisian fifty-five years old, tells his story to the president of the military tribunal by which he is being tried as an insurgent. His father had been fatally shot in the uprising of 1830. " By his side, on the litter was his gun.

" ' Take it,' he said to me; ' I give it to you — and whenever there shall be an insurrection against the government — always, always, always ! ' " — and died.

The boy was fifteen and in frame a mere child, but he offered himself to the Commune, and from that moment became what he remained for forty years — an insurgent. He was the first to climb the iron fence of the Louvre under fire of the Swiss in 1830 — but monarchy still prevailed. In 1832 he distinguished himself again, and was wounded in a chapel of the church of St. Méry. After ten years in prison he used to return to the chapel, not to pray, but to see the stains of his blood which still marked the stones. In prison he had missed the rising of 1834. In 1848 he failed again as an insurrectionist and was sent to Cayenne, but after four years — in 1852 (having missed the revolt of 1851) — he was pardoned for saving a French officer from drowning. Back again in Paris, he married the widow of an old comrade, and a son was born. Under the Empire all was peace, but he reared his son in the ideas his own father had given him. At length Martin took part in an assault against La Villette, and was again imprisoned, but was soon released by a change of government. All through the risings of 1870 and 1871 he was prominent. "I loved revolt for the revolt itself. An insurgent, I told you at the start; I am an insurgent. I can't see a political club without going in, an insurrection without running to it, a barricade without taking my stone to it."

But after forty years of devotion to revolt, he complains, "Now you tell me that this insurrection was not lawful. That is possible, but I don't quite see why. I am getting muddled between these insurrections which are a duty and these which are a crime." He gets medals and applause for the one, and for the other, prison, exile, death. He is confused and discouraged. All he asks is that they deal gently with his son, who is not responsible for his father's teachings.

"As for me, you've got me; don't let me go — that's the advice I give you. I'm too old to change, and besides, what would you have? Nothing can alter what is; I was born on the wrong side of the barricade."

12. A LIGHT MAN, by Henry James (1843-1916); about 13,000 words; *The Galaxy*, July, 1869. A character study, with little action, but handled with the subtlety characteristic of the author (13).

Returning from long residence abroad, Maximus Austin (who tells the story in the first person and in diary form) receives a letter from his old-time friend, Theodore Lisle. The letter bears an invitation to spend a month at the home of an aged millionaire, Frederic

Sloane, who had known Austin's mother years before. Austin accepts and finds Theodore Lisle settled as secretary to Sloane, who is an interesting but battered old worldling. Three weeks suffice to show Lisle that Austin is really "a light man," and that Sloane has set up the newcomer in his affections to the detriment of himself — Lisle. Being in need of the situation, Lisle struggles to maintain his hold upon his patron, but Sloane finally begs Austin to remain with him to the end, offering to destroy his will, which Austin finds is in Lisle's favor. Upon being pressed, Austin goes to get the will from Sloane's desk, and finds Lisle standing with the will and some other papers in his hand. The latter asserts his ignorance of the contents of the will, but reads it at Austin's request. Knowing now that he is about to lose the fortune, Lisle regrets much more the loss of his faith in Austin, and so himself destroys the will, and bids farewell to the friend he has lost. All this moves Austin but a little, and while the men are still together the valet announces the death of Mr. Sloane — now intestate. The heir-at-law, as nearest of kin — a Miss Meredith — telegraphs that she is coming to the funeral. "I shall remain till she comes," resolves Austin, with characteristic coolness. "I have lost a fortune, but have I irretrievably lost a friend? I am sure I can't say. Yes, I shall wait for Miss Meredith."

13. ON THE STAIRS, by Arthur Morrison (1863–   ), about 1,600 words. A realistic tragedy, told by suggestion (25).

On the stairs of a grimy, ugly, eight-family tenement in the East End of London, a gaunt woman pauses as a door opens, and a tottering old woman stands in the doorway. Her name is Mrs. Curtis, and Mrs. Manders, her gaunt neighbor, asks after her sick son. No, he is no better. She need not ask the doctor to find that out for she heard three spirit raps last night, a sure omen —" 'E's goin,' " said the old mother.

Mrs. Manders rehearses with pride the oft-repeated details of the " 'an'some funeral " she had given her husband with the twelve pounds received from the Odd Fellows, and the old dame declares that her son shall also be " put away decent "— though she is doubtful if the insurance will permit her to afford both hired mute mourners and " plooms." At this the doctor's assistant comes. When he leaves the sick-room he insists that the patient's only chance of recovery is in good port wine, but the old mother complains that it is " sich a expense." The assistant then gives her five shillings from his own small resources, not knowing that the doctor himself had given a like sum the day before. But the woman puts the money away, and " nothing left the room all night. Nothing that opened the door . . ."

The next morning the gaunt neighbor is the first visitor. " Ah, 'e's a lovely corpse," said Mrs. Manders. " Like wax. So was my 'usband." And now the old woman feels able to hire the mutes — " and the plooms too. They ain't sich a great expense, after all."

14. TENNESSEE'S PARTNER, by Bret Harte (1839–1902); about 4,000 words; written about 1870. A humorously pathetic character study, of Western local color (15).

After showing how such appellatives as " Dungaree Jack " and " Saleratus Bill " came to be applied to the California gold-seekers, the author takes up his story.

Tennessee's Partner leaves Poker Flat to procure a wife. At Stockton he is suited, and in a week marries and returns to Poker Flat. Presently Tennessee makes off with his partner's wife, but somebody else soon takes her from him. He returns to Poker Flat, and his injured partner shows no resentment but takes the double steal philosophically.

" Meanwhile a popular feeling against Tennessee had grown up on the Bar. He was known to be a gambler; he was suspected to be a thief. In these suspicions Tennessee's Partner was equally compromised; his continued intimacy with Tennessee after the affair above quoted could only be accounted for on the hypothesis of a copartnership of crime."

At last Tennessee is detected in a plain " hold-up," is pursued, captured and tried before " Judge Lynch." He refuses to say anything for himself, but his partner — simple, serious, direct and loyal — comes into the improvised trial-room, and haltingly speaks for Tennessee. At length he pulls out of an old carpet-bag his entire " pile "— seventeen hundred dollars in coarse gold, and a watch — which he offers as compensation, to " call it square." But the gold is indignantly refused by the "court," and Tennessee is convicted. "For the first time that evening the eyes of the prisoner and his strange advocate met. Tennessee smiled, showed his white teeth, and, saying, 'Euchred, old man!' held out his hand. Tennessee's Partner took it in his own, and saying, 'I just dropped in as I was passin' to see how things was gettin' on,' let the hand passively fall, and adding that 'it was a warm night,' again mopped his face with his handkerchief, and without a word withdrew."

After the lynching Tennessee's Partner is seen near by with his donkey-cart. Asking for the body, he places it in a coffin he has made, and the bystanders join in the funeral procession. He buries Tennessee without help and then says a few memorial words — full of character and simple pathos. Tennessee's Partner does not long survive. As he is dying his eyes light up with the vision of Tennessee — " 'coming this way, too — all by himself, sober, and his face a shining. Tennessee! Partner!'

"And so they met."

15. WHERE LOVE IS, THERE GOD IS ALSO, by Lyof Tolstoy (1828-1910); about 5,500 words; written about 1890. A didactic story, told with conviction and simplicity. *The Outlook,* March 28, 1908.

Martin Avdyeeich was an honest Russian cobbler whose children and wife had died, leaving him with but one child, a small boy, upon whom he had set his heart.

But that child also died, and Martin reproached God.
A Pilgrim monk, however, directed him to the gospels
and he became a devout follower of their teachings. One
day he heard a voice which bade him look to-morrow
into the street, for Christ would come to him. But He
did not appear, only a chilled old snow-sweeper, to whom
Martin gave hot tea to drink, as he explained the gos-
pel; and then the grateful old man left. Martin continued to look for Christ, but He did not come, though
he saw a poorly clad woman with a little child, whom
he fed and warmed, hearing her story and giving her an
old jacket to cover her thin summer garments. He next
acted as mediator between an old woman and a mischievous boy who had stolen her apples; and to her also
expounded the new truth which has possessed him —
the doctrine of love. All day long he had looked for the
Christ and had not seen him, but now as he returned to
his cellar a Presence declared itself as He who had
said, "Inasmuch as ye have done it to the least of these
My brethren, ye have done it unto Me." "And Martin
then understood that his dream had not deceived him,
and that the Saviour had really come to him that day,
and he had really received Him."

16. ANOTHER GAMBLER, Paul Bourget (1852–   );
about 6,000 words; published in 1889. A dramatic,
psychological study of morbid remorse, done in semi-
realistic style (21).

Two young men of good family, Claude and the narrator, are discussing the suicide of Claude's cousin Lu-

cien, which has just ended his career of gambling and dishonesty. Claude tells the narrator the following story, as illustrating the gambler's faith in fetiches:

When Claude was a boy he passionately desired a sabre which hung in the window of a Parisian toyshop. Ten francs would buy it, but how should he save so large a sum! One day his cousin Lucien gave him two francs as a gift, and at the same time a ten-franc piece, which he charged him to give to the first beggar he should meet — to insure gambler's luck for Lucien that night. The ten francs, he reflected, would buy the sabre! The boy yielded, in spirit, and gave a blind beggar the silver coin, keeping the gold piece for the coveted sabre. But he suffered torments of conscience. He felt that he had brought misfortune — perhaps suicide — to Lucien, so he arose in the night, stole out of the house, and started off to give the coin to the blind beggar. On the way he slipped in the snow and lost the gold piece. That night Lucien lost heavily at baccarat, cheated, began his vicious career, and ended a suicide.

17. THE FATHER, Björnstjerne Björnson (1832-1910); about 1,500 words; written in 1860. A realistic story of pathos and lofty spirit, exhibiting compression and the power of suggestion (16).

Thord Overaas was the first man of his parish. One day he presented himself at the priest's and asked baptism for his newborn son, requesting that he be baptized alone. As Thord left the pastor prayed that the child might prove a blessing to his father. Sixteen years later he came to the priest to arrange for the lad's confirmation, and this time he is proud that his boy will head the list. Eight years more, and Thord comes to the priest with the request that he publish the bans for his son — he is to marry the richest girl in the village. A fortnight later the young man is drowned before his father's eyes. A year passes and for the fourth time Thord comes to the priest. He has changed from a robust man to one of bowed form and white hair. He lays upon the table half of his wealth, to be invested in his son's name as a legacy for the poor.

"They sat there for a while, Thord with downcast eyes, the priest with his eyes fixed on Thord. Presently the priest said, slowly and softly:

"'I think your son has at last brought you a true blessing.'"

"'Yes, I think so myself,' said Thord, looking up while two big tears coursed slowly down his cheeks."

18. MATEO FALCONE, by Prosper Mérimée (1803–1870); about 5,500 words; published in 1829. A tragedy, exhibiting local color and marked climax (25).

Mateo Falcone was a well-to-do sheep-raiser, living in the open plateau country of Corsica, whose thickets were often the resort of fugitives from justice. One day Mateo and his wife set out early to visit one of their flocks, leaving their little son Fortunato at home. Several hours later a bandit, limping painfully from a wound received from the pursuing soldiery, claims protection because of his friendship for Falcone. Fortunato hesitates, but at sight of a five-franc piece hides the man under a haystack. Soon the soldiers come, but threats cannot make the boy betray the bandit. A silver watch, however, proves an effective bribe. Just as the wounded bandit is dragged from the haystack, Falcone returns and learns the truth. When the soldiers have gone, bearing their prisoner on a litter, the father takes out little Fortunato and shoots him as the first traitor in the family.

19. THE DAMNED THING, by Ambrose Bierce (1842–); about 9,000 words. From " In the Midst of Life," 1898. A fantastic story of the supernatural, with pseudo-scientific conclusion (14).

The setting is a small Western community, during a coroner's inquest. William Harker, newspaper man, who has been visiting Hugh Morgan, the deceased, is summoned as a witness, and he introduces in his testimony a copy of the description of the tragedy, which he has sent to the newspaper he represents. He and Morgan were out after quail, when he heard a sound as of a heavy body dragging itself through some nearby bushes, and Morgan became violently agitated. He ascribed the noise to what he called " The Damned Thing," and when a moment later some wild oats not far away were bent as though some animal was passing through them, though nothing was visible, he fired at the spot, then turned to flee. Harker was thrown down by the sudden impact of a large, soft body flung against him with great force. When he arose, he saw his friend on the ground some distance away, writhing in an apparent struggle with something, though nothing was visible. He hurried to his assistance, but Morgan was dead, his throat horribly lacerated. Harker then noticed the same motion among the wild oats as he had seen before, only this time the Thing was evidently going away. A diary kept by the dead man speaks of " The Damned Thing " as a huge, savage creature which cannot be seen. Morgan's solution of the mystery was that, just as there are sounds which cannot be heard by mortal ears, so there are colors which we cannot see. " The Damned Thing," he asserted, must have been of such a color. The verdict of the coroner's jury was, " We, the jury, find that the remains come to their end at the hands of a mountain lion, but some of us thinks, all the same, they had fits." [2]

20. WHAT WAS IT? A MYSTERY, by Fitz-James O'Brien (1828–1862) ; in condensed form about 5,000 words; written in 1859. A realistic story of unexplained mystery (15).

The narrator, Harry, was one of a group of boarders who agreed to go with his landlady if she would remove to a spacious house reputed to be haunted. For some weeks nothing happened, but one night, after a long dis-

[2] Compare with the next plot.

cussion of ghostly matters with his friend Hammond, Harry was trying to fall asleep, when a Something dropped upon his chest and clutched his throat. A struggle of horrible intensity followed, in which Harry was at last victorious. He bound the unseen Thing and turned on the light — but saw nothing, though he still had one arm around "a breathing, panting, corporeal shape." Hearing the noise, Hammond entered the room and also touched the Thing, but could not see it. They then fastened it more securely and threw it upon the bed — which creaked under the weight. Then followed prolonged observation of its movements, as shown by the bed-clothes. It slept, but neither ate nor spoke. At last they secured a plaster mold of the Enigma by giving it an anæsthetic. It was in form like a misshapen man. For two weeks its heart-beats grew daily feebler, until it died. They buried the invisible Horror in the garden, and rumor had it that the plaster-cast was to be exhibited in a well-known museum.

APPENDIX D

I. Diction — The Right Use of Right Words

(a) *Pure Words*
1. Use neither obsolete words nor words too new to be standard.
2. Avoid the needless use of localisms and technical terms.
3. Rarely employ a foreign word until it has become naturalized.

(b) *Proper Words*
4. Be too alert to use the wrong word even if it sounds like the right one.[2]
   Do not use the same word in more than one sense in the same paragraph.

(c) *Precise Words*
6. Among synonyms, choose the word that conveys exactly your shade of meaning, both in kind and in degree.
7. Avoid general words when specific words will convey your idea.

[1] Adapted from the author's *How to Attract and Hold an Audience* (Noble and Noble, New York).
[2] As, *discomfort* for *discomfit, demean* for *bemean.*

414

II. SENTENCES

Kinds

8. Short sentences should be used for vigor, emphasis, rapid movement, and impassioned discourse.

9. Too many short sentences produce a disconnected, jerky effect.

10. For detail, smoothness, rhythm, and beauty, use longer sentences.

11. Use care lest long sentences obscure the meaning.

12. Use balanced sentences to bring out contrast.[3]

13. To sustain interest, use periodic sentences.[4]

14. For easy and informal discourse use loose sentences.[5]

15. Learn to use all kinds of sentences and so avoid monotony.

[3] "If the flights of Dryden therefore are higher, Pope continues longer on the wing. If of Dryden's fire the blaze is brighter, of Pope's the heat is more regular and constant. Dryden often surpasses expectation, and Pope never falls below it. Dryden is read with frequent astonishment, and Pope with perpetual delight."— JOHNSON's *Lives of the Poets:* Pope.

[4] Grammatically incomplete if ended before the last words. "By a curious irony of fate, the places to which we are sent when health deserts us are often singularly beautiful."— STEVENSON: *Ordered South.*

[5] May be ended earlier and yet be grammatically complete.

III. Essential Properties of Style

(a) *Grammatical Correctness*

16. Keep your tenses congruous.[6]
17. Use the subjunctive only when the condition is doubtful.[7]
18. Use shall and will, should and would, with care.
19. "Do not let intervening words disturb the agreement of verb and subject."— GENUNG.[8]
20. Rarely place an adverb between the parts of an infinitive.[9]
21. Let the sense rather than grammar govern your treatment of collectives.

(b) *Clearness*

22. Place adverbs and adverb modifiers close to the words they modify. Beware especially of "only."

"Often, too, they are places we have visited in former years, or seen briefly in passing by, and kept ever afterwards in pious memory; and we please ourselves with the fancy that we shall repeat many vivid and pleasurable sensations, and take up again the thread of our enjoyment in the same spirit as we let it fall."— Passage immediately following the foregoing extract.

[6] "I never *was* so long in company with a girl in my life — trying to entertain her — and succeed [succeeded] so ill."— JANE AUSTEN, *Mansfield Park*, ii, p. 160.

[7] Note the difference in conditions in these sentences: "If I *be* dishonest you are to blame;" "If I *am* dishonest, you are to blame."

[8] "In these expressions *were* shadowed out the *whole* of that course subsequently developed."— H. L. BULWER, *Historical Characters*, ii, p. 336.

[9] Called a "split infinitive," as "to sweetly sing."

Clearness

23. Arrange relative and restrictive modifiers so that there may be no doubt as to what they modify.[10]

24. " Between a word and its modifier do not put anything that can steal the modification."— GENUNG.

Clearness (Continued)

25. Be careful to use " whom " only as an objective, never as a nominative.[11]

26. A clause should not be used instead of a noun, or a pronoun as the antecedent of a relative pronoun.

27. Let there be no doubt as to which, of two or more nouns of like number and gender, a personal pronoun relates.

28. Omit no parts not evidently implied (understood).[12]

(c) *Unity and Coherence*

29. During the course of a sentence do not change its subject or shift the standpoint.

[10] Obscure: " I went to see the assistant to the physician *that you recommended.*"

[11] Wrong case: " The younger Harper, *whom* they agree was rather nice-looking."— DISRAELI.

[12] Error by omission: " The domain of the husband *to whom* she felt that she had sold herself, and [by whom she] had been paid the strict price — nay, paid more than she had dared to ask."— *Daniel Deronda.*

30. The sentence should be completely dominated by one main thought, and upon that directly should each subordinate thought depend.

31. Do not crowd together conflicting ideas, nor thoughts unnaturally related.

(c) Unity and Coherence

32. Rarely attach relative clauses to other clauses which are themselves dependent.

33. A too free use of parenthetical expressions tends to switch thought away from the subject.

34. Rarely attach a supplementary expression to the end of an already complete sentence.

IV. SPECIAL PROPERTIES OF STYLE

(a) Emphasis

35. For emphasis, accord a conspicuous place in the sentence to the main idea, using the other parts as a background.

36. Invert the position of the modifier to give it emphasis.[13]

37. An inverted sentence-order will emphasize the logical subject, or principal idea.

[13] "A forehead high-browed and massive."

Emphasis

38. By putting subsidiary matter first, the logical subject will be emphasized (periodic sentence).

39. Repetition of sentence-forms sometimes adds emphasis.

40. Observe proportion, sequence, and climax for emphasis.

(b) *Force*

41. Plain, specific, short, and strong words give vigor to sentences.

42. Avoid the repetition of ideas, and the use of unnecessary words, especially connectives.

43. " End with words that deserve distinction."— WENDELL.

44. For weighty force, cut out modifiers, condense clauses and phrases into equivalent words, and choose the most emphatically direct words.

45. Do not depend upon italics and exclamation points to strengthen weak thoughts, weak words and weak arrangement.

(c) *Harmony*

46. To secure harmony suit the sound of words to the sense.

47. Select synonyms when it is necessary to repeat ideas.

48. Use alliteration sparingly.

(c) *Harmony*

49. Arrange your material with an ear to the prevalence of harmonious sounds.

(d) *Vitality*

50. To give vitality to discourse, use direct, idiomatic English.
51. Distinguish between an idiom and a worn-out stock expression.
52. Avoid the too free use of poetic forms.
53. Beware the pitfall of a stilted and exaggerated style.
54. Rapid movement is secured by suppressing details, and using epithet to portray the characteristic points.

(e) *Variety*

55. Occasionally affirm a thing by denying its opposite (litotes).[14]
56. Used guardedly, circumlocution gives variety.
57. Study the art of recasting sentences.
58. Figures of speech afford variety.
59. Use epithet — sparingly.
60. Use suggestion to relieve description.

[14] "A citizen of no mean city."— PAUL.

(e) Variety

61. Vary declarative and interrogatory with exclamatory forms.
62. Expression may be varied by changing the voice of the verb.
63. Study the inversion produced by introducing sentences with " there " and " it."
64. Learn to change from direct to indirect quotation (discourse).
65. Employ the historical present, sparingly, if at all.
66. Learn how to paraphrase poetic into prosaic language, and contrariwise.
67. Practice contracting clauses into phrases and into words; as well as expanding words and phrases into clauses.

(f) Figures of Speech

68. For condensed and vivid description, use simile, metaphor, allusion, and personification.
69. Interrogation, exclamation, and hyperbole are used for impressive assertion.
70. Apostrophe, and vision (the historical present), are suited to dramatic narration.
71. For illustration, study the use of figures of comparison.

(f) *Figures of Speech*

72. Do not use figures except where you desire to add clearness, force, or beauty.
73. Figures should harmonize with the general character of the story.
74. Vary the use of figures by studying many different objects for suggestions.
75. Do not in the same sentence mix figures of speech with literal language.
76. Figures should neither be carried so far as to be incongruous, nor used to excess.

V. THE THOUGHT-DIVISIONS

Relation of Thoughts

77. Each division of the whole story should be dominated completely by one main thought, and upon it directly should each subordinate thought depend.
78. Each such thought-division must preserve its unity by including only its own logical material.
79. The several divisions must follow one another progressively, each growing out of its predecessor, so that the entire series may move toward a climax.

Relation of Thoughts { 80. The transition from one division to another must be smooth and unforced.

VI. THE WHOLE STORY

Entire Effect {
81. Let your style be determined by the type of the story.

82. Do not sacrifice earnestness, individuality, and directness, to gain literary finish; you really need not.

83. Subordinate each part of the story to the effect of the whole.

APPENDIX E

ABBREVIATIONS OF PUBLISHERS' ADDRESSES

American........ American Book Co...... New York

Appleton.........D. Appleton & Co..... New York

Baker........... The Baker & Taylor Co... New York

Barnes...........A. S. Barnes Co.......... New York

Bobbs........... The Bobbs-Merrill Co.... Indianapolis

Boni.............Boni & Liveright......... New York

Brentano........Brentano's. .... New York

Century.........The Century Co......... New York

Collier...........P. F. Collier & Son...... New York

Dillingham.......The G. W. Dillingham Co. New York

Dodd............Dodd, Mead & Co...... New York

Doubleday....... Doubleday, Page & Co.... New York

Duffield.........Duffield & Co............ New York

Funk............Funk & Wagnalls Co.... New York

Ginn............ Ginn & Co................. Boston

Grafton..........The Grafton Press...... New York

Harcourt........ Harcourt, Brace & Co... New York

Harper.......... Harper & Bros.......... New York

H. C. S..........Home Corr. School, Springfield, Mass.

Heath........... D. C. Heath & Co.......... Boston

Hinds........... Hinds, Hayden & Eldredge. New York

Holt.............Henry Holt & Co........New York
Houghton........Houghton Mifflin & Co.......Boston
Jacobs...........George W. Jacobs & Co..Philadelphia
Lippincott........J. B. Lippincott Co......Philadelphia
Little............Little, Brown & Co..........Boston
Longmans........Longmans, Green & Co....New York
Lothrop..........Lothrop, Lee & Shepard Co...Boston
Macmillan........The Macmillan Co........New York
McClure.........The McClure Co.........New York
McClurg.........A. C. McClurg & Co........Chicago
Moffat...........Moffat, Yard & Co.......New York
Noble...........Noble & Noble...........New York
Oxford..........Oxford University Press..New York
Page............The Page Co................Boston
Putnam..........G. P. Putnam's Sons.....New York
Reeve...........James Knapp Reeve....Franklin, O.
Review..........Review of Reviews Co....New York
Scott............Scott, Foresman & Co.......Chicago
Scribner.........Charles Scribner's Sons...New York
Small...........Small, Maynard & Co........Boston
Stokes..........Frederic A. Stokes Co....New York
Taylor..........J. F. Taylor & Co.......New York

NOTE: Some of the foregoing publishing houses that have either merged with others or have gone out of business have been retained in this list so as to enable the student to identify their books as referred to. This is not intended as a full list of book publishers, but is given merely to interpret the abbreviations. A complete list of publishers is to be found in *Where and How to Sell Manuscripts,* William B. McCourtie, Home Correspondence School, Springfield, Mass.

APPENDIX F

1. *The New International Dictionary,* G. & C. Merriam Co.; *The Standard Dictionary,* Funk and Wagnalls Co.
2. *The Working Principles of Grammar,* Genung; Home Correspondence School.
3. *The Working Principles of Rhetoric,* Genung; Ginn & Co.
4. *The Study and Practice of Writing English,* Lomer and Ashmun; Houghton, Mifflin Co.
5. *Synonyms and Antonyms,* Allen; Harpers.
6. *Psychology,* Gordy; Noble and Noble.
7. *Studying the Short-Story,* Esenwein; Noble and Noble.
8. *The Art of Story Writing,* Esenwein and Chambers; Home Correspondence School.
9. *The Technique of the Mystery Story,* Wells; Home Correspondence School.
10. *Today's Short Stories Analyzed,* Neal; Oxford University Press.
11. *The Stories Editors Buy, and Why;* Wick; Small, Maynard.
12. *The American Short Story,* Jessup; Allyn & Bacon.
13. *The Study of a Novel,* Whitcomb; Heath & Co.
14. *Where and How to Sell Manuscripts,* McCourtie; Home Correspondence School.

APPENDIX G

BIBLIOGRAPHY

1. *Books on the Short-story*

1. Albright, Evelyn May; *The Short-Story.* Macmillan, 1907.
2. Barrett, Charles Raymond; *Short Story Writing.* Baker, 1900.
3. Canby, Henry Seidel; *The Short Story;* Yale Studies in English. Holt, 1902.
4. Hart, W. M.; *Hawthorne and the Short Story.* Berkeley, Cal., 1900.
5. Matthews, Brander; *The Philosophy of the Short-Story.* Longmans, 1901.
6. Quirk, Leslie W.; *How to Write a Short Story.* Editor, 1904.
7. Smith, Lewis Worthington; *The Writing of the Short Story.* Heath, 1902.

See also numbers 1, 2, 5, 7, 8, 9, 10, 11, 15, 16, 17, 18, 24, and 25, in *APPENDIX A;* and also the references given in *APPENDIX H.*

2. *Books Referring to the Short-Story*

8. Anonymous; *How to Write a Novel.* London, 1901.
9. Bainton, George (Editor); *The Art of Authorship.* London, 1898.

10. Baldwin, Charles S.; *College Manual of Rhetoric*.

11. Besant, Walter; *The Art of Fiction*.   London, 1884.

12. Cody, Sherwin; *How to Write Fiction*.   London, 1895.

13. Cody, Sherwin, and others; *On the Art of Writing Fiction*.   London, 1894.

14 Dye, Charity; *The Story-Teller's Art*.   Ginn, 1898.

15. Gosse, Edmund; " Kipling's Short Stories," in *Questions at Issue*.   Appleton, 1893.

16. Hamilton, Clayton; *Materials and Methods of Fiction;* Introduction by Brander Matthews.   Baker, 1908.

17. Hawthorne, Nathaniel; *American Note Book*. Works, Houghton.

18. Heisch, C. E.; *The Art and Craft of the Author*. Grafton, 1906.

19. Howells, W. D.; *Criticism and Fiction*.   Harper. 1891; *Literature and Life*.   Harper, 1902.

20. James, Henry; " The Art of Fiction," in *Partial Portraits*.   Macmillan, 1888.

21. Matthews, Brander; *Aspects of Fiction*.   Scribner. 1896.

22. Maupassant, Guy de; Introduction to *Pierre et Jean*. Paris, 1888.

23. Norris, Frank; *The Responsibilities of the Novelist* (and other papers).   Doubleday, 1903.

24. Pain, Barry; *First Lessons in Story Writing*.   London.

25. Poe, Edgar Allan; *The Philosophy of Composition*. Works.

26. Stevenson, Robert Louis; *Vailima Letters; Memories and Portraits*. Works. Scribner.

27. Bates, Arlo; *Talks on Writing English*. First Series. Houghton, 1897.

28. Winchester, Caleb T.; *The Principles of Literary Criticism*. Macmillan, 1899.

29. Bates, Arlo; *Talks on Writing English*. Second Series. Houghton, 1901.

30. Maxcy, Carroll Lewis; *The Rhetorical Principles of Narration*. Houghton, 1911.

31. Bennett, Arnold; *The Author's Craft*. Doran, 1914.

32. Quiller-Couch, Sir Arthur; *On the Art of Writing*. Putnam, 1916.

33. Phillips, Henry Albert; *The Universal Plot Catalog*. H. C. S., 1916.

34. Kilmer, Joyce; *Literature in the Making*. Harper, 1917.

35. Hawkins, Willard E.; *Helps for Student Writers*. Student Writer Press, 1917.

36. Upham, Alfred H.; *The Typical Forms of English Literature*. Oxford, 1917.

37. Trent, W. P., and Others; *The Cambridge History of American Literature*. Sections on the Short Story. Putnam, 1917.

38. Hamilton, Clayton; *A Manual of the Art of Fiction*. Doubleday, 1918.

39. Hearn, Lafcadio; *Talks to Writers*. Dodd, 1920.

40. Stevenson, Robert Louis; *Learning to Write*. Selections of advice from his works. Scribner, 1920.

41. Klickman, Flora; *The Lure of the Pen*. Putnam, 1920.

42. Lubbock, Percy; *The Craft of Fiction*. Scribner, 1921.

43. Slosson, Edward E., and Downey, June E.; *Plots and Personalities.* Century, 1922.

44. Polti, Georges; *The Art of Inventing Characters,* translated from the French by Lucile Ray. Reeve, 1922.

45. Chunn, Culpeper; *Plotting the Short Story.* Reeve, 1922.

46. Robinson, Mabel L.; *Juvenile Story Writing.* Dutton, 1922.

47. Bedford-Jones, H.; *The Fiction Business.* Student Writer Press, 1922.

48. Holliday, Robert Cortes, and Van Rensselaer, Alexander; *The Practical Side of Writing.* Doran, 1922.

49. Wildman, Edwin; *Writing to Sell.* An expansion of a brochure published in 1914. Appleton, 1923.

50. Hoffman, Arthur Sullivant; *Fundamentals of Fiction Writing.* Bobbs, 1923.

51. Hoffman, Arthur Sullivant; *Fiction Writers on Fiction Writing.* Bobbs, 1923.

52. O'Brien, Edward J.; *The Advance of the American Short Story.* Dodd, 1923.

53. Pitkin, Walter B.; *How to Write Stories.* Harcourt, 1923.

54. Pattee, Fred Lewis; *The Development of the American Short Story.* Harper, 1923.

55. Uzzell, Thomas H.; *Narrative Technique.* Harcourt, 1923.

56. Wharton, Edith; *The Writing of Fiction.* Scribner, 1925.

NOTE: Many helpful articles on the art of the short-story are constantly appearing in *The Writer's Monthly.*

APPENDIX H

NOTE: Since this book was published, in 1909, many more books and articles dealing in whole or in part with the short-story have been brought out than had theretofore appeared since the day of Poe. It is believed that all the important volumes on the subject published within succeeding years have been included in this supplementary list. No attempt, however, has been made to list the later magazine articles on the short-story—they are now too many for inclusion in a treatise of this scope. Those who wish to use to a complete periodical bibliography are referred to the cumulative indexes to be found in the periodical departments of all large public libraries.

BOOKS DEALING MORE OR LESS DIRECTLY WITH THE TECHNIQUE OF THE SHORT-STORY

Canby, Henry Seidel; *The Short Story in English*. Holt, 1909.

Gerwig, George W.; *The Art of the Short-Story*. Werner, 1909.

Ransome, Arthur; *A History of Story Telling*. Stokes, 1909.

Peck, Harry Thurston; *Studies in Several Literatures.* Dodd, Mead, 1909. Chapters on "Poe," and "The Detective Story."

Chester, George Randolph; *The Art of Writing* (also issued under the title, *The Art of Short Story Writing*). The Publishers Syndicate, 1910.

Cooper, Frederick Taber; *The Craftsmanship of Writing.* Dodd, Mead, 1911.

Young, Duncan Francis; *The Fiction Writer's Workshop.* Reeve, 1911.

Edwards, John Milton (pseudonym); *The Fiction Factory.* Reeve, 1911.

Esenwein, J. Berg; *Studying the Short-Story.* Noble and Noble, 1912.

Pitkin, W. B.; *The Art and Business of Story Writing.* Macmillan, 1912.

Smith, C. Alphonso; *The American Short Story.* Ginn, 1912.

Lieberman, Elias; *The American Short Story.* Reeve, 1912.

Phillips, Henry Albert; *The Plot of the Story.* Home Correspondence School, 1912.

Esenwein, J. B., and Chambers, Mary D.; *The Art of Story Writing.* Home Correspondence School, 1913.

Wells, Carolyn; *The Technique of the Mystery Story.* Home Correspondence School, 1913.

Phillips, Henry Albert; *The Art of Short Story Narration.* Home Correspondence School, 1913.

Neal, Robert Wilson; *Short Stories in the Making.* Oxford University Press, 1914.

Grabo, Carl; *The Art of the Short Story.* Scribner, 1914.

Notestein, Lilian, and Dunn, Waldo H.; *The Modern Short-Story*. Barnes, 1914.

Bennett, Arnold; *The Author's Craft*. Doran, 1914.

Conrad, Joseph, *The Art of Writing*. Doubleday, 1914. Preface to "The Nigger of the Narcissus."

Baker, Harry T.; *The Contemporary Short Story*. Heath, 1916.

Pain, Barry; *The Short-Story*. Doran, 1916. Reprint of Earlier English edition.

Quiller-Couch, A.; *On the Art of Writing*. Putnam, 1916.

Polti, Georges; *The Thirty-Six Dramatic Situations*. Editor Co., 1916.

Williams, Blanche Colton; *A Handbook on Story Writing*. Dodd, Mead, 1917.

Esenwein, J. Berg, and Stockard, Marietta. *Children's Stories and How to Tell Them*. Home Correspondence School, 1917.

SHORT-STORY COLLECTIONS—MOSTLY PREFACED BY INTRODUCTIONS DEALING WITH THE FORM

Trent, W. P., and Henneman, J. B.; *The Best American Tales*. Crowell, 1907.

Dawson, W. J., and Coningsby; *The Great English Short Story Writers*. Harper, 1910.

Patten, William; *International Library of Fiction*. Collier, 1910.

Hawthorne, Julian; *The Lock and Key Library*. 10 Vols. Reviews of Reviews, 1912. This is an expansion of the six-volume edition of *Mystery and Detective Stories*.

Ransome, Arthur; *The World's Story-Tellers*. 9 Vols. T. C. & E. C. Jack (London), 1912.

Esenwein, J. Berg; *Short-Story Masterpieces*.. French, 2 vols.; Russian, 2 vols. Home Correspondence School, 1912 and 1913.

Pittenger, L. A.; *A Collection of Short Stories*. Macmillan, 1913.

Canby, Henry S.; *A Study of the Short Story*. Holt, 1913.

Sherman, Stuart P.; *A Book of Short Stories*. Holt, 1914.

Ashmun, Margaret; *Modern Short Stories*. Macmillan, 1914.

Cross, E. A.; *The Short-Story*. McClurg, 1914.

Heydrick, Benjamin A.; *Types of the Short-Story*. Scott, Foresman, 1914.

Hale, E. E., Jr., and Dawson, F. T.; *Elements of the Short Story*. Holt, 1915.

Mikels, Rosa M. R.; *Short Stories for High Schools*. Charles Scribner's Sons, 1915.

Moulton, Leonard; *Short Stories*. Houghton Mifflin, 1915.

Masson, T. L.; *Short Stories from "Life."* Doubleday, 1916.

Baker, Emilie K.; *Short Stories and Selections, for Use in Secondary Schools*. Macmillan, 1916.

Sherman, Stuart P.; *A Book of Short Stories*. Holt, 1914.

O'Brien, Edward J.; *The Best Short Stories of 1915, etc. The Yearbook of the American Short Story*. Small, Maynard, 1916, and similar volumes annually.

Hart, Nina, and Perry, Edna M.; *Representative Short Stories*. Macmillan, 1917.

Firkins, Ina Ten Eyck; *Index to Short Stories*. Wilson.

OTHER TREATISES AND COLLECTED STORIES

Gowans, Adam L.; *Famous Ghost-Stories by English Authors*. Leroy Phillips, Boston, 1910.

Gowans, Adam L.; *The Twelve Best Short Stories in the English Language*. Phillips, 1910.

Maxcy, Carroll Lewis; *Representative Narratives*. Houghton, 1911.

Waite, Alice Vinton, and Taylor, Edith Mendall; *Modern Masterpieces of Short Prose Fiction*. Appleton, 1911.

Milford, H. S.; *Selected English Short Stories*, 2 vols., XIX and XX Centuries. Oxford, 1914 and 1921.

Lodge, Henry Cabot, and five other critics; *Prize Stories from "Collier's."* Collier, 1915.

Dorchain, Auguste; *The Twelve Best Short Stories in the French Language* (translated). Phillips, 1915.

Benecke, Else C. M.; *Tales by Polish Authors*. Longmans, 1915.

Smith, C. Alphonso; *Short Stories, Old and New*. Ginn, 1916.

Atkinson, W. Patterson; *The Short Story*. Ginn, 1916.

Wright, Willard Huntington; *Great Modern French Stories*. Boni, 1917.

Seltzer, Thomas; *The Best Russian Short Stories*. Boni, 1917.

Campbell, Oscar James, and Rice, Richard Ashley; *A Book of Narratives*. Heath, 1917.

Neal, Robert Wilson; *Today's Short Stories Analyzed*. Oxford, 1918.

Williams, Blanche Colton; *A Book of Short Stories*. Appleton, 1918.

Atlantic Narratives, First and Second Series, 2 vols. Atlantic Monthly Press, 1918.

Schweikert, Henry C.; *French Short Stories*. Scott, 1918.

Law, Frederic Houk; *Modern Ghost Stories*. Century 1918.

McSpadden, J. Walker; *Famous Ghost Stories*. Crowell, 1918.

O. Henry Memorial Award Prize Stories. Doubleday, 1919. Similar volumes annually.

Pattee, Fred Lewis; *Century Readings for a Course in American Literature*. Century, 1919.

Williams, Blanche Colton; *How to Study "The Best Short Stories."* Small, 1919.

Schweikert, Henry C.; *Russian Short Stories*. Scott, 1919.

Schnittkind, Henry T.; *The Best College Short Stories*. Stratford Co., 1919.

Laselle, Mary A.; *Short Stories of the New America*. Holt, 1919.

Jessup, Alexander; *The Best American Humorous Short Stories*. Boni, 1920.

Nicoll, W. Robertson, and eleven other critics; *The Masterpiece Library of Short Stories,* 20 vols. Educational Book Co., 1920.

Howells, William Dean; *The Great Modern American Stories.* Boni, 1920.

Heydrick, B. A.; *Americans All.* Harcourt, 1920.

Williams, Blanche Colton; *Our Short Story Writers.* Moffat, 1920.

O'Brien, E. J.; *The Great Modern English Stories.* Boni, 1920.

Ragozin, Zénaïde A.; *Little Russian Masterpieces.* 4 vols. Putnam, 1920.

Hrbkova, Sarka B.; *Czechoslovak Stories.* Duffield, 1920.

Vaka, Demetra; *Greek Stories.* Duffield, 1920.

Popovic, P.; *Jugo-Slav Stories.* Duffield, 1920.

Laselle, Mary A.; *The Joy in Work.* Holt, 1920.

Edgar, Randolph; *The Miller's Holiday.* Stories from the "Northwestern Miller." The Miller Pub. Co., 1920.

Wick, Jean; *Stories Editors Buy, and Why.* Small, 1921.

Edgar, William C.; *The Bellman Book of Fiction.* The Bellman Co., 1921.

Ramsay, Robert L.; *Short Stories of America.* Houghton, 1921.

Clark, Glenn; *A Manual of the Short Story Art.* Macmillan, 1922.

Macklin, Alys Eyre; *Tales From the French.* Harcourt, 1922.

Rhys, Ernest; *English Short Stories.* Everyman's Library. Dutton, 1922.

O'Brien, E. J., and Cournos, John; *The Best English Short Stories of 1922.* Small, 1923, and annually.

Georgian Stories. Putnam, 1923.

Jessup, Alexander; *The American Short Story.* Allyn and Bacon, 1923.

Pence, R. W.; *Stories by Present Day Writers.* Macmillan, 1923.

Pitkin, Walter B.; *As We Are.* Harcourt, 1923.

Polti, Georges (Lucile Ray, translator); *The Art of Inventing Characters.* Reeve, 1922.

Robinson, Mabel L.; *Writing Juvenile Stories.* Dutton, 1923.

Frederick, John T.; *A Handbook of Short-Story Writing.* Knopf, 1924.

Hastings, W. T., Clough, B. C., and Mason, K. O., Editors; *Short Stories.* Houghton, 1924.

Joseph, Michael; *Story Writing for Profit.* Small, Maynard, 1924.

Williams, Blanch Colton, Editor; *Thrice Told Tales.* Dodd, Mead, 1924.

Bercovici, Konrad, Editor; *Short-Stories of the World.* Stratford, 1925.

Harper Prize Stories. Harper, 1925.

Clark, B. H., and Lieber, M., Editors; *Great Short Stories of the World.* McBride, 1926.

Goodman, Theodore; *Narrative Structure and Style.* Appleton, 1926.

Leeming, Benjamin Christopher; *Plot and Idea Psychology.* Schroeder, 1926.

Conrad, L. H., and Lovett, R. M.; *Descriptive and Narrative Writing.* Houghton, 1927.

PART VI
SUPPLEMENTAL CHAPTERS

Having decided . . . what moves himself most, or what he believes to have the most nearly universal appeal, the author should gather such attendant conditions and motivations as will strengthen the appeal of his concrete choice. Nor should he forget that he must address himself to the intellect in order to reach the emotion. Unless the reader "believes" or is convinced of the truth of what he reads, it cannot move him greatly. And, finally, it must be admitted that having striven through his own feeling, the feelings of his characters, and through employment of all technical "tools of emotion," the writer may not quite succeed. He may achieve technical correctness, and fall short of the "contagion" or ignition which takes place only when he discovers the wee bit of under- or over-emphasis, and evaluates correctly the infinitely minute degrees. Otherwise, he may interest by his skill, but he does not move.—BLANCHE COLTON WILLIAMS, *A Handbook on Story Writing.*

An error into which the beginning author easily falls is the too lavish use of coincidences. While perhaps the majority of detective stories are founded upon coincidences, they must be made so plausible, so seemingly inevitable, that they shall not appear to be mere coincidences. A modern fiction detective thus frankly admits the value of coincidences in his work:

"Don't forget the fortunate coincidences," replied Average Jones modestly. "They're about half of it. In fact, detective work, for all that is said on the other side, is mostly the ability to recognize and connect coincidences."

But the reader cannot agree that a frankly announced coincidence makes as good a mystery problem as one where that element is left out. . . . Work up to the coincidence until it seems to occur naturally. Invent causes to produce the effects that otherwise would have seemed pure coincidence.—CAROLYN WELLS, *The Technique of the Mystery Story.*

440

PART VI

SUPPLEMENTAL CHAPTERS

CHAPTER I

MAKING THE STORY CONVINCING

The fundamental problem of the dramatist . . . is the problem of plot-and-character harmony—which, being reduced to its lowest terms, amounts merely to a strict observance of natural logic. Observation may be most just and acute, and as a result men and women in plays may be exhibited with all manner of skill in contrast and grouping, as well as with sympathetic individual portraiture; and yet, if what they are fails to accord with what they do, they will most likely amount to no more than wasted effort. In spite of this fact, however, a common defect in drama is the tendency to "plot-ridden" personages, who, for the sake of the fable, are forever belying their own selves.
—CHARLTON ANDREWS, *The Technique of Play Writing.*

It is worth while asking what, precisely, an editor means when he tosses a manuscript aside and exclaims, "Unconvincing!" or regretfully sighs, "Mighty good story—if only that final scene were more convincing!"

In the parlance of the magazine office, a "convincing" story is one that seems real—root, stock, branch, leaf and fruit. Even though the foundation facts—the premises—strain belief, as in many wonder stories and in much humorous fiction, and especially farce, when once we play the game with the author and accept his premises, we are

441

convinced—provided all the conclusions he draws are logical and real-seeming.

An experienced editor views in more than one mood every story manuscript that challenges his interest. Well he knows that he must scrutinize his own feelings as he reads, or at least after he has done reading, because the flaws that are glossed over or even do not at all appear while he is in the glow of a well-written story are pretty sure to emerge to view in the cold grey calm of after-analysis. And it is this sober second thought that saves many an editor from buying a story that at first laid hold upon him ardently. Naturally, it is only the subtler errors in convincingness that are not at once apparent to the editor; the others do not get by him for a moment.

Wherein lie the weaknesses in all such failures to convince the reader? In hazy or in absolutely bad character drawing, of course, and in misfit combinations of story material in general, we find fruitful sources of unreality of presentation, but *the chief trouble is inadequate motivation.*

In the preceding chapters I have frequently touched upon offences against reality, naturalness and plausibility in both character and plot, but now it seems necessary to consider in a single chapter the causes of and the cures for weak motivation. Let it be said in passing that the published short-stories cited are for the most part examples of good motivation, because it would be needless, for my purpose, to pillory a writer by name simply to name a bad example. Further, most of the stories used are available for examination either in plot form in this volume or in my *Studying the Short-Story.*

1. *The Nature of Motivation*

The word "motivation" will not be clearly understood at once by all, because critics of the short-story have only lately begun to employ it freely, and even then not always with identical meanings in mind. For the moment, it will be enough to say that motivation has to do with the use of cause and effect in the story.

Poe used the term "causation" as we now use "motivation." Other critics of the drama and of fiction have preferred various other words—R. Zimmerman expressed much the same idea in "causality"; Gustav Freytag in "motiving" and, for one phase of motivation, "exciting cause"; William Archer in "logic" and "obligatory scenes"; and Charlton Andrews in "logic." Both Selden L. Whitcomb in his *The Study of a Novel* and Robert Wilson Neal in his *Short Stories in the Making* define and explain "motivation" quite adequately, though briefly.

Motivation is causation, together with its result. Its fundamental rule is that each effect in the story, whether in the plot or in character delineation, must be founded in an adequate cause, and each cause must have an effect that is consistent with the power of the cause. For example, in a manuscript read recently a burglar comes upon a sleeping child. Somehow the child reminds him of a neighbor's little boy in whom he took an interest long ago, and he slips quietly away—and reforms. Such things may occur in real life, but aside from the triteness of the theme, the average reader would feel that the cause was too slight for the effect.

Again, in another manuscript story a son unexpectedly returns to his mother in France after long years in

America. But the mother, who is shown as being otherwise most affectionate, goes on about her tasks as if she were quite unimpressed. The effect is unconvincingly slight for the cause. In neither case was the character in question previously shown to be of the sort that would act so unusually.

2. *Kinds of Motivation*

(a) *The whole story may be motivated by a single idea.* Of such are stories that demonstrate a thesis. A good example is "Where Was Wych Street,"[1] in which a London "pub" dispute over the location of a street leads on and on, involving violence and murder among the arguers and extraordinary consequences to judge, counsel and several others. The theme of this story, like that of "The Necklace" (page 326), "The Piece of String" (page 393), and many another classic, might be crystallized in the Biblical exclamation, "Behold, how great a matter a little fire kindleth!" And this thesis theme not only motivates the initial situation, but runs like a scarlet thread of tragedy through the whole story.

Critics like Francisque Sarcey have called attention to the petering-out effect of plots that either do not make good the demonstration of their theses or allow new ideas to bob up and divert the original trend—as a red herring dragged over the trail spoils the scent, to use William Archer's expressive figure. Thesis stories are more exacting in their demand for logical motivation, and for satisfying climax, than any other in the whole category.

[1] Stacy Aumonier, *Saturday Evening Post,* Nov. 4, 1921

(b) *Each separate incident in a story demands adequate motivation.* This is true, obviously, whether the incident is the opening one and constitutes the fundamental story situation, or any of the minor events of the story.

Yet a word of warning is needed here. Motivation may be made too inevitable—by which I mean that for the purposes of struggle, complication and suspense there would better be more than one possible way out of a difficulty. Else where were the anxiety of the reader for the outcome, which means so much to the prosperity of the fiction? True, many good stories clearly forecast the denouement almost from the start, and for their interest depend upon the strength of the situation, the vividness of character portrayal and the power of the treatment. The modern French and Russian writers have given us admirable models of this type. But as a plot-device the foregone conclusion is for the master, not for the tyro. In most stories, inevitableness would better be shown not in the beginning, but in the ending. Only the genius of Halévy could compass the inevitableness of "The Insurgent" (page 402).

(c) *Any vital emotion, decision, or action in the plot demands a satisfying motivation,* as will presently appear. So motivation extends beyond the mere causation of situations and of incidents.

3. *The Sources of Motivation*

The causation that brings about emotions, decisions and actions in a story spreads its roots everywhither: to the subsoil of the fundamental situation, and to the top-soil—the environment of the characters, the time, place and conditions of action, and all the rest; but the one prime source of motivation lies in the characters themselves. If Madame Loisel had not been altogether such as she was by upbringing, ideals and surroundings, she could not have worked out so terrific a penalty for her coveting the necklace and losing it. If Mateo Falcone (page 410) had not lived in the Corsica of a century ago, with its patriarchal devotion to the laws of kinship and of sanctuary, he could not have executed— he would never have said "murdered," as would we of today—his son Fortunato; just as Abraham must needs be a Jewish patriarch of early ages to be willing to act upon the fanatical belief that Jehovah could be pleased by the father's living sacrifice of his own son Isaac. Go down the list of great stories and see how every decisive turn in the plot is pivoted deep in the nature of one leading character.

Consistency is the *sine qua non* of all good motivation of character in its emotions, decisions and acts. But pause here. I do not mean consistency to character so much as to the forces that move that character. We could have no fiction if every honest man acted with consistent honesty and every rogue were impervious to motives of sacrifice, generosity or other lofty feeling— in such a case we can scarcely say "principle." In *variations from the normal* we find most of our drama in real life as in fiction. Therefore the problem of character-motivation is twofold: (a) To make the characters seem so natural to us that when they (b) act thus and so under stress of a given force in given circumstances we are convinced. To what a man is we must add the emotion (or whatever other force may move him) and the circumstances in which the testing comes; then the sum will inevitably be the correct "answer" in the story-problem. The shifts from scornful virtue to complacency, and back to sniffing virtue, by the stranded passengers in Maupassant's "Tallow Ball" will serve to illustrate.

Think of the tremendous range of forces that play upon a character. They are as wide as life. The virtuous woman in the grip of social ambition, of jealousy, of revenge, of petty spite, of sudden unreasoning hatred; the mean man under the power of an uplifting emotion; an untested youth possessed by rank self-conceit brought up with a jolt by self-revelation—the endless combinations challenge beginner and artist alike. And always three or four factors enter into the problem: the fundamental nature of the character—built up as it has been by all his past,—an emotion or a sequence of emotions, the environment, and, sometimes, some force from without exerting a strong moving influence.

So variation constitutes a chief element in the actions and reactions of characters in fiction as in life. Yet it absolutely must lie *in* the character to do the unexpected thing. There are two kinds of "can't"—the normal and the super-normal. There stands my friend. Physically, I *can* strike him in the face. But can I? No, something bigger than my physical ability makes it impossible. The old theologians used to say that the distinction between *non possere peccare* (not having the power to sin, in free translation) and *possere non peccare* (having the power not to sin) was a vital one, and it is exactly this difference, yet in countless variety, that must govern us in motivating character. Life is not coldly logical, but swept here and there by forces within and without the human soul. Hence there can no more be a formula for the actions of a character in fiction than a real man can be measured by a yardstick.

The difference between sentiment and sentimentality is that the former is based soundly while the latter is not. Sentiment may weep, but its tears are respectable because they are justified. Sentimentality snivels, and earns our laughter or our contempt. Only the superb workmanship of Bret Harte in both "Tennessee's Partner" (page 406) and "The Outcasts of Poker Flat" (page 82) saved him from the charge of sentimentality. It was not natural for Tennesse to show no change toward his old partner—who had eloped with Tennessee's wife—when the partner returned to their camp. No more would a group of people from the underworld be likely to prove so angelic as they turned out to be in the other story. But all this is cold criticism. Read the stories again and the unreality falls away—until you are again in a critical mood.

4. *The Revelation of Motivation*

Of course it will not be assumed that the motivation of a plot must, or even as a rule should, be apparent to the reader early in the story. That would be fatal to suspense, where suspense is needful, as mostly it is. No one can advise you as to when in the process of narration "the secrets of all hearts shall be revealed." One thing, however, is certain: when that time does come the reader must be satisfied that, in the nature of your story people, in the circumstances in which you have shown them

acting out the plot, under the emotions and other forces
—motives, it may be, or forces from without—that move
them, the outcome is convincingly real and natural.

In order to attain to this naturalness it is the custom of
many writers to work forward, while others work backward—that is, while Henry James held that one should
first conceive a character and then let him work out his
own salvation—or damnation—while the reader supplies
the fear and trembling, other writers begin with a result
and work back to an act or a decision or an emotion, and
then motivate it by building up a causal force sufficient
to account for the emotion, decision or action, and the
eventual result. Each man to his own method.

The motivation of conflict, and motivation *by* conflict,
are vital steps in plot building—statements that explain
themselves. Character and situation both lead to conflict
and result from it. It is a recognition of this truth that
sets the author free from the tyranny of mere coincidence
as a plot device.

5. *Coincidence*

Maupassant once said, "The number of people who die
by accident every day is considerable, but we cannot
make a tile fall on the head of the principal character or
throw him under the wheels of a carriage in the middle
of the story, under pretext that it is necessary to introduce an accident."

Now coincidence—the unpremeditated coming together
of two elements in such a way as to produce a complication or to solve a difficulty—is an entirely necessary thing
in the mechanics of fiction. In fact, few great plots do

not use either the accidental (one thing happening without the volition of the person affected) or the coincidental (two persons, or one person and a thing, being brought together without plan). It is in the abuse of these devices that the fault lies.

The whole story of Kipling's "The Man Who Was" (page 390) is based on coincidence, yet it is entirely convincing, because when the motivation is disclosed to the reader it is plain that the wretch did not just happen to do as he did or just happen to recognize the words of the Russian. In the end, every step of the plot is logically accounted for. This is the only justification for the use of coincidence in plot. We are unconvinced when the old lady who is going to the city to hunt up her recreant son finds herself seated by chance in the train beside her boy's employer and learns by chance who her seat companion is—whereupon things at once take a start for the better. But, sooner or later, show us that the employer had been to see the old lady about her son, missed her, barely had time to take a taxi and make the train, and so plumped himself down in the first vacant seat, and we have probability as a basis for the coincidence. Let anybody happen to be anywhere or do anything, so as to tie up or untie the complication, only be certain to "plant" the reasons for the coincidence earlier in the story. But do it unobtrusively.

In humorous stories, especially in farce, we are less critical. In Richard Harding Davis's "The Man Who Could Not Lose," we have a character whose every gamble proved successful, whether he wished it or not. Coincidence and improbability abound; but, given such a condition, which the reader smilingly accepts for the fun of the thing, and all is forgiven because the story amuses. In perusing serious fiction the reader is in a different mood. The *deus ex machina*—the god who descends in a car out of the sky to rescue the hero—doubtless convinced the patrons of the early Greek drama because their world was crowded with deities, but such devices are unacceptable today, though amateurs refuse to believe it, It simply shows poverty of invention when, to perpetrate a bull, the author shows that the only way to untie his knot is to cut it.

QUESTIONS AND EXERCISES FOR CLASS OR INDIVIDUAL STUDY

1. From the plots on pages 211-215 and 389-413 select three. Study the motivation (a) of the whole story and (b) of the several incidents; then briefly name the motivating forces, of whatever sort, so clearly that we may see the working of cause and effect.

2. Are any of the foregoing plots unconvincingly motivated? If so, (a) point out specific instances, and (b) suggest stronger motivation.

3. From a magazine or a collection of short-stories select a story of inadequate motivation and handle as in question 2.

4. Take one of your own stories and, applying the tests set forth in this chapter, analyze the motivation, defending it as if from criticism.

5. What happens to the reader's interest when the motivation of a plot intended to produce suspense, or surprise, or both, discloses the motivation of the final crucial situation early in the story?

6. Criticise favorably or unfavorably, and completely, the motivation of any one of the following well-known stories: "Without Benefit of Clergy," Kipling; "The Monkey's Paw," Jacobs; "Markheim," Stevenson; "The Siege of Paris," Daudet;

"Moonlight," Maupassant; "Monsieur Beaucaire," Tarkington; "The Duchess at Prayer," Wharton.

7. Try to find a story in which the use of coincidence betrays weakness of invention.

8. Select a story in which coincidence is used justifiably—by being well though unobtrusively prepared for.

CHAPTER II

Looke in thy heart and write.—Sir Philip Sidney.

Without the objective point of view, a writer must fail of any worthy achievement. You must stop studying yourself; you must project your personality into the world, and incorporate it with whomever you meet or see. You must not turn from one because his face repulses you, nor over-appreciate another because his nature is like your own. You must try to realize how others look at the world; you must see through their eyes, and think with their minds. In short, you must look out at the world and not in at your own soul.—*The Writer's Book.*

The several popular and technical meanings that lie in the terms "point of view" and "viewpoint" were briefly noted on page 124; these deserve a more expanded treatment here.

1. *Point of View as the Author's Attitude toward his Story*

Both meanings of this word "attitude" apply to the author's point of view in relation to his story: a position assumed for a purpose, and a position truly expressive of the author's views of life, his personal philosophy. This is to say that for the time being the author may be a satirist, treating his story from that angle, or a humorist, a moralist, what not; yet this particular attitude may not be typical of his philosophy of life, but predominant only for the moment. How far he will depart from his characteristic general attitude toward life, in assuming a special point of view, will depend on the degree of seriousness with which he looks upon his story, his art in general, and his responsibilities as a writer. The whole question is a subtle one and not to be decided by a set of rules. The conscientious writer will not wish his story to teach, even if only by implication, lessons that he believes to be vicious, yet on the other hand he knows that the reader cannot justly hold him responsible for the views of his characters—unless he handles them in such a way as unintentionally to allow or purposely to make his own point of view to crop out.

The pure realist demands that the author's personal philosophy shall never color his treatment of a story—in other words, that, for fictional purposes, he shall *have* no personal philosophy. (See pp. 175, 185, 284.) But how often is this severe standard attained to? However, the short-story is a poor field in which to ride a hobby, and, in turn, a hobby horse makes a ridiculous substitute for a charger in either tournament or battle. Let the characters do their own fighting for a cause that the author may wish to promote. All in all, when the author's personal viewpoint obtrudes in the story the interest is likely to suffer. The story is a vehicle; when it is overloaded with opinion, or sermon, or spite, or derision, or any purpose-material or propagandum whatsoever, its wheels will creak, and perhaps break down.

2. *Point of View as the Author's Attitude Toward His Characters*

This is but a subtle variation of the sort of viewpoint just discussed, but it is worth considering for a moment. Contrast Maupassant's cold, dissecting treatment of Mme. Loisel in "The Necklace" with the sympathetic viewpoint maintained by Daudet toward his characters in "The Last Class." True, the latter story is told in the first person, and so portrays the viewpoint of the fictional narrator, but the love of human kind and the patriotism depicted are obviously not mere sentiment put into the mouth of the narrator but spring from the author's own heart. He sympathizes with his characters because they speak his own thoughts.

It will perhaps go without saying that there should be no shift of the author's attitude toward his characters throughout the story. If he finds the tone of his treatment inevitably shifting, let him go back and bring the whole into harmony. We may gently laugh at our characters and yet be sympathetic, just as a mother laughs at her adored children; but that is not satire. Satire and sympathy are incongruous when applied to the same story people.

3. *Point of View in Description*

This phase of viewpoint—remote from the main subject of this chapter—is sufficiently treated on pages 158-159, and is mentioned here (as on page 124) merely to avoid confusion with the technical uses of "viewpoint" and "point of view" now being considered.

In each of the three foregoing kinds of viewpoint, it

seems well to reiterate, the author's purpose is best served when he succeeds in causing the reader to see things, whether spiritually or physically, from his own angle, and experience reactions similar to his own.   In fact, that is at once the prime purpose and the supreme test of the spinner of yarns.

4. *Point of View as Governing the Characters*

The actors in a story are real—or they are not.   If to the reader they are actually alive, they are subject to the same limitations as circumscribe his own being.   True, he permits a romantic super-man to accomplish astounding feats, but he demands plausibility even in the midst of the improbable.   In the heat of reading he believes in the ability of the hero to defeat his opponent against great odds, but he insists that the hero must be properly informed of, or be able shrewdly to infer, the whereabouts of his enemy.   The hero, be he never so heroic in gifts, must submit to the common laws of mankind in this respect.   He may, like the colored preacher, "bust the incombustible and unscrew the inscrutable," but he cannot unassisted know the unknown.

Something of this has been said in the foregoing chapter on "Making the Story Convincing."   Just now the particular phase of motivation insisted on is point of view. *How* does the heroine know that her brother is waiting to rescue her?   If she is not in a position to know of herself, or to guess, she must learn the facts in some plausible way, for she is only human.

Constantly in the stories of amateurs—and, really, of experienced writers now and then—the authors pass over the trifling matter of what can or cannot be known, seen, of heard from the vantage point that a given character occupies, and, of course, the effect is proportionately unconvincing. There is no more firmly established principle in fiction writing than this: *Everything that a character knows and acts upon in a story must be accounted for plausibly.* In other words, a fictional character must be in a position to know, see, hear, or find out all that the writer assumes that the character does know, see or hear.

There is another phase of the character's viewpoint that demands consistency—his attitude toward other characters in the story or toward a given fact of life. Any change must be motivated clearly, even if not openly. For example, a woman's attitude toward children does not change without a reason. Though that reason may be unreasonable—a whim, an obsession, a touch of madness —it must lie in the character, in the circumstances, in the emotional stress to which she is subjected, if it is strong enough to make her change. For the author merely to say that such a shift of moral, intellectual or emotional viewpoint occurred, is arbitrary and weak; show us why, let us feel that such a reversal is natural.

5. *Point of View as Applied to the Central Character*

In the chapter on "How Stories are Told," pages 109-124, we examined the various sorts of first-person and third-person story-telling. No further discussion is needed here except to say that these several methods have a real bearing on viewpoint, because the author's decision as to whether a story is to be told in one or the other of these ways hinges in large part on whose story it is—whether that of one character or another. Equally, this factor governs the viewpoint, for the personality of the chief actor will give it color, characteristic tone.

Coming still closer to the heart of the matter, we see that it is the *story itself* that thus has a viewpoint, and not merely the author and the characters, as in the preceding sections. It is as if the story were telling itself to a hearer, and the personality whose special story it is were being centralized and elevated to make the narrative effective.

Both in the title and in the story itself Mérimée leaves us not at all in doubt—"Mateo Falcone" is not the story of Fortunato, the son, vital as he is to the plot, but the story of the tragic necessity, from Falcone's viewpoint, of a father's executing his boy.

A less skillful literator might easily have been led into a confusion of effects in telling such a tragic story. Indeed, many a writer has begun his narrative with the purpose of telling it from one point of view—that is, looking at the story so as to see one character dominating the action—and gradually shifted his attitude until another character overshadowed the first. It is as if the "second man" insisted on usurping the spotlight and ousted the "star." In such a case two courses only are open, and both mean revision—re-vision, seeing the whole matter again: Either recast the opening section so as to harmonize with the ending, or vice versa; in no case is it wise to permit this kind of shifting viewpoint to go uncorrected.

For purposes of his own, an author may not bring the chief character out of the shadows until the last—often an effective device; but in such a case let him remember that he may unintentionally awaken so much interest in a minor character that when the true leading man or woman steps out on the stage the reader will be disappointed, and "never get over it." This, of course, is quite a different matter from centering interest at a certain point in the story upon one or another of the lesser characters. Even then, the proportion must be held rigidly in hand lest the little chap run away with the story.

6. *Point of View as the Angle of Narration*

One final phase of the subject remains: the skillful and the bungling shift of the angle of narration, and this point needs but a few words.

When the author decides that he will look upon his story and his story people as a reporter does, that is one point of view. When he decides that he will enter into the very hearts of his characters and reproduce for the reader their thoughts, feelings and motives, that is quite another. When these two methods are combined, the shift calls for skill in order to avoid a jolt to the sense of reality. It can be done, but it must be done with the greatest care. In Maupassant's "Moonlight"—which is the abbé's story—the author minutely depicts the austere priest's philosophy of life, and then sits down inside of the abbé's soul and tells us about the shifting emotions that work out so great a transformation. The whole story is psychological. In Stevenson's "A Lodging for the Night" we see François Villon objectively, all through the story; virtually all that we know of him we discern from his words and his actions. In Kipling's

"Without Benefit of Clergy" we have a masterly illustration of how one may shift from one point of view to the other without a single jar. Barrie slips in telling his delightful dialect story, "The Courting of T'nowhead's Bell," for throughout he omnisciently tells what his characters think and feel, yet once or twice he lapses into the personal narrator—who *could* not read all hearts—and says "I" and "you."

In the use of indirect discourse—indirect quotation of thoughts almost as if they had been put into speech—we have one valuable device that the writer uses to shift the viewpoint from the dramatic reporting of action and dialogue to a view of the character's mind. For example:

> Tommy was puzzled. This looked like a friendly little kitten, but why did he hump up his back in that odd way? Old Tabby's kittens *liked* to be stroked, and they always cuddled and purred when Tommy held them up close. This one—
> Suddenly Tommy let out a startling yell.

The shift from the indirect analysis to the direct dramatic narration is obvious.

QUESTIONS AND EXERCISES FOR CLASS OR INDIVIDUAL STUDY

Note: In the following exercises use the plots on pages 211-215, 389-413, the stories in "Studying the Short-Story," or any good stories you may find available.

1. Name one example of each of the several sorts or phases of point of view, taking either plots or stories for your examples.

2. In your fictional reading, be on the alert to find any unjustified shift in the narrator's attitude toward his characters. Report any instances you find.

3. Try to find an example of an unmotivated shift of a

character's attitude toward another character or toward a fact of life—such as honesty, gambling, etc.

4. Briefly state the plot, and yourself supply the necessary motivation to account for the shift.

5. Examine one of your own plots or complete stories for shifts of viewpoint. Test them for entire plausibility, remembering that the improbable may be made plausible by adequate motivation, and point out how you propose to improve the weak spot, if you find any.

CHAPTER III

The writer, when tempted to depart from the time order,
should make certain that he has cogent reasons therefor, . . .
If he does depart from it he must be doubly careful that the
time relation of events is perfectly clear to the reader.
—CARL H. GRABO, *The Art of the Short Story.*

To the beginner, the sequence in which the events of
a story may best be told seems often a trivial matter. But
the strict chronological order of incidents must sometimes
be interrupted—though never without the best of reasons
—in order to make clear some prior foundation fact or
condition upon which an understanding of the story-action
rests. In fact, it is not merely the time-sequence of incidents that is involved in the order of narration, but the
effective grouping of all the elements of the story, the
integration of the parts into a whole—a whole that shall
produce a unified impression upon the reader.

The author's problem involves the combination of plot-
elements under conditions of purpose, time, and method.
Now let us see, in brief, how this result is obtained.

1. *The Elements of the Plot*

The materials that the writer uses for building his story
are *exposition, characters, situation, setting, incident,
twist, emotion, narration, dramatic action and dialogue,
minor and major crises, minor and major climaxes, and*

462

ending. Obviously, he will not use all of these elements in every story, hence each plot presents its own problem.

2. *Purpose in Using the Story-Elements*

The story-elements do not exist for themselves, but for the plot. More than this, in many instances they are used by the author to bring about certain effects aside from the plot proper, but directly contributory to it. The following story-effects have all been discussed in the preceding chapters, so a mere mention of them here will suffice.

The purpose of exposition is to acquaint the reader with all necessary facts and conditions prior to the main action.

Some characters may be used for the purpose of acting out the story, others for the purposes of setting, and others to provide information, contrast, humorous relief, and so on.

Situation gives us the basis for the action, in whole or in part.

Setting is used to create the atmosphere of reality.

Incident gives plot-development, dramatic effect, suspense, surprise etc.

Twist produces mystification, or surprise, or humor, etc.

Emotion has an almost universal purpose.

Dramatic action and dialogue give vividness to the plot by evoking mental images.

Narration is used to state facts and conditions, analyze the moods and motives of the characters, etc.

Crisis produces suspense.

The purposes of climax and denouement are self-evident.

Naturally, the lines of these purposes will cross and recross; for example, perhaps an incident will constitute a twist, and also will almost surely be developed with dramatic action and dialogue; narration may be used to give the setting, and so on.

3. *When to Use the Story-Elements*

Here is where the wisdom of the story-teller is displayed. Just where to begin—whether with foundation facts, in the center of the situation, or, as in many detective and mystery stories, near the end and then back-track—is the author's peculiar test. Whichever course he chooses, the effect must be cumulative, and the let-down for back-tracking must not lower suspense. The short-story is much more exacting in this respect than is the novel. One word here is enough: Never leave the direct order of narration to back-track without making sure that you have already sufficiently gripped interest and created enough suspense to carry the reader's absorbed attention over the period of retrograde action. Naturally, the simpler the plot the less need will there be for going back to lay your foundation.

Three typical arrangements of story-elements follow, to illustrate how they may be handled in endless variety.

First Example

Exposition.

Foundation situation as basis for the main crisis to be developed later.

Character revelation.
Incident to create suspense.
Narration to show motives.
Incident to introduce a twist.
Sudden development of real crisis.
Climax of the action.
Denouement.

Second Example

Setting.
Statement of the thesis-theme, more or less openly, in dialogue.
Characters delineated in action.
Incident points to main situation and lays foundation for motivation to be disclosed later.
Main situation develops.
Minor crisis.
Minor climax.
Exposition of earlier events.
Incident produces main crisis.
Twist by use of incident mystifies reader.
Climax shows true trend of the action, and the denouement reveals the motivation.

Third Example

Tragic incident shows mystery to be solved and gives setting and situation.
Characters introduced.
Incident provides character delineation.
Exposition.
Narration of chain of events leading up to the mystery.

Incident shows unsuccessful effort at solution; mystery deepens.

Twist to mystify reader still further.

Incident for suspense—deceptive crisis.

Minor climax reveals the false clue.

Incident produces new suspense.

Dialogue and character revelation heighten suspense.

Sudden introduction of main crisis.

Climax.

Denouement unravels mystery.

In the chapters on "How Stories are Told" and on "Point of View" we saw how the elements just discussed may be brought into the story. While it is needless to discuss them here, it seems well in closing to say that the author's decision as to how to tell his story—whether in the third person: (a) as a reporter viewing the story objectively and telling it dramatically; (b) as an analytical recorder who enters into the motives and emotions of his characters and adopts the viewpoint of one and perhaps each of them; or (c) by a combination of methods (a) and (b); or whether in the first person: (a) as an unnamed onlooker; (b) as a participant in the action; (c) as a diary or letter writer—will be governed largely by a careful examination of his materials (his story-elements) and in what order he can present them most effectively. The careless or obscure use of the time-element has spoiled many a good story, hence in choosing the order of narration keep the question of time always before you.

QUESTIONS FOR CLASS AND INDIVIDUAL

Study

1. Analyze "The Necklace," page 326, showing the order of story-elements as illustrated in this chapter.

2. Do the same with one of the stories given in Esenwein's *Studying the Short-Story*, using one of the stories not analyzed by the author. If this volume should not be available, select a story from some magazine, being sure to choose one that has a well-complicated plot.

3. Analyze in similar manner a story of mystery, or a detective story, observing particularly how the back-tracking is handled.

4. Invent at least three outlines of story-elements as shown in this chapter.

5. Choose the outline that you like best of those developed for question 4 and write the plot of the story. Do not hesitate to change the outline if you can see an improvement.

6. Write out the full story outlined in question, after perfecting the plot.

CONDENSED HINTS FOR FICTION WRITERS

Touching the Most Common Errors

1. Don't over-punctuate. The modern way is to use no more commas than the sense really demands—yet be sure to use enough to make your thought unmistakably clear.

2. Unless either an exclamation point (!) or an interrogation point (?) is required, use a comma and not a period after a remark in dialogue when it is followed by an explanatory or interpretative comment; thus: *"A very dull performance," shrugged Myra.* However, when the succeeding sentence is plainly detached from the speech, a period is proper; thus: *"I don't believe a word of it." Washburn's lip curled in derision.*

3. Put a comma before a name used in direct address; and also after it if the sentence continues; thus: *"Good morning, Daddy." "Jerry, are you going to town?" "Hello, Jim, how are the folks?"*

4. Dashes may be used instead of commas when the expression set off by dashes—as this one is—is used as an example, or is thrust into the sentence—that is, without a close grammatical connection. A single dash is used before an explanatory or illustrative expression that closes the sentence, as in the foregoing; or to mark an abrupt shift of thought. Don't form the habit of using dashes when you are in doubt as to what else to use.

5. Be careful to use quotation marks where they are needed, otherwise the reader may be confused as to when a speech ends and the author's comment begins.

6. When a quotation is introduced within a quotation use double quotes outside and single quotes inside; thus: *"Why," she said, "I don't see what you mean. His very word was 'prig'—that's exactly what he said,"* and *Jean flashed at her sister an indignant look.*

7. Don't use a pair of "quotes," as editors call them, for each individual sentence of an uninterrupted speech in dialogue—if the speech contains more than one sentence—but only for the entire speech. However, if the speech uninterruptedly extends over more than one paragraph, place quotes only at the beginning of the speech, at the beginning of each other paragraph that is included in that one speech, and at the end of the last paragraph.

8. Indirect quotations require no quotation marks, as: *She told me what you said—that you don't like Billy.* Direct quotations do require quotes: *"I don't like Billy." Those were her very words.*

9. Notwithstanding the tendency of certain "futuristic" writers, such as May Sinclair and James Joyce, to ignore English grammar (albeit with intention and full knowledge), do not punctuate as a complete sentence a group of words having no predicating (asserting) verb, but merely a present participle, like: *His generous nature paving his way.*

10. Capitalize "Mother," "Sister," "Doctor," "Honey," "Dear," etc., when used as proper names, particularly in direct address; but not when used as mere general terms; thus: *"I hate to, Father." "Have you spoken to the General?" "Run for a doctor, Dear."*

11. Examine a good magazine to see how dialogue is punctuated and capitalized.

12. Don't use two qualifying words that convey substantially the same idea, as: *He was a virile, manly fellow.*

13. Preferably use "Oh" for exclamations, as, *"Oh, I'm so glad!"* and "O" for the direct address (the vocative), as, *"O Lord, I am Thy Servant."* Note where the exclamation point is used.

14. Don't write it "alright," but "all right"—two words.

15. Better not allow yourself to split infinitives. "To sing sweetly" is better English than "to sweetly sing," though sometimes the split infinitive is not really awkward.

16. Don't overlook the value of "that." To omit it may make it necessary to revise the first impression received in reading a sentence, and that violates the important law of economy of attention. For example: *She knew her son's wardrobe, from collars to hose, needed replenishing.* "She knew her son's wardrobe, from collars to hose," gives us an impression that must be immediately altered when we read "needed replenishing." Insert "that" after "knew," and the meaning is instantly clear.

17. Study variety in the way you begin your sentences, especially when they are in sequence. Also mingle short sentences with longer. Monotony hurts a story.

18. To begin many sentences, and particularly adjacent ones, with "and" is an unpleasant mannerism.

19. As a rule, call things by their names. Use epithets ("the famous detective," meaning Sherlock Holmes) sparingly, and never in close sequence. Never call the chief character of a story "our hero," "our friend," "our

poor Donald," and the like. To speak of the Devil as "his Satanic Majesty" is trite, and no longer even remotely humorous. If a man is searching for a will, do not call it "a legal document." The epithet style of writing, when it becomes a habit, tends to cheapen the style, and it is not really clever.

20. A free use of well-known sayings or quotations should be avoided.

21. Simplicity is best. Don't use an ornate expression when a simple one will serve. Over-elaborate writing has killed many a good story, and high-sounding words smack of amateurism.

22. Be suspicious of the easy phrase that comes first to your pen-point. It is likely to be commonplace from much use. "Trite," we call such expressions. Re-dress old phrases so as to make them new, but do not *strain* after originality.

23. Set in (indent) the first word of every paragraph about one inch from the left margin of your manuscript.

24. Start a new paragraph for each new and separate speech by a different speaker in dialogue. Note how this is managed, by examining a good magazine. (See 7.)

25. Don't let your paragraphs be either habitually very long or very short. A paragraph should contain only that which strictly belongs to one idea, but it should continue until the idea is completed or a new speaker speaks.

26. Abrupt transitions of topic are sure to break up the smooth progress of narration. When such a sudden shift is required, be careful to make the reader see, by what precedes and by what follows, that the transition is natural and intended and not caused by careless, dis-

orderly thinking or is the result of an afterthought. If you put each thought precisely where it belongs in a paragraph, and each paragraph in its proper place in the whole manuscript, the transitions will carry the reader forward without jerks anl lapses.

27. Use contractions like "I'll," "there's," "he'd" only in dialogue or in a very informal article.

28. Loosen up your dialogue by the use of contractions like "he's" and "they'll." Don't let your characters talk stiltedly—make their speech natural and, usually, colloquial. Above all, let your characters talk consistently with their own natures all the time and not only part of the time. Read your story aloud to test the naturalness and informality of the dialogue.

29. Never misspell a word in dialect unless the sound is thereby materially altered. "Iz" sounds like "is," and "sed" like "said." Dialect is for the ear—not for the eye. Dialect that is at all heavy or slows up the reading because it is even slightly difficult is likely to bring about a rejection. Use dialect sparingly.

30. Don't use "he," "she," "they" too often. Vary by the use of names and terms that stand for names. The constant use of pronouns is confusing.

31. Name your character very early in the story and use the name consistently throughout. Don't say "Jim Jennings," and then "Jim," and later "Jennings." Use the full name as often as you will, but if you use only one, let it be always the same, unless you have a definite reason for doing otherwise.

32. In fiction, don't be content with the very common names, such as Jones, Smith, Brown. Don't name your characters in a symbolic way, as Gouge, Smart or Trim

—the method is out of date, except in broad humor. Use natural names in preference to "fancy" ones, like Montague and Montmorency, except in farce.

33. Don't put in your character delineation in chunks, especially in the opening of the story. Weave it in gradually, in comments by other characters and in a word here and there. We want to see a character as shown in his own words and actions, and also through the eyes of other characters, not merely as the author describes him.

34. Unless your fictional character is designed by you to be dense, don't make him show surprise at, or appear too dull to understand, a point in the plot-action which in the eyes of the reader seems perfectly clear. Surprise or ignorance or lack of understanding should appear to be *natural* in the circumstances, and not asserted or suggested in a story obviously because it suits the author to have it so in his handling of the plot. A character stultified by the plot is what we call "plot-ridden."

35. A "slender" story demands a more brilliant treatment than one with a fuller plot. By a slender story we mean one that consists entirely or almost entirely of one event, without the use of developing incidents or additional plot incidents. A good full plot is likely to include *action, reaction, twist, suspense, surprise, and climax.*

36. Be sure that surprise in your story has been "planted" in some earlier scene—that is, has its foundation in some fact or condition that will make the surprise seem natural when it is sprung.

37. In choosing the main struggle, don't take the line of least resistance—that leads to triteness.

38. By opening your story in the midst of action you

will compel the reader's attention. Long foundation explanations do not make for interest.

39. It is impossible to build a strong plot out of mere general situations, such as: "Margaret gradually came to doubt Billy's love." Here nothing is visualized. If her doubts came gradually, you should at least let us see dramatically what definite incident brought her doubts to a head. What did she do as a result? How did her doubts react on Billy? etc. Be pointed. A good plot does not slide along—it progresses by definite steps.

40. The way to avoid general situations is to think of your story as being acted on the stage. Crystallize each separate incident or situation into an actable scene. Each scene must contain something dramatic enough to justify its use. Each scene must logically prepare for, without disclosing, the next scene. The whole series of scenes must rise in interest—perhaps by means of suspense—until the "big" scene. Give space to that big scene; then plan to end swiftly while interest is intense.

41. Center your scenes about definite incidents. Don't simply *tell about* your story. Invent incidents to show us why Frank is jealous of Ted, how he shows his jealousy, what important results follow, etc. Motives and feelings and decisions work out in action, and action makes incidents.

42. Use a pen to correct every omission or error in your typing. We cannot expect editors to think well of our manuscripts if we ourselves do not respect them enough to make them letter perfect. Carelessness is the earmark of the amateur. This statement is severe, but true.

43. Number your pages clearly, and consecutively. A

manuscript dropped by a careless clerk or an awkward editor, or scattered by a mischievous wind, may cause the reader much trouble—and an annoyed editor is not in a frame of mind to be more appreciative than your manuscript compels him to be.

44. The moment an editor discovers a sheet placed out of its natural order he naturally suspects that you doubt whether he intends reading your manuscript entire and have set a trap for him. Even when you have misplaced a page by accident the impression is the same, so be careful. Only amateurs play this trick, and it always works to their hurt, for it shows that the writer is afraid of his own work and also places a low estimate on the honesty of a manuscript reader. It displays an equal disregard for the time of an editor to send in your story with the pages in reverse order—due, of course, to your having misplaced them in that way when giving the manuscript a final reading.

45. Never send a letter to an editor or a publisher announcing that you are sending him "under separate cover" a manuscript for his decision—if the manuscript is a short one; and even a long manuscript would better be accompanied by the letter—a short one, of course. To keep editors or clerks on the lookout so that letter and manuscript may finally be placed together results in annoyance; and it may mean a lost manuscript. If the manuscript is a bulky one it should be sent short distances by express, and bear both inside and outside the name of the sender. In such a case, do not enclose a letter in the express package. But if the manuscript is sent by first-class mail—*manuscripts cannot lawfully be sent by parcel post*—enclose the letter with the manuscript.

CONDENSED HINTS ON PUNCTUATION

Many writers do not punctuate correctly because they have not learned to reason in terms of what punctuation really stands for. Without a thought of covering the entire ground, which would be quite impracticable in such a treatise, the fundamental reasons for the use of these distracting little marks are here set forth. It will be remembered that a few specific directions have been given also on pages 468-469.

It is a matter of common knowledge that in centuries gone by books were printed with the letters all run together, our present-day points and spacing being virtually absent. That naturally made reading an intricate process in which the commonalty, for more than one reason, could not engage. So when "points" were devised and spacing was used so as to group the letters and the words that belonged together, and thus enable the mind readily to cognize what the author meant, it was a natural thing to call these symbols punct(point)uation marks, because they pointed off the parts of a piece of writing.

As punctuation progressed in accuracy, and became as standardized as it is ever likely to become, writers came to see that the mastery of a few simple principles would serve to enable them to punctuate clearly even when a full knowledge of technical usage seemed unattainable, or at least impracticable.

The basic principle is that a writer wishes by the use

of these symbols to show that he is aiding his readers to separate the various elements of his story or what not, by inserting longer and shorter thought-spaces, as it were. Speaking loosely, these space-indicators correspond to the time that a careful reader would pause at these stops when reading aloud.

Here are the points arranged in time- or space-order, beginning with the longest:

The period (.) indicates a full stop, and is used at the close of a sentence. It is aside from the purpose of this brief attempt at simplification to discuss its use at the end of an abbreviation (Mr.) and with certain numbers (2.; $109.50).

The interrogation (?) marks the close of a question, even when it is a single word—just as the period may be used after a single word (Yes? No.) when a complete sentence is suggested but not expressed.

The exclamation (!) is used in precisely the same way as the interrogation, only it is used at the close of an exclamatory word, expression or sentence.

So, with regard to the period, the interrogation point and the exclamation mark, all that we need absolutely to know is *what a sentence consists of,* and then set after it the mark that suits our purpose—a period for a statement, an interrogation for a question, and an exclamation for an ejaculation. These three are of the same value, so far as the time of the pause is concerned.

The colon (:) is the next in order of pause-length. It has two uses only: to precede a formal summary or an example; as, "The following gentlemen were present: Senator Johnson, Judge Calderwood, etc." See also its use after "only," preceding. Its second use is to mark a sentence-division somewhat shorter than is indicated by the period. This latter function is now very rarely employed, so that it may virtually be dismissed by the present-day fiction writer.

The semicolon (;) marks a pause shorter than is indicated by the period or the colon, and longer than the comma. Its chief value is to set off parts of a sentence one or both parts of which contain a comma or commas; as, "I was, at the moment, greatly confused; what is more, I was actually annoyed." As is evident, the clauses of the foregoing example are rather loosely related; in fact, one might make separate sentences of them instead of showing their relationship by using a semicolon.

The semicolon is very useful in keeping long sentences absolutely clear by throwing the meaning of a phrase evidently backward or forward, as the writer may desire. It is also used to precede an example introduced by "as". Observe its use before the preceding passage enclosed within quotation marks, and also in the sentence that follows almost immediately after this one.

The dash (—) has two uses, and they are very definite. The first is to mark a break in the ordinary flow of a sentence; as, "I—er—I—to tell the truth, I just don't know." Notice that the last dash has much the same value as a colon used before a summary, or an explanatory statement—though a colon would look awkward after "I." The dash is often substituted for the colon: "I am now referring to the principal deciduous trees—the maple, the oak, etc." Of the same force is the break marked by the dash in the following: "Please find enclosed ten dollars—if you can"; but the idea of a summary is, of course, not suggested in this example. So the dash and the colon are really not quite interchangeable.

The second main use of the dash is similar to the first, but in this case they hunt in pairs, serving to set off the enclosed expression as being interjected as an explanation, but not *structurally* one with the sentence—that is, not necessary to its grammatical unity. Here is an example: "Pennsylvania's mineral resources—so far as we now know—exceed those of any other state in the Union."

Many writers use the dash with a gay nonchalance whenever they are uncertain as to what mark to insert. It is a bad habit, and never fools an editor; he can spot ignorance on the instant.

Parentheses ( ) are used precisely as dashes are used in pairs, as illustrated in the foregoing paragraph. They have therefore a pause-value about equal to that of a pair of dashes. However, the presence of parentheses somehow suggests to the discriminating reader that the inserted (parenthetical) passage is connected with the main thought of the sentence in an explanatory, or perhaps undertone, sort of way. For this reason it is better not to form the parenthesis habit, for it tends to loose structure.

Brackets ([ ]) really mark a pause longer than is indicated by either dashes in pairs or parentheses, but it has seemed to make for clearness of treatment to discuss brackets immediately after the other two interjectory signs. They clearly indicate an insertion of an explanation or interpretation *from the outside,* as it were; hence their chief use is to show that an editor has inserted something to make clear a matter that otherwise might seem incomplete or obscure. Thus, suppose that an author is making a statement which the editor cannot allow to go unchallenged, but which for one reason or another he does not wish to omit. He might then use brackets to enclose his own comments and by these signs clearly show that the author had nothing to do with the interpolation. For example:

"The editorial fraternity is as venal to-day as it always has been. [Surely the author cannot be making this serious charge seriously—EDITOR] Their opinions are formulated and proclaimed for revenue only. There is not an editor to-day who does not write with his tongue in his cheek."

The comma (,) marks the lightest, briefest pause in a sentence. It has more uses than any other mark, but they differ not at all from each other in value fundamentally —they all denote slight thought-pauses. The following are the chief values of this busy little punctuation mark, together with simple examples:

1. To set off words of similar force in a sentence; as, "It was a bitter, vicious day." Note that the close relation of "bitter" to "day" is interrupted by the insertion of "vicious," which equally modifies "day." Therefore the comma marks the omission of the word which is directly modified—"day." The full form would therefore be, "It was a bitter day. It was a vicious day." More briefly, it would read: "It was a bitter day, a vicious day"; and, still more briefly, a form almost like our first example: "It was a bitter, a vicious day."

2. To mark an omission, as in the foregoing examples. Note that the comma in this instance might be regarded as being used in place of "and," though a more

precise form would then be, "a bitter and a vicious day."

3. To set off one clause from another: "There is no such thing as an absolutely perfect climate, for the absence of frost is a cordial invitation to the various members of the bug family to make themselves at home."

4. To mark an inserted (parenthetical) expression; as, "This, of course, is only my own idea of the thing."

5. To precede or to follow a name used in direct address in dialogue; as, "No, Father, I can't admit anything of the kind." "Yes, Doctor."

6. To precede or to follow a remark in dialogue, when accompanied by the author's explanatory comment:

She replied archly, "Well, you are not quoting me quite correctly."

"No, I admit that," he grinned, "but isn't that just what you meant?"

On the other hand, when the author's comment is not an explanation closely connected in *form* with the speech of the character, but may stand as a separate sentence, a period is used to precede the speech, or to follow it. Examine the varied methods used in these two passages:

Jeremy was evidently perplexed. "But, I don't understand you, really." He flushed painfully and looked to Helen for further enlightenment.

"I—I don't understand you, really." Jeremy was evidently perplexed. He flushed painfully and looked to Helen for further enlightenment.

There is, of course, much more to punctuation than these few pages could possibly show, but the whole subject is simple enough if one will take pains to resolve his thoughts into elements, make these elements stand out clearly in his own mind, and then use the punctuation symbols to show his reader just what relation one thought-element bears to another.

GENERAL INDEX

Names of authors whose words or titles are quoted, are printed in small capitals; titles of books and stories appear in italics; while topics and persons referred to are set in plain type. The authors and titles referred to in the chapter on *Titles* and in the *Appendices* are not included in this Index.

483

ENGLISH

Composition, Grammar, Literature, Punctuation, and Spelling.

Barbe's Famous Poems Explained (*School Edition*) $1.00
Barbe's Great Poems Interpreted.............................. 2.00
Boylan and Taylor's Graded Drill Exercises in Corrective English:
    Book 1—Grades 4 and 5 (*Teacher's Edition* .90) .... .50
    Book II—Grades 6 and 7 (*Teacher's Edition* .95) .... .58
    Book III—Grades 8 and 9 (*Teacher's Edition* 1.00) .... .65
Clark's English Composition Completely Analyzed............ 1.50
Clark's English Classics Completely Analyzed................. 2.00
Dillon's Journalism for High Schools........................... 1.25
Esenwein's Writing the Short Story............................. 2.00
Esenwein's Studying the Short Story........................... 1.75
Flint's Newspaper Writing in High Schools................... 1.00
Hanna and Taylor's 1600 Drill Exercises in Corrective English (Grades 6A-9B), (*Teacher's Edition* .90) .... .50
Hart's Composition and Rhetoric (*Revised Edition*).... 1.50
Hart's Punctuation and the Use of Capital Letters...... .60
Heydrick's How to Study Literature (*Revised Edition*) .85
Heydrick's One Term Course in Eng. and Amer. Lit. 1.30
Heydrick's Short Studies in Composition..................... .60
Hix's Fifty English Classics Briefly Outlined................. 2.00
Hix's A Brief Outline of the Books I Have Read........ .44
Irish's American and British Authors......................... 1.25
Irish's New Orthography and Orthoepy........................ .60
Keyes' My Reading Outlines...................................... .30
Keyes' Recommended Eng. Readings for High Schools .35
Kirkland's 1000 Classified Subjects for Composition Writing .... .35
Massee's Merchant of Venice (*Completely Outlined*).... .50
Murphy's Patriotic Poems Explained........................... 1.00
Radford's Composition and Rhetoric........................... 1.52
Rigdon's Language and Grammar for the Grades........... 1.00
Rigdon's Grammar Essentials for the High School........ 1.25
Rigdon's The English Sentence................................. 1.50
Rossman-Mills' Graded Sentences for Analysis............. .50
Seachrest's Child Life Composition Pictures (*32 Pictures*), (*Teachers' Manual* 1.50).......................... .50
Sheran's Handbook of Literary Criticism..................... 2.40
Smith's Grad. Exer. in Punctuation and Use of Capitals .40
Webb's Model Definer.. .60
Webb's Model Etymology.. .90
Webb's Manual of Etymology.................................... 1.30
Willis' 2000 Sentences for Class Drill in Analysis........ .50
Deming and Bemis' Pieces for Every Day the Schools Celebrate 2.00
Lovejoy and Adams' Pieces for Every Month of the Year 2.00
Shurter and Watkins' New Poems for Oral Interpretation 2.00
Blackstone's The Best American Orations of Today 2.00
Blackstone's New Pieces That Will Take Prizes (*Rev.*) 2.00
Esenwein's How to Attract and Hold An Audience.... 1.50
Neil's Sources of Effectiveness in Public Speaking.... 2.60
Pearson & Hicks' Extemporaneous Speaking................. 2.00
Scott's Psychology of Public Speaking (*Revised*) 1.60
    Any of the above books will be sent subject to approval.

NOBLE & NOBLE, *Publishers,* **76 Fifth Ave., New York**

Speaking! Debating!

Declamations, Recitations, Reading; Dialogues, Debates,
Prize Speaking, Orations, FOR ALL OCCASIONS.

Barbe's Famous Poems Explained	$1.50
Barbe's Great Poems Interpreted	2.00
Craig's Both Sides of 30 Public Questions Completely Debated (Pros and Cons), (*Revised Edition*)	2.25
Shurter's Both Sides of 100 Public Questions Briefly Debated (*Revised Edition*)	2.00
Henry-Seeley's How to Organize and Conduct a Meeting	1.50
Howe's Hand Book of Parliamentary Usage	.75
Nichols and Pearsons' Intercollegiate Debates (*8 Volumes*), each	2.50
Palmer's New Parliamentary Manual	1.00
Shurter's The Science and Art of Effective Debating	2.00
Brownlee's "Patriotic Speaker"	1.75
Blackstone's The Best American Orations of Today (*Enlarged Edition*)	2.00
Blackstone's New Pieces That Will Take Prizes (*Revised Edition*)	2.00
Coomb's A Ten Weeks' Course in Elocution	2.00
Craig and Gunnison's Pieces That Have Taken Prizes	2.00
Davis' Model Commencement Parts, Orations, Essays, Addresses	2.50
Davis' Three-Minute Readings for College Girls	2.00
Davis' Three-Minute Declamations for College Men	2.00
Deming and Bemis' Pieces for Every Day the Schools Celebrate	2.00
Esenwein's How to Attract and Hold An Audience	1.50
Fenno's New Science of Elocution	2.00
Fry's Educational Dramatics	.75
Fry's A Midsummer Night's Dream (*A Dramatic Cast Reading Arrangement*)	.60
Gunnison's New Dialogues and Plays (*Primary, Intermediate and Advanced*)	2.50
Hix's Poetry for Each School Year Grades 1 to 8 (*Approved Selections for Memorizing*) each	.72
LeRow's Pieces for *Every* Occasion	2.00
Lewis' Selected Readings from Popular Novels	2.00
Lovejoy and Adams' Pieces for Every Month of Year	2.00
McHale's Pieces That Have Won Prizes in Speaking Contests	2.00
Neil's Sources of Effectiveness in Public Speaking	2.60
Pearson & Hicks' Extemporaneous Speaking	2.00
Pearson's Humorous Speaker	2.00
Pearson's The Speaker Series (*Eight Volumes*), each	2.50
Reynold's Graded Poetry for Memorizing, Book I, Book II, Book III, each	.75
Reynold's Graded Poetry for Memorizing, for Junior and Senior High Schools, 7th and 8th Years, each	.85
Ross' A Southern Speaker	2.00
Scott's Psychology of Public Speaking (*Revised Ed.*)	1.60
Shurter's Winning Declamations—How to Speak Them	2.00
Shurter and Watkins', Poetry for Oral Interpretation	2.00
Shurter and Watkins' Masterpieces of Modern Verse	1.50
Shurter and Watkins' New Poems That Will Take Prizes in Speaking Contests	2.00
Yendes' Entertainments for Every Occasion	1.50

Any of the above books will be sent subject to approval.

Noble & Noble, *Publishers*, 76 Fifth Ave., New York